Linda T. Sanford, LICSW is a social worker and licensed psychotherapist who teaches at the Simmons College Graduate School of Social Work. She began working with survivors of sexual assault in 1973, with youth who have sexual behavior problems in 1983, and currently provides training and consultation on a national basis. She is also the author of *The Silent Children* and is co-author of *Women and Self-Esteem*. In 2002, Linda Sanford received the Massachusetts Chapter of the Nation' ·sociation of Social Workers Award for Outstanding Contribu·   cial Work Practice.

First published in 1990, NEARI P   ⌐ of the classics in the literature about su.   ⌐ie stories of twenty survivors who know th.   is living well". Prevailing over a childhood of sexua   ⌐use, neglect, parental substance abuse and witnessing don   ⌐ence, Linda Sanford asks them to look back and help us all under. ⌐d how they fared so well. One of the first popular books on resiliency, *Strong at the Broken Places* was written for every survivor, friend, family member, mentor or helping professional who seeks the path towards self-forgiveness and healing.

LINDA T. SANFORD

STRONG
AT THE
BROKEN
PLACES

Building Resiliency
in Survivors of Trauma

NEARI Press

Strong at the Broken Places:
Building Resiliency in Survivors of Trauma

Published by
NEARI Press
70 North Summer Street
Holyoke, MA 01040
413.540.0712

Distributed by
Whitman Distribution
10 Water Street
PO Box 1156
Lebanon, New Hampshire 03766
603.448.0037
800.353.3730

ISBN# 1-929657-25-0

First Published by Random House, Inc., 1990

For my daughter Grace —
love you forever
like you for always

*The world breaks everyone
and afterward
some are strong
at the broken places.*

—ERNEST HEMINGWAY
Farewell to Arms

AUTHOR'S NOTE

All of the survivors described and quoted in this book are real individuals whom I interviewed in depth for the book, with their consent. In order to protect their privacy, however, all their names and the names of their family members have been changed, and identifying details such as geographical locations and specific occupations have been altered or omitted.

CONTENTS

PREFACE

Since 1973 I have worked with victims and survivors of sexual violence. While my work has been rewarding, I have been frustrated by the scarcity of hope that traditional psychological theories have to offer survivors of abuse. Most of the existing literature—and the assumptions behind much clinical practice—seem to suggest that my clients' rough start in life has forever doomed them to be "damaged goods." Widespread media sensationalism has amplified the professionals' sense of gloom and doom, by portraying survivors as uniformly deranged, violent, suicidal, chemically dependent or abusive.

My work with victims and survivors of abuse has not borne out conventional psychological wisdom or the lurid headlines. I know from experience that many survivors are far from defeated by childhood trauma. Often their general functioning is quite good, and the very reasons that bring them into treatment suggest an impulse toward and capacity for health: they are having specific problems, or have reached important developmental milestones—the death of a parent, commitment to an intimate relationship, struggles with an authority figure at work or school, decisions about having or raising children—and want help in reaching a full resolution of thoughts and feelings about their childhood trauma that these events have evoked.

Whatever the problems or circumstances that brought them into therapy, there are strong commonalities among many of the survivors I have worked with. Despite popular and professional expectations, these survivors have not inflicted trauma on themselves or others. Their thoughts and feelings about childhood trauma are normal, given the abnormality of their experience. Their problems are not radically different in scope or intensity from those of many others I have worked with who were *not* traumatized as children. They leave therapy having resolved the issues that brought them and continue to live useful and rewarding lives.

In 1983 the focus of my work as a social worker and licensed psychotherapist shifted to the evaluation and group treatment of court-involved juvenile sex offenders, many of whom had themselves been abused. I braced myself for the relative hopelessness of their situations, expecting at least among this group to see the experts' predictions fulfilled. But this has not always been the case. I have discovered that the relatively young age at which they have been identified as offenders greatly increases their chances of successful treatment. For every one who seems unable or unwilling to prevail over childhood trauma, there is another who responds to group and individual psychotherapy.

Given my experiences, I came to wonder what it is that allows one chronically abused child to grow up to be a good friend, responsible citizen and reasonable person with a few "normal" emotional problems, and causes another to become incarcerated because of violent behavior by the time he reaches his teens. While gender, class and race account for some of the differences, they do not explain them all. There is no shortage of middle- and upper-class white male sex offenders or female sex offenders, for example. And it's clear that poor and minority offenders are more likely to be identified because of inequities in our criminal justice and child protection systems.

It seems that with comparably traumatic beginnings, child victims eventually come to the proverbial fork in the road. Some go on to be survivors, while others take the downward path to violence and destruction. What makes the difference?

The more I have studied the problem, the more convinced I have become that there are *many* roads to survival. Moreover, there are an endless number of U-turns; even well into adulthood, traumatized people can make their way back to the fork and set out on a better course.

The old adage "We all teach what we need to learn" is true for me. I never fully subscribed to the "damaged goods" theories. In 1983 I read Gloria Steinem's essay "Ruth's Song (Because She Could Not Sing It)," in which Steinem described her mother's struggle with mental illness and the impact it had on her childhood. One passage was particularly meaningful to me: "I once fell in love with a man only because we both belonged to that large and secret club of children who had 'crazy mothers.' We traded stories of the shameful houses to which we could never invite our friends."[1] I had suspected the club was large, but why was it secret? We had done nothing wrong, yet we treated our pasts as something to be concealed. Steinem's essay planted the seeds for this book.

Then I became aware of the theoretical work of Israeli medical sociologist Aaron Antonovsky. In 1970, while conducting research on how women of different ethnic groups adapt to menopause, he found that 51 percent of the women in his control group were "in quite good overall emotional health," as compared with 29 percent of the women who were concentration camp survivors. "Focus not on the fact that 51 is far greater than 29," he suggested, "but consider what it means that 29 percent of a group of concentration camp survivors were judged to be in reasonable mental health."[2] The physical data, he said, told the same story.

This experience led to Antonovsky's 1979 book, *Health, Stress, and Coping,* in which he introduced the *salutogenic* approach to disease.

> A pathological orientation seeks to explain why people get sick, why they enter a given disease category. A salutogenic orientation focuses on the origins of health and poses a radically different question: Why are people located toward the positive end of the "health ease/disease" continuum? Or, why do they move toward the health ease end, whatever their location at any given time?[3]

This book is based on salutogenic questions. It is a nonempirical and descriptive study of twenty healthy adults, each of whom extensively experienced at least two of the following five childhood traumas: physical abuse; sexual abuse; parental substance abuse; extreme neglect; and the witnessing of domestic violence.

Some people believe that only forcible rape or injurious assaults count as child abuse. What could be *so* bad about these other experiences?

If you've ever seen a person who had passed out on the street, you may recall the shock it gave you. Or remember the last time you saw a chronically mentally ill person, raging in gibberish against anyone who happened by. Have you ever seen drivers and passengers injured in a car accident while you stood by, filled with anxiety and repulsed by the violence, but helpless to prevent it? Now imagine that these unconscious, erratic, threatening, violent, or injured people are adults you love and depend on.

Imagine further what it would feel like if you went to the emergency room, very ill but without knowing why, and waited for hours without receiving medical attention or even having your presence acknowledged. After a while you would be as upset over the blatant lack of interest in your existence, let alone your needs, as over being sick. Why doesn't anyone pay attention? you'd wonder. Can't they see I need help? This is how neglect feels to children.

Finally, imagine that each of these incidents happens to you over and over again for years—every month, every week, every day. This is what it is like for countless child victims of abuse and neglect.

Remember, too, that all of these traumas happen within the larger context of emotional abuse, an "attack by an adult on a child's development of self and social competence, a *pattern* of psychically destructive behavior" in the form of rejecting, isolating, terrorizing, or ignoring the child, or "corrupting" him into "destructive, antisocial behavior" that "makes the child unfit for normal social experience."[4]

Most books on childhood trauma have limited themselves to one kind of trauma, and few have made the connections among the various types. But when we study and treat them as if each trauma were discrete and unique, we parcel out recovery, isolate survivors from one another and slow the healing process. I believe that the similarities are far more striking than the differences.

A word about language: In an attempt to overcome the sexism of our language, I have alternated between "she" and "he" throughout the text when referring to child or parent, victim or abuser.

I often refer to "troubled parents" or "abusive or neglectful parents." Often, however, abuse is perpetrated by siblings, relatives, baby-sitters, teachers and others. Usually, these abusive and neglectful people are in a position of authority over the child, and often the child trusts and depends on them. Therefore their abuse also represents attachment exploitation and an abuse of power, as is more fully explained in Chapter Three. Readers who have been abused and neglected by people other than their parents will most likely find here resonances of their own experiences. Moreover, many of the survivors I interviewed had been abused and neglected by people other than their parents, and they give voice to the aftermath of those experiences as well.

When referring to a child, I use the terms "child" and occasionally "child victim." It is generally accepted that children still living with abusive or neglectful parents are "victims," and adults who have left those parents and are no longer being actively abused are referred to as "survivors." When referring to the many survivors who specifically belie the myth of "once damaged goods, always damaged goods," I use such phrases as "survivors who have fared well in life." Conversely, a phrase like "survivors who have not fared well in life" refers to formerly abused and neglected people who, at this particular point in time, have not prevailed over the injuries of trauma.

The twenty healthy survivors I interviewed in depth specifically for this book I refer to as "the survivors I interviewed," "the survivors I spoke with" and so on. I thought long and hard about coining a special term for them, because they have done so much more than survive; they have triumphed. "Survivor" connotes nothing of the vibrant colors and textures of their lives today. They have transformed their childhoods into adulthoods that are rich with strength, courage, compassion, wisdom, humor and impressive self-awareness.

In the end, I settled on the straightforward term "survivor." I hope it is appropriately respectful; I would not want to impose a rigid standard by which "good" survivors transform their experiences into a healthy life and "bad" survivors merely endure.

If we are to learn more about the possibilities of transformation, we must open our hearts and minds. Perhaps someday we will learn enough to improve our language to the extent that it will reflect the hope and health that "survival" alone does not capture.

ACKNOWLEDGMENTS

First and foremost, I am very grateful to Steve Bengis, Robert E. Longo and Diane Langelier of NEARI Press for giving this book a second chance. My literary agent, Frances Goldin, has known me since I was a "girl writer." I am so grateful to her, not only for her mighty talents as an agent but also for her generosity of spirit and clarity of thought. She continues to be one of my most valued friends. Each book strengthens and deepens our connection, and for this alone I could keep on writing.

I feel very fortunate to have had Becky Saletan as my editor at Random House. Early on, she inherited this project from my first editor, Pat Mulcahy, and saw it through with competence and vision. This book has been greatly influenced by Becky's wisdom and humor, and I especially appreciate her hard work and compassion in the "eleventh hour."

Many thanks to my administrative assistant, Kate Darling-Shur, who spent many hours making changes in the final manuscript. Hers was a tedious job, but she did it with grace and good humor.

Larry Rothstein helped me to organize the work. After I completed my research and interviews, he provided needed line editing and helpful comments on several of my drafts. Last, but not least, Larry introduced me to my new passion—Boston Celtics basketball games.

This book was written at the Writers' Room, which is sponsored by the Artists Foundation of Boston, Mass. I am thankful for the workspace and collegial atmosphere. Lewis Hyde, the foremost organizer of the Room, deserves special thanks. I enjoyed my camaraderie with the other writers: Nadya Aisenberg, Ruth Butler, David Eddy, Gail Fenske, Ivan Gold, Suzanne Gutman, Barbara Helgott Hyett, Sandra Jaffee, Cecily Morse and Pam Painter. My bonds of friendship with Debra Spark and Paul Tucker will reach far beyond the walls of the Room.

Within the Transportation Building, where the Writers' Room is located, I found much friendliness and support. Thank you to Toby Pearlstein, Irene Guthrie and George Sanborn of the State Transportation Library; Tim Salvesen of Mail Boxes Etc.; and Evelyn Freeman and Gerri Carrington of the Transportation Station.

Every book needs readers who comment on theory and narrative in the draft stages. James Hurley-Bruno and Phyllis Barajas donated much time, expertise and caring to this project, and my "most excellent" friend Maggie Close read the manuscript and provided stimulating discussion of the theories. Maggie is a great personal and professional teacher for me.

Bessel van der Kolk helped by giving Chapter Five an early reading. James Ritchie generously contributed his knowledge and constructive criticism to fine-tune the chapter. Bessel leads the Harvard University Trauma Study Group, which was a source of relevant thought and discussion during this project. My thanks to my colleagues there.

Several colleagues helped by sending the fruits of their research, referring survivors to be interviewed or consenting to being interviewed themselves. My gratitude to Suzanne Anderson, Jean Shinoda Bolen, John Briere, Tina Buchs, Anne Cohn, Joe Cruse, Sharon Wegscheider Cruse, Nick Etcheverry, Sherry Fine, David Finkelhor, Pam Freeman, Terry Hunt, Michael Hussin, Terry Kellog, Krishnabai Kee MacFarlane, Dusty Miller, Jane Middleton-Moz and Roland Summit.

In my work with juvenile sex offenders I have been privileged to work with two cotherapists. Kevin Creeden was the first, and he has greatly influenced my thinking and enjoyment of this work. Craig Latham and I have worked together since 1986, and our relationship provides me with much warmth and intellectual challenge. Thank you, Kevin and Craig.

I have been blessed with much love and friendship in my life and I appreciated it more than ever during the arduous months it took to complete my book. Thank you to Fran Adams; Cordelia Anderson; Walter Bera; Claudia Black; Linda Canfield Blick; Clara Bolden; Liza Brooks; Bill Devaney; Joe Doherty; Ed and Michael Fleming; Danny French; Cathy Ferguson; Mike, Mary Ann and Julie Germann; Georgia Green; Nick Groth; Fran Gutterman; Ginny Houston; John Humleker; Mary, Joshua and Ryan Hurley-Bruno; Sandy Lorentzen; Trudi Lanz; Bob McMackin; Kathy, Michael and Rachel Mathews; Joe, Adam and Matthew Mendola; Barbara and Sherman Okun; Tom O'Malley; Frank Pescosolido; Dianna Petrella; Jori Ross; Florence Rush; Skip Sauvain; Lee Schwartz; Paula and Jeffrey Stahl; Judy Starr; Sara Theiss; Cheryl,

Ben, Lisa, Tom, Phil and Irene Tschirhart; Andy Ward; Abby Weinberg; Ron Witmer; and my first love, John DeGolyer.

Freada Klein and Linda Getgen deserve special mention as extraordinarily good friends who have been especially supportive of me. What would I do without you?

I have had many guides in my journey and it is time, once again, to thank them: David Brittain, Susan Bandler, Thomas Davidow, Sharon Polk-Sadnowik, Cheryl Qamar Laham and Leona Koppel. Jim Kilpatrick is both an anchor and a beacon for me. Also, my love to the Monday morning gang: Bill, Dorothy, Eleanor, Marni and Sandy.

Although it is unusual to acknowledge people one does not know, thanks to Robert Parish and the Boston Celtics and to Bruce Springsteen and the E Street Band for the diversion their work has given me from mine.

Finally, I would not have missed the year of interviewing the twenty survivors whose experiences are recounted in this book for anything in the world. Each of you touched my life and inspired me with hope. Thank you for your honesty, courage, self-awareness and passion to heal. We are in this together.

CHAPTER ONE

"Once Damaged Goods ..."

Life is not a matter of holding good
cards but of playing a poor hand
well.

—ROBERT LOUIS STEVENSON

Rachel sits in a training session with other employee assistance staff from around Connecticut as a social worker like herself lectures on employees from dysfunctional families. He lists their characteristics: they could be work-addicted or totally unreliable; often they are substance abusers; they have problems with authority figures, seeing their mother or father in every supervisor; having lied to survive as children, they are frequently dishonest. They have one redeeming quality: they are fiercely loyal to their organization.

He's preaching to the converted, Rachel thinks to herself. Having grown up with parents who physically abused each other and Rachel and her two sisters, she understands the troubled family's legacy of pain. But what strikes her is the speaker's conviction that the survivor's situation is hopeless.

Rachel wonders why her therapist never told her she was at risk to physically abuse her adopted son and daughter. Or why she focused on Rachel's capacity to be a loving, persevering and optimistic person. Was I missing or denying in therapy? Rachel asked herself. Perhaps I was even *lying* to myself and everyone else, she worries.

By the middle of the afternoon session, Rachel can't take the speaker's endless negative comments. She raises her hand, stands up and says in a shaky voice, "You told us this morning that statistically almost half the adults in America have been affected by family violence, that *those* people, in turn, beat their kids, mainline heroin or go on food binges. First of all, some of that half is in this room. Secondly, I know there's a way out. Good people can come from bad families. That's true for our employees and it's true for us. We are everywhere." Rachel sits down to scattered applause.

The speaker defends himself: "I can only talk about what is statistically proven and these are the outcomes we know. I'm sorry if you have a problem with that."

Kenneth doesn't sleep well one summer evening. Waking in the morning with flu symptoms, he stays home from his carpentry job. He drifts in and out of sleep. After a while he becomes absorbed in a television talk show featuring male incest offenders. One by one, they recount their own sexual abuse as children, which they point to as the cause of their subsequent offenses: "That's where I learned it." "If it hadn't been for what they did to me, I wouldn't be in prison today." "It seemed normal to me."

Kenneth's fascination with this talk show extends beyond passing idle time. His father was a daily marijuana smoker and his mother used amphetamines to control her weight. They often left Kenneth in the care of a male baby-sitter who sexually abused him.

In the show's audience are many female sexual abuse survivors who angrily denounce the sex offenders' behavior and rationalizations. "Where are the female offenders, or the male survivors?" Kenneth wonders. While he agrees with some of the women, he wishes male survivors like himself were there to speak. The talk-show host, the offenders and their group therapist repeatedly stress that little-boy victims grow up to be adult sex offenders. Kenneth's wife, Darlene, also grew up in a substance-abusing family. When they met, Kenneth was concerned about what kind of parent he would be—"I didn't have the best of examples, you know." He told her of his sexual victimization. He and Darlene were married ten years before they had children. They now have a newborn son, David, and Kenneth wonders if his son is at risk to be molested by his own father.

The images of the sex offenders stayed in Kenneth's mind for days. Was he helpless too? After a few days he told Darlene about his fears. She assured him that he was not a sex offender. For years, she pointed out, he'd been around children, and he'd never been remotely interested in them sexually. Darlene added that she'd read in an infant psychology book that children stir up sexual feelings in both parents. "When this happens," she explained, "we should let each other know so we can transform these normal feelings into tenderness or admiration. It won't be so difficult. You'll see."

Yet, Kenneth's doubts linger, and he feels isolated. Is he the only abused man in the world who has not metamorphosed into an offender?

Kenneth has been going to an Adult Children of Alcoholics meeting for three years. He has made friends there, and has seen that those friends are good parents. At the next meeting Kenneth tells how the talk show has disturbed him. A friend, Bill, speaks of being sexually abused as a child. He admits that he, too, feels oppressed by the misconception that he must be an offender. Andy, a newcomer to the meetings, declares, "I'm a survivor too. I don't know if you do this at these meetings or not, but would the men who were sexually abused as children mind raising their hands?" It wasn't usually done, but they look around at each other, and slowly eight of the twenty-two men raise their hands. Kenneth and two other men begin to cry.

Rachel and Kenneth are ordinary adults with extraordinary childhoods. They belie the pernicious myth that all survivors of childhood trauma are doomed to inflict trauma on others or themselves, to become criminals, addicts or abusive parents, to repeat patterns of self-destruction or mental illness. Rachel and Kenneth would be the first to tell you they were hurt as children, but they have not passed on the violence to the next generation.

When I explained to people that the book I was writing would be based on interviews with healthy adults from abusive and neglectful families, many asked, "Are there any?" and expressed sympathy for the difficulty I must be having finding subjects. In fact I had more qualified interview volunteers than I knew what to do with. As Rachel said, they are everywhere. And they are unanimous in feeling that it is crucial for others to know that there is hope, that even given a rough childhood a normal adult life is possible.

To date, most studies have examined the psychopathology of survivors who came to the researcher's attention by way of criminal justice, mental health, chemical dependency treatment or social welfare agencies. Survivors not in need of or identified by those services were automatically excluded. Survivors who have the economic resources to be seen in private psychotherapy practices have also been excluded. As a result, our popular notions of what survivors of childhood abuse and neglect are like have been based on highly biased samples.

Previous researchers have also failed to analyze the roles of timing and motivation in the survivors' attempts to get help. Almost all the survivors I interviewed benefited from psychotherapy and participation in self-help groups. All went through difficult times in their twenties. The prognosis for them might have been guarded at that time, but by mid-life they had transformed themselves into healthy adults. Identifying one's problems and reaching out for help may be indicative more of health than of pathology.

This book is based on the salutogenic approach; that is, the question I asked was "What are the origins of health in survivors of family violence?" Most of the survivors I interviewed were at one point in their lives closer to the "disease" end of the continuum. How were they able to move steadily toward and eventually to secure their place at the "health ease" end? What went *right* in these survivors' lives, and what had they done right for themselves?

My belief that many adults overcome childhood abuse and neglect is based on more than the study of the survivors I interviewed. Psychologist Sarah Moskovitz extensively interviewed twenty-four adults who had been children imprisoned in Nazi concentration camps or forced into hiding to fend for themselves during World War II. She found twenty-two of these survivors living, loving and working well, a challenge to "the concept that early deprivation unalterably determines the course of life."

Contrary to previously accepted notions, we learn powerfully from these lives that lifelong emotional disability does not automatically follow early trauma, even such devastating, pervasive trauma as experienced here. Apparently, what happens later matters enormously. Whether it is the confidence of a teacher, the excitement of new sexual urges, new vocational interests, or a changed social milieu, the interaction can trigger fresh growth. We come to respect anew how children vary in their resilience, strengths, charm and ability to get affectionate care from those nearby. And we appreciate more deeply how unique is each person's struggle for competence, search for love, and making of a place for himself.[1]

In a forty-year longitudinal study of 456 youths at high risk for social and mental health problems, Dartmouth Medical School psychologist J. Kirk Felsman and psychiatrist George Vaillant found "evidence that the things that go right in our lives do predict future successes and the events that go wrong in our lives do not forever damn us."[2]

Projected Deficiency

If you are affected by the gloom and doom that permeates the media and the cluckings of helping professionals, it's hard to form an optimistic picture of a survivor's future. This lack of perspective and optimism has culminated in a sociological and psychological condition I term "projected deficiency," a malaise that in itself can diminish the quality of a survivor's life.

Projected deficiency begins in the family of origin. Abusive or neglectful parents rely heavily on the psychological defense of *projection:* "unacceptable impulses, attitudes, or feelings are attributed to others rather than the self."[3] Unconsciously the parent treats the child as a blank screen upon which he projects all of his inadequacy and unhappiness in an attempt to be rid of them. "If it weren't for this kid, *I* might be OK." "This kid—*not me*—is rageful, empty, disgusting, stupid, not good enough." The child is defenseless and too young to understand such a twisted, powerful dynamic.

Unfortunately, the media and helping professionals constantly reinforce this projected image, by continuing to disseminate the "Once damaged goods, always damaged goods" myth. When we hear of how pervasive and hurtful child abuse and neglect are, we often feel rageful, confused, sad, helpless and, most of all, inadequate to stop them. These are many of the feelings child victims have. When we do not know how to express those feelings constructively, we may project them onto the victims and survivors: *"Those* people must grow up to be rageful, con-fused, sad, helpless and inadequate adults. What else can we expect?" We have given away feelings too uncomfortable for us to bear.

As one of the survivors I interviewed put it, "You know, it wasn't enough that I had to hear from my family what a terrible, sick, damaged person I was for the first twenty years of my life. Now I no longer live with my family, but everywhere I turn, I am told people with my experiences are the scourge of this society, damaged beyond repair, human time bombs waiting to go off. I just can't get away from it."

With such overwhelming messages from both family and society, many survivors internalize the belief that they are damaged and un-worthy human beings. After all, if enough people call you a jackass, you might just go out and buy yourself a saddle. Like Kenneth and Rachel, many survivors "project" their deficiency into the future. "Sure, I look good now, but when am I going to hit bottom? Will I become an addict in my forties? If I have children, am I guaranteed sooner or later to beat them? Isn't it amazing I haven't been institutionalized—it must be a matter of time before I need to be." With forecasts of gloom and doom hanging over their heads, it's tough for survivors to rest easy, to be secure in their sense of inherent worth. On their deathbed, perhaps, they'll be able to look back on their lives and say, "Well, I never dumped abuse onto the next generation—I guess I was OK after all."

Sexual abuse researcher David Finkelhor eloquently reminds us:

> In the rush to draw public attention to the seriousness of the problem of child abuse, we have had the tendency to overstate the inevitability of its traumatic effects. Those who were abused as children also need reassurance that they are not permanently maimed, that many of their efforts to cope and put their past behind them have made them strong and capable individuals.[4]

Yet we tend to seek simplistic explanations, searching for the formula that will help to tame what overwhelms us and give us distance from what repulses us. When we are disturbed by a criminal, addicted or abusive parent, for example, we may say, "If it weren't for his abusive childhood, he wouldn't be acting this way." Unfortunately, such formulas can become life sentences. Where do they leave room for free will, the right and responsibility of chosing one's own behavior? By excusing abusive behavior from those who've been abused (including ourselves), we are denying them hope and health.

Projected deficiency and its corollary, the pernicious "once damaged goods" myth, are fueled by the misapplication of three psychological theories. Let us look at each in turn.

Intergenerational Transmission of Violence

The first and best known of the three theories holds that children who are victims of parental abuse or neglect inevitably follow in their parents' footsteps.

What Kenneth didn't know was that the much publicized statistic in the statement "80 percent of sex offenders were sexually abused as boys" was taken from studies of *incarcerated* offenders only.[5] Three groups of men were excluded from the study: convicted sex offenders who were not in prison, sex offenders who had not been arrested and *male survivors of sexual abuse who never become sex offenders.* Given that the more violent and repetitive the offender, the more likely he is to have been imprisoned, the study had examined a largely self-selecting group. In fact, the group had dramatically higher rates of *many* traumatic childhood circumstances, from bed-wetting to frequent relocations. It may be that each problem contributes separately, or it may be the *constellation* of problems that increases a person's chances of becoming an incarcerated sex offender.

Besides lacking such information, we also often mishear statistics. Many people scramble the conclusion, believing that "80 percent of boy victims will grow up to be sex offenders." I've often heard this misquote from parents of boys who were sexually abused by someone not in their family. The parents' knowledge of this "fact" compounds the immediate trauma they are struggling to cope with.

In fact, studies of adult sex offenders who can be treated on an outpatient basis with minimal risk to the community report a range of 0 percent to 50 percent rate of sexual victimization.[6] Many offenders in my psychotherapy groups tell me that they learned their abusive behavior from observing sexual abuse, being exposed to violent media images and pornography or being influenced by their peer group.

When a family court attorney told psychology professor Edward Zigler of a parent who "was denied custody of her children in a divorce case solely because she had been abused as a child," Zigler and a graduate student of his at Yale, Joan Kaufman, became concerned that "adults who were maltreated have been told so many times that they will abuse their children, that, for some, it has become a self-fulfilling prophecy." They reviewed the methodology and results of over forty studies. "The studies reported widely differing rates of abused children who become abusive parents—from 18 percent to at least 90 percent." Their own finding is that "between 25 percent and 35 percent of abused children maltreat their own offspring. Parents who did not repeat the cycle of abuse tended to have more extensive support from family and friends and were more openly angry about the abuse they experienced as children."[7]

Half of the survivors I interviewed in depth for this book have children; none have physically or sexually abused their children. As we will see, all of them have made a conscious effort to understand fully their troubled childhood and its effects. They have taken lessons from their traumas and developed sensitivity and skills that a nontraumatized parent might be less likely to have. Those with children displayed greater acceptance of their own and their children's vulnerabilities and were acutely aware of their impact on their children. All had done a remarkable job of unlearning their parents' bad examples. As Rob, the father of two daughters, put it, "It's like a bad movie. I know how it turns out. I'll never go back to see it again."

Abusive and neglectful behavior is not a contagious or terminal disease; it is learned. To be sure, parents are powerful role models, teaching children what constitutes "normal" family life, discipline, problem solving and expression of feelings. Not all children, however, blindly follow their parents down the path of destruction. Abusive and neglectful behavior can be unlearned and replaced with nonabusive behavior.

Children are taught not to swear, smoke or torment their siblings. In spite of our best efforts, they ignore or unlearn those norms and rules. The same is true for abusive and neglectful parental behavior.

Learned Helplessness

Between 1965 and 1969, psychologist Martin Seligman conducted experiments on approximately 150 dogs.[8] Each dog was put into a Pavlovian hammock (a device that restrains all movement) and given moderately painful shocks. The dogs were absolutely helpless—unable to anticipate, avoid or escape the shocks.

Twenty-four hours later Seligman put each dog into a chamber divided by a shoulder-high barrier. One side of the chamber was electrified; the dogs could escape being shocked only if they jumped the barrier. Each dog was tested on ten separate occasions.

Sixty-six percent of the dogs repeatedly endured the painful shocks, never learning to jump the barrier to escape the shock. However, *"33% of the dogs readily learned how to escape and repeatedly did so* [emphasis mine]."[9]

Both psychological theorists and therapists have extrapolated this study to human behavior—particularly that of women—theorizing that the experience of repeated victimization with no escape teaches helplessness. When nonabusive options are available, the victim fails to take advantage of them, resigned to her "fate" as a victim. As sociologist and domestic-violence researcher Edward Gondolf summarizes, "Battered women, as the theory goes, typically are conditioned to tolerate the abuse as a result of persistent and intermittent reinforcement from the batterer. The community lack of response to the abuse, and frequent accusation that the woman contributed to the abuse, furthers the helplessness. The cage door is shut, so to speak, and the women have no apparent way out."[10] Furthermore, early victimization supposedly predicts "career" victimization: little-girl victims grow up to be battered women, rape victims, self-mutilaters, drug addicts and prostitutes.

But Seligman's conclusion largely ignores the substantial number of dogs—a third—who escaped immediately and never returned to the electrified chamber. And Gondolf and his colleague Ellen Fisher believe that "learned helplessness" has been far too broadly ascribed to battered women. In their comprehensive survey of more than six thousand women in fifty Texas shelters they found that "the battered women appeared more as 'survivors' than as victims of 'learned helplessness.' They have actively tried to get help; in fact, they have contacted on average five different types of helping sources. Over half the women had contacted the police, and 20 percent had previously sought legal assistance prior to becoming a shelter resident. Nearly a third of the women had visited an emergency room at some time. Moreover, the more severe the abuse and antisocial behavior (substance abuse, arrests and general violence) from the batterer, the more different help sources were contacted. *The abuse that women experienced as a child and other background variables do not appear to significantly influence her helpseeking* [emphasis mine]."[11]

Unfortunately, belief in the inevitability of learned helplessness colors the attitude of too many helping professionals. Their lack of optimism and confidence in their clients can be psychologically contagious, undermining the survivors' belief in their own fundamental resiliency. In essence, the helper's attitude can "shut the cage door."

The survivors I interviewed had learned help*ful*ness. As children, most cared for brothers and sisters and tried to please their parents, hoping they could prevent the abuse. Being a caretaker earned them the esteem of people outside the family. Of course, any coping strategy will have both its strengths and weaknesses. Many of them acknowledge that their preoccupation with caring for others has at times been at the expense of developing other parts of themselves. But in the aftermath of a troubled childhood, they did "not give up, give in or give too little."[12]

Identification with the Aggressor

Finally, there is the widely held theory that posits that victims, unable to bear their helplessness and powerlessness, imitate the offender's abusive behavior to gain mastery of the trauma. In the child victim's experience, there are only two kinds of people in the world: victims and offenders. When he can no longer stand being a victim, his only choice is to become an offender.

Sex-role stereotyping distorts our understanding of this powerful dynamic. We tend to ascribe it almost exclusively to men, overlooking women who, through identification with their aggressors, become physically or sexually abusive. But we also overlook *men who never stopped identifying with the victim* and continue to hurt themselves or relate only to those who will hurt them.

The survivors I interviewed are aware of both the victim and aggressor within themselves. They struggle to accept both, yet they no longer identify with either. They have learned that most adults are neither victims nor offenders, and several have transformed their experiences as victims into meaningful work. Jenny, a pastoral counselor, says, "I can relate to the psychological dynamics of violence from the inside out. Because I've experienced the terror, degradation, self-disgust and I've come out onto the other side with self-respect, I can reach a hand back more skillfully and empathically. And at the same time, having survived, I can also be more objective. I *know* people can prevail over childhood abuse."

Predicting the Future

These three theories—intergenerational transmission of violence, learned helplessness and identification with the aggressor—are useful as psychological biopsies or postmortems. They can help us to trace the origins of problematic behavior. For survivors who momentarily or chronically exhibit victimizing behavior (of the self or others), these theories can be descriptive, accurate and helpful.

They do not, however, accurately *predict* the aftermath or dynamics for the *majority* of victims and survivors. Based on some of the alternative studies cited above and on my fifteen years of clinical experience, my estimate is that they apply to between 25 and 40 percent of children raised in abusive and neglectful homes. What the theories do best is help identify *potential* psychological issues that need to be addressed in treating child victims.

Those who share a common experience do not necessarily react in the same way. But if we study and discuss only the most negative outcomes, we will be blind to any other possibilities. An old Yiddish saying sums it up best: "When you are a worm in horseradish, the whole world is horseradish."

The "Bad Enough" Childhood

All theories and conclusions are subject to misinterpretation, and it is extremely important that the material in this book be considered with care. In particular, it is necessary to bear in mind that the childhood experiences of the survivors I interviewed were particularly—though not unusually—abusive. Moreover, each of these survivors had learned, in the course of recovery, to remember more fully and give voice to those experiences. If you know yourself to have been abused but find yourself minimizing or denying your experience, you might want to consider the possibility that you are doing so because, for the time being, you need to protect yourself.

Pioneering psychoanalyst D. W. Winnicott developed an important phrase in psychological thought: the "good enough" mother.[13] Early psychoanalytical theory held that parents could make their children neurotic through any number of subtle, often indiscernible mistakes. Winnicott contended that children need only a "good enough" mother—from which, of course, we can extrapolate also a "good enough" father. Such a parent has the child's best interests at heart, tolerates if not encourages the child's separation from himself and basically loves the child without shaming, neglecting or abusing her. Parents make mistakes, but if there is a core of health and unconditional love in the parent-child relationship, the child eventually takes the parent's mistakes and shortcomings in stride.

Given the epidemic scale of child abuse and neglect, I believe we are in need of a corollary concept: the "bad enough" parent, one who consistently puts his needs above the child's and demands that the child meet those needs at the expense of her own growth. The "bad enough" parent shames and ridicules the child, often blaming her for his own shortcomings. A "bad enough" parent's love is conditional, and his protection is in short supply. The "bad enough" parent does not always injure the child in dramatic or obvious ways. Infliction of any of the five traumas (physical abuse, sexual abuse, parental substance abuse, extreme neglect and the witnessing of domestic violence) qualifies.

As we've seen, the documented health and happiness of survivors of childhood trauma does not fit neatly into a simplistic "if . . . then" scheme. We must not therefore assume that the "exceptions" occurred because the trauma "wasn't so bad." Unfortunately, many survivors who love and work well today internalize this faulty thinking, failing to give themselves credit for healing. Others deny themselves the gifts of recovery, supposing they haven't suffered enough to earn them.

In his classic *Man's Search for Meaning,* philosopher and psychiatrist Viktor Frankl recounts his imprisonment in Nazi concentration camps. He believes that the enormity of his horrible experience in no way diminishes the pain of others who are not survivors of concentration camps: "A man's suffering is similar to the behavior of gas. If a certain quantity of gas is pumped into an empty chamber, it will fill the chamber completely and evenly, no matter how big the chamber. Thus suffering completely fills the human soul and conscious mind, no matter whether the suffering is great or little. Therefore the 'size' of human suffering is absolutely relative."[14] As a Chinese proverb says, "Nobody's family can hang out the sign 'Nothing the matter here.' "

If you have suffered, your suffering matters. My hope is that in reading this book, no matter how great or small the trouble you are seeking to overcome, you will discover strengths you didn't know you had.

It is also worth pointing out that in no way do I intend to suggest that abuse is good for children. One researcher concluded from his study of children with schizophrenic parents that "one is left with the impression that pain and suffering can have a steeling—a hardening—effect on some children."[15] This implies that being hard as steel is desirable. The survivors I spoke with say that being hard as steel is a difficult state to live in, particularly in their intimate relationships. Make no mistake about it: they've fared well in life *in spite of* troubled childhoods, not because of them.

In recent years, numerous celebrities have disclosed abusive childhoods. They have been courageous and effective in raising our awareness of child abuse and neglect, but we must guard against using these examples to minimize the impact of abuse: "How bad can it be if people turn out this creative and successful?" Maybe, we may imagine, they wouldn't have turned out to be so good at what they do if they hadn't been abused.

Psychologist J. Kirk Felsman and psychiatrist George Vaillant take issue with the label "invulnerable" that is so often used to describe survivors like the ones I've interviewed:

> One repeatedly reads and hears misguided reports of "superkids" and references to "invulnerability." The term "invulnerability" is antithetical to the human condition. Kierkegaard was right when he said, "Fear and annihilation dwell next door to every man." Perhaps it is this inner knowing that adds to our eager, even blind propensity for exaggeration and misinterpretation. If unqualified, our vision becomes my-

opic; human vulnerability is equated with weakness and invulnerability equated with strength. In bearing witness to the resilient behavior of high-risk children everywhere, a truer effort would be to understand, in form and by degree, the shared human qualities at work.[16]

Foremost "invulnerable children" researchers Lois Barclay Murphy and Alice Moriarty clarify further:

Along the continuum of vulnerability, children may be distributed in different numbers: few if any are so robust, so completely lacking in small as well as moderate or major handicaps as to be totally free from some zone of vulnerability. Most children have a *checkerboard of strengths and weaknesses, or an Achilles heel,* or a cluster of tendencies that interact in such a way as to produce one or another pattern of vulnerability as well as strength [emphasis mine].[17]

All human beings, traumatized as children or not, are "checkerboards of strengths and weaknesses." Perhaps with trauma the strengths are a little stronger and the weaknesses a little weaker.

We must not forget that before they could become strong, survivors were simply broken at the broken places. I can hear them reminding me that they are now and always will be mending. Mending means growth and health—they would never want to be finished with it.

To call them "invulnerable" denies the healthy and natural vulnerability of a child. To call them "resilient" brings to mind images of rubber bands being stretched to their limits, then bouncing back to their original shape. But what if the original shape was painful? And the stretching more painful still?

I am reminded of Rabbi Harold Kushner's loss of his fourteen-year-old son, Aaron, to a prolonged terminal illness:

I am a more sensitive person, a more effective pastor, a more sympathetic counselor because of Aaron's life and death than I would ever have been without it. And I would give up all of those gains in a second if I could have my son back. If I could choose, I would forgo all of the spiritual growth and depth which has come my way because of our experiences and be what I was fifteen years ago, an average rabbi, an indifferent counselor helping some people and unable to help others, and the father of a bright, happy boy. But I cannot choose.[18]

None of us can choose our parents or our childhoods. And none of us are responsible for the way we were treated—good or bad—as children. We are, however, responsible for what we do with our childhoods. Do we chose to heap our experiences on the next generation? Or perpetually heap abuse upon ourselves? Or do we rise above it, embrace both the strength and vulnerabilities, and get on with our lives?

It is possible not to be responsible for a problem yet still to be responsible for its solution. Above all, it is the sense of personal responsibility, self-awareness and belief in choices and courage that distinguish survivors who have fared well in life in spite of the trauma of their childhoods.

Esther, one of the most seriously abused survivors I interviewed, puts it best: "I feel so proud of myself for not letting the abuse kill me. From knowing other survivors as well as my own experience, I am so impressed with the courage and spirit it takes to come out of this childhood. It's not just that we function, that we are not all in institutions. We've managed to maintain a sense of life as being precious and wonderful. I am proud of who I am."

Trauma

> When on all sides assailed by
> prospects of disaster . . . the soul of
> man . . . never confronts the totality
> of its wretchedness. The bitter drug
> is divided into separate draughts for
> him; today he takes on part of his
> woe; tomorrow he takes on more;
> and so on, till the last drop is
> drunk.
>
> —HERMAN MELVILLE
> *Pierre*

So many people look up to Amy. She is warm, quick-witted, compassionate and smart—she seems to be one of those women who "have it all." Amy is a successful stock broker: last year her commissions were the second highest in the established Wall Street firm where she works.

Amy doesn't bask in the respect and caring people show her, however. She describes herself as having "everything I want but nothing I need." She dates only occasionally, even though she meets plenty of men. When a relationship becomes more than casual, she "turns into the wicked witch of the West," flaring up over the smallest decision—who does the dishes or where to go for the weekend. Her outbursts escalate until the man dumps her. At first, Amy feels relieved—the pressure's off, but after a while she lapses into depression. On some level she suspects she'd have some of what she wants if only she could tolerate being close to a man, but she understands little of why she feels and behaves the way she does.

Amy believes she has left her "sick and perverted family behind forever." She never contacts her alcoholic and sexually abusing father or her two violent brothers. The last time she was home was for her mother's funeral. Rose had overdosed on hundreds of hoarded nerve pills, tranquilizers the family doctor had been prescribing for over twenty-five years.

Yet Amy has not escaped her past. She's plagued with "home movies," unwanted mental images "in Technicolor with Dolby Sound" of her father battering her mother or her father or brothers sexually and physically abusing her. Before her mother's funeral, Amy could turn off the "home movies"—she'd read, study stock market reports or repeat a childhood ritual, reciting the alphabet to herself backward. But lately these distractions haven't worked as well, and the movies now contain scenes of Amy killing her father and brothers. Amy feels as if she were "going crazy. I've got a serial killer inside of me, waiting to get out."

If Amy's waking hours are bad, her nights are worse. No matter how exhausted she is, she wakes up, startled, forty-five minutes after she goes to sleep. This timing is not coincidence. Her mother was obese and had to sleep on her back. Amy's brothers or father would wait until the snoring started—about forty-five minutes—before they would come in to force Amy to have sex with them. When Amy finally manages to get back to sleep, her nightmares begin.

On the morning of her thirtieth birthday, Amy woke up and thought, What now? As a child, she never expected to live to thirty: "I was sure my father or brothers would kill me. I assumed I had to accomplish as much as possible in the few years I had."

Relationships and intimacy were the "What now?" for Amy. This was new territory, harder to conquer through willpower and perseverance. Amy did have good women friends but none knew about the "home movies," or even that she had been a victim of childhood abuse.

Amy felt worn out. She was having increasing difficulty controlling her thoughts and sleeping; for the first time, she began to think about suicide. So when her best friend, Jane, invited Amy to vacation in the Caribbean, Amy thought the change of scene might do her good.

As Amy relaxed she began to talk to Jane about her recent listlessness, and slowly she revealed the dark secrets of her past. When Amy got back from vacation, she began to see a therapist. At first she would talk only about her mother, but after a year she finally answered her therapist's periodic questions about physical and sexual abuse. He told Amy he was sorry about her abuse, and she knew she could trust him. It mattered that someone finally apologized to Amy for the violence done to her.

Amy worked with the therapist for two years, then entered group therapy with other survivors of abuse. She has begun to feel much better about herself. A few friends now know about her past. On the anniversary of Rose's death, Jane and two other friends surprised Amy by bringing dinner over to her condo. The home movies still run, but not as frequently. "It's been like putting the pieces of a jigsaw puzzle together—connecting the memories at night with the panic or despair during the day, and all of that to my fears around men. With each 'showing of my home movies' to my friends, therapist or group, my past has less power over me. Someday I will be able to tolerate, even enjoy, closeness with a man without being reminded of my own family. I have all the time in the world. Right now, I am more accepting of myself and my past. What happened to me was wrong, but there is nothing wrong with me."

Trauma

Amy is a survivor of the five types of childhood trauma listed in the Preface. I have focused on these traumas because of what they have in common—the abuse of parental authority and the exploitation or misuse of children's dependence on adults for survival.

Trauma specialist and psychotherapist Frank Pescosolido believes that "what is most tragic about child abuse and neglect is the exploitation of the child's attachment to the parent."[1] To be sure, it is far easier to abuse one's own children, precisely because their love and loyalty to the parent render them much more compliant than they would be to a stranger. It is exactly this attachment exploitation that teaches children they are not safe in relationship to other human beings.

As psychiatrist Brandt Steele reminds us in his article "Notes on the Lasting Effects of Early Child Abuse Throughout the Life Cycle":

Physical abuse itself does not necessarily cause trouble. Most people have had physical injuries, fractures or burns during childhood due to purely accidental causes and they have not been harmed by it because they have been comforted and cared for by good caregivers at the time of the incident. Damage comes when the injuries are inflicted by those to whom one looks for love and protection, and there is no relief from the trauma. The same is true of sexual abuse in some ways. It is not the simple sexual act itself, except in cases of forcible, physically damaging rape to young children, that causes the trouble. It is the emotional and psychological setting in which the sexual maltreatment occurs, and with whom it has occurred, that makes the difference and causes lasting damage. If simple sexual contacts of touching, fondling, or even intercourse were seriously damaging in themselves, most adolescents who have been through high school and college would be in much more serious difficulty than we commonly see. At such times sexual activity is more age-appropriate and involves conscious consent. Sexual activity is abusive when a child of any age is exploited by an older person for his own satisfaction while disregarding the child's own developmental immaturity and inability to understand the sexual behavior.[2]

Children are born into the world absolutely helpless and dependent on others for food, warmth, cleanliness and protection from threat. Children's natural and healthy helplessness is transformed into terror and despair when those needs are ignored or when a parent plays "Let's make a deal" with the child's needs—"I will tolerate your dependence on me *only* in exchange for sexual abuse of you or for your silence about violence in our family."

Childhood should be a time of no-risk dependency. The five types of trauma we will examine create high-risk dependency. Many children, in desperation, learn to care prematurely for themselves—at the expense of their trust in others, emotional growth and self-acceptance. Unfortunately, try as they might, such children can never absolutely ensure their survival, simply because it is never absolutely within their control.

What Didn't Happen Afterward

Try as they may, parents cannot always protect their children from trauma. A relative dies. The house burns down. Bigots attack the family's ethnic origins or religious beliefs. The child witnesses a fatal car accident or street shooting. The child is molested by someone outside the family and terrorized into keeping the secret. Yet children can survive intact emotionally if adults provide them with a sense of safety and well-being in the aftermath of traumatic events.

Realistic, protective and compassionate treatment by adults can become more meaningful than the trauma itself, thus lessening its long-term effects. However, when the source of the trouble is within the family, realism, protection and compassion are usually in short supply. It is often not so much what actually happened that causes the "persistent negative effects" of trauma as the absence of healing responses, what *didn't* happen afterward.

Most important are responses that validate the reality of the trauma: "I believe you. Yes, you perceive reality correctly. Something terrible and wrong did happen to you and it wasn't your fault." In troubled families, the abuser or abusers are unlikely to admit to misdeeds. Often, as in Amy's case, there is a neglectful or nonprotective parent who denies the trauma as well, not wanting to "rock the boat" and incur the abuser's wrath.

Suppose that in the midst of a tornado a child sought comfort and protection from his parents and was told, "What tornado? It's a beautiful day. Go out and play." That's how crazy and unsafe the world seems to some children. Some of the survivors I interviewed had tried to tell the truth about the abuse and were called liars or accused of being responsible for the abuser's behavior. "It never happened," they were told, or "That isn't so bad," "It could be worse, you know," "It was for your own good."

Rita had been physically abused by her mother for as long as she could remember. Her father began to abuse her sexually at age eleven. "One day, I ran into the bathroom and locked the door to get away from him. He called for my mother, who ordered me to open the door. When I did, she hit me for disobeying my father. That day, I realized there would be no safety in my house."

As a college student, Rita began to see a counselor for severe depression. "She never asked me anything about abuse, which made me feel ashamed, like 'This must be *really* horrible if we can't even speak of it.' Finally, I couldn't bear the secret. I had to tell someone and she was it. Her only response to my disclosure of five years of sexual abuse by my father was 'That happens sometimes.' We never discussed it again."

When a victim or survivor is disbelieved, shamed, threatened into silence, or when the disclosure is minimized or becomes cause for punishment, the trauma inflicted by willful ignorance compounds the original trauma. Children can withstand a lot with the help of other people; conversely, the denial or rejection of children's normal thoughts and feelings about trauma can cause as much pain as the original trauma.

In the aftermath of trauma, children also need encouragement to express their feelings and to have those feelings affirmed. "Tell me how you feel," or "Of course you're scared, hurt, angry, confused. I would be too if I were in your shoes." As Thoreau put it, "It takes two to tell the truth: one to say it and another to hear it." Yet, too often, no one wants to hear about the child's feelings, and persistence in expressing them can bring about more abuse.

Christina was diagnosed at age four as having neurosensory loss, a condition that made her progressively deaf. She was in speech therapy several times a week from age five to eighteen. "You know, speech therapy is a very intimate process. We touch one another's face and neck and it is about successful communication. I often say I made it through the hell at home because of my connection to my speech therapists."

Christina's "hell at home" was made up of a psychotic and sexually abusing mother, a father ashamed of her deafness who beat her for disobeying orders she could not hear, and a schizophrenic older brother who constantly grabbed at her breasts. "Neither our neighbors nor our relatives came to visit us. Still, I hoped and prayed someone would *see* some of the abuse and help me, ask me about it. When I was thirteen, I had a speech therapist named Eva. One night, when she dropped me off, her car broke down near our house. The next day, she came back with her husband, a psychologist, to pick up the car. They were outside fussing with the car when my brother flew out of the house with my father in pursuit. My father didn't see them. He picked up a fallen branch and hit Wayne in the head, cutting his scalp open. Eva and her husband grabbed Wayne, put him in their car and took him to the hospital, where he got eleven stitches. I wanted so much for them to come to me and say, 'That was awful, that was wrong. Has that happened to you? I feel terrible about that. How do you live with it?' The least Eva could have done was to ask me how I felt. But she never said anything. I was frozen inside and couldn't say anything to her. The therapeutic relationship felt phony after that."

Today, someone in the professional position of Eva or her husband could be in serious trouble for not making a mandated report to the local child protection agency. Prior to 1973, however, no one was required to report child abuse or neglect. Still, historical context does not lessen Christina's sense of betrayal.

To minimize the damage of trauma, children also need protection from further harm. But in a troubled family it is not in the abuser's best interest to teach the child how to prevent further abuse. The nonprotective parent who denies or minimizes the abuse is usually passive. The child is usually left on his own to figure out the best way to protect himself, as Rita was: "Both of my parents were alcoholics. When my Dad was sober, he was sheepish, and when my mother was sober, she was arrogant, nasty and violent. Conversely, when my father was drunk, he was violent and sexually abusive and my drunk mother would be quiet and sullen. I mixed drinks for them at six years old and I figured out to put less liquor in my father's drink and three times the liquor in my mother's drink. I knew enough to keep my father sober and my mother drunk."

Finally, trauma is mitigated when children have time to heal from one trauma before they are subjected to another. The survivors I interviewed considered themselves "lucky" if they had a week or month between traumatic family episodes. Like Daryl, many lived in neighborhoods marked by violence, racism, religious persecution or class oppression, which compounded the domestic strife. Daryl's segregated housing project had three buildings for blacks and ten buildings for whites. When the white teenagers weren't "rocking" (having rock fights) with Daryl and the other black youths, Daryl "was the butt of constant jokes and bullying from other blacks" because he was by far the darkest. "This was the 1940s, before 'Black Is Beautiful.' " Daryl's father was an alcoholic who became so agoraphobic that he could not work. Conflict between his parents often erupted into violence, which Daryl had to break up in the middle of the night. Yet his "most painful memory of childhood is being tormented by the other kids and being ashamed of how I looked."

One of Vinnie's worst memories is of public humiliation: "On Tuesdays we had to bring an extra dime for milk and a cupcake. Most weeks, my family just didn't have it. I can still hear it, in front of the class, the nun saying loudly, 'Vincent Abruzzi—do you mean your family doesn't even have a *dime*?' "

The survivors I interviewed rarely if ever benefited from the compassionate and reasonable reactions that would have lessened the effects of their troubled childhoods. Given the enormity of what *didn't* happen after their traumas, it isn't surprising that they entered adulthood numb or anxious or both. Protective numbing and reactive anxiety are, after all, normal reactions to abnormal situations.

Dissociation: When the Heart and Mind Go Numb

Clearly, people were not meant to be physically or sexually abused. Human beings are not equipped to understand abuse as it happens, nor to feel the full force of their physiological and emotional response at the time. And they cannot, at that moment, find meaning in the experience of the abuse. Each of these important elements of *accommodation* can happen only later, in distinct stages.

A relatively insignificant experience as an adult gave me new insights into the challenges of accommodation for children. One night I was rushing to a support group for women directors of sex abuse treatment units in the Boston area. I was late, exhausted and not being careful. The meeting was at a Harvard Square restaurant located in a basement. At the top of the outside stairs, I tripped and fell headfirst down the stairs. I lay stunned, facedown on rough brick, my skirt wrapped around my upper body. Three strangers rushed over to help. One man asked if I could move my hands and legs. Disregarding his question, I noticed that my right shoe was missing. I spotted it at the top of the stairs and began to crawl after it. All I could think was "Somebody is going to steal that shoe if I don't get it, and then how will I get home?" I was unaware of physical pain or emotional fright or embarrassment, which would have been normal responses to such an experience. Unable to comprehend what had just happened, I found myself obsessed with an irrelevant detail.

As it turned out, I had seriously injured my right ankle and would need months of physical therapy to repair the damage. Within a few minutes, I began to become aware of what had happened and of a constant throbbing pain in my ankle. I talked out my feelings about the

fall with my friends inside the restaurant and later with the X-ray techni-
cian in the hospital emergency room. A few days later I was able to find
some meaning in the event. Clearly, on both a real and a symbolic level,
I needed to slow down. (And, incidentally, while in a wheelchair for
two weeks I discovered how inaccessible most "accessible for the handicapped" buildings are.)

Living in a violent family is like falling down the stairs every day, every
week, every month.

Survivors commonly speak of how they endured trauma by pretending that their mind and spirit had gone to a safer place, leaving the body
behind to endure the abuse:

"I pretended it was happening to someone else and I was just a
spectator."

"I pretended I was asleep."

"I did my math problems in my head."

"I counted the flowers on the wallpaper."

"I played music in my head."

"I counted the number of blows so I wouldn't cry."

"In my mind, I would carry on both sides of a very pleasant conversation while my father was raping me."

Abused children abandon reality, dissociating mind from body so
that they won't be overwhelmed and their ability to cope won't be
shattered. Even a relatively minor trauma like my falling down the stairs
can provoke dissociation: I worried about my shoe being stolen (instead
of feeling hurt, afraid or embarrassed) and my body was numb until
later, when I was better able to integrate the experience. "Later" in the
case of chronic abuse, particularly where the child victim has no support, may mean years later.

In the short run, dissociation is a very effective defense, walling off
what cannot be accommodated. I think of dissociation as the cryonics
of trauma, designed to put parts of the trauma into deep freeze until
a "cure" can be discovered. Sometimes the actual memory of the abuse
goes into deep freeze. An incident in the present may trigger strong
feelings that really belong to an incident in the past that the survivor
is unable to remember. The survivor may become enraged by what
merely annoys others, devastated when others are momentarily sad,
panicked when others are just worried. Present events tap into a deep
well of feelings whose source remains elusive.

Until recently Joan did not understand "those inexplicable waves of sadness" she would feel when she saw pink hem tape: "Now I've always remembered sleeping alone in the attic on a metal cot, terrified of the dark. My stepmother would try to catch me with the light on and would hit me if she caught me. In this last round of therapy, I remembered tying my pink hem tape from seventh-grade home economics class to my big toe and then tying the other end to the light chain. When I heard her footsteps, I'd give the hem tape a yank and quickly turn the light off."

When asked what her worst memory from childhood is, Christina replied, "My worst memory has yet to surface."

Sometimes only the feelings about the trauma go into deep freeze. Some survivors have perfect, excruciatingly detailed recall of the abuse itself but are numb to their feelings. Their hearts are in deep freeze. They do fine when they are not provoked to feel much. They may avoid friendships and romance, or enter into them only on their own terms. They believe their feelings are as troublesome and overwhelming today as their parents once told them they were. They are numb to feelings as a way to keep control.

Glen is a model of self-restraint and has prevailed over a childhood in which he was profoundly neglected and witnessed scenes of murderous rage between his parents. He believes his "emotional flatness" contributed to his recent divorce. "Feeling vulnerable feels like being pre-verbal again. I'm giving myself a break from relationships because whenever I become vulnerable to the other person, I feel like a helpless toddler."

For others, both memories and feelings are in deep freeze. Survivors find their bodies reacting or behaving in ways that were life-giving at the time of the trauma but have outlived their usefulness now that the threat is gone. They may find themselves curled up in a fetal position, protecting their heads with their arms, and not know why they are behaving like this. They have no recollection of a time long ago when they needed to protect their heads from life-threatening blows and punches.

Elaine was knocked unconscious several times as a child. "Today, I don't have memories. I have re-experiences. I'll be minding my own business when my body will go limp and tremble. My mind is blank and I can't control my muscles."

Many survivors ask, "If I don't remember the trauma, or if I don't have strong feelings about it, isn't that better? Shouldn't I let sleeping dogs lie?" Therapist Janet Yassen, my colleague, asks rape victims and incest survivors who pose this question, "What would you do if I demanded, *'Don't* think about the word "elephant"? Whatever you do, just don't think about it!' You would probably think about it more, or obsessively think about how you are not supposed to be thinking about it." And so it goes with attempts not to think or feel about childhood trauma. Dissociation eventually takes far more psychic energy than it is worth. The more we try not to, the more thoughts and feelings assert themselves, unconsciously demanding our attention. It takes an enormous toll to keep perfectly legitimate memories and feelings about childhood trauma in deep freeze. In the long run, one is better off letting the thaw happen and, with the support of others, participating in some manner of "cure" that will allow life to go on.

Post-traumatic Stress Disorder

What Amy—so poised, self-confident, productive and goal-oriented on the outside, so fearful on the inside that she might "go crazy"—didn't know was that she had a highly recognizable and treatable anxiety disorder called post-traumatic stress disorder (PTSD), which has been associated with survivors of the Vietnam war, the Holocaust, mass murders, natural disasters, rape, kidnapping, accidents, torture and other extraordinary events.

In the late nineteenth century Sigmund Freud published accounts of the prevalence and long-term damage done by family violence to his patients. Unfortunately, psychiatrists learned too much, too quickly about the horrors of trauma. Historically, whenever people in authority give others permission to talk about family violence, the floodgates open. The unhappy truth is that child victimization was and is commonplace. Psychiatrists realized that if what Freud's patients told him about their childhoods was true, nothing short of a total overhaul of the structures of family life was in order. Freud buckled under the pressure of his colleagues' criticism (often anti-Semitic in nature) of his early trauma theories, and retreated into denial and misinterpretation of his patients' early victimization;[3] physical and sexual abuse must be fantasy born of the patient's sexual desire for one parent and jealous aggression against the other.

Survivors like Amy who are coming to terms with their childhoods and fear they are "going crazy" are too often told, "That's right—you are crazy. The abuse is all in your head." Fortunately, Amy's therapist recognized the symptoms of PTSD, knew how to ask questions about trauma and patiently sat with her until she developed enough trust so she could talk about her father and brothers. By self-report or their therapist's diagnosis, the majority of the survivors I interviewed suffered from PTSD as adults.

Because different diagnoses indicate different paths of treatment, Amy's therapist was thorough and cautious in his assessment of Amy's problems. He relied on *The Diagnostic and Statistical Manual of Mental Disorders (III-R),* [4] the authoritative reference for psychotherapists. Let's examine the criteria for Amy's disorder.

First, a person with PTSD must have "experienced an event that is outside the range of usual human experience [that] would be markedly distressing to almost everyone." Amy's childhood certainly qualified.

Second, people with PTSD often reexperience the trauma in their minds, involuntarily recalling it. Amy experienced both intrusive recollections ("home movies") and nightmares. When the memory brings on a physiological response or a feeling this is called an *abreaction:* "the release of emotional tension through the recalling of a repressed traumatic event" [5] Often the situation that brings on the abreaction is reminiscent of the original trauma. Joan's reaction to pink hem tape is a good example. Thelma is embarrassed by the tenacity and "poor manners" of her childhood demons: "Friends and I were driving along in the most beautiful parts of the French Riviera. We'd missed lunch by a couple of hours and the weather was a bit damp. My hunger pangs turned me into the street urchin I'd been *fifty* years before, growing up in the Depression without enough to eat or warm clothes. Not only did I demand food and vilify my friends, but my panic didn't subside until after I'd gotten a hot meal."

An abreaction could be triggered by something someone says ("Do it or else" or "Who do you think you are?"—even said jokingly), circumstances such as the press of a crowd, being left totally alone, a darkened room or a particular season of the year, smells, touch, tastes or the like associated with the trauma. Suddenly, the survivor is transported as if in a time machine to the event of the original trauma and reacts with the emotional intensity that would have been appropriate then though not now. During an abreaction it is difficult to distinguish "what was" from "what is."

Herein lie some of the Achilles heels for the survivors I interviewed. They function well in many aspects of life *until* they encounter the events or circumstances that are likely to trigger abreactions: emotional vulnerability, physical illness and invasive medical procedures like surgery, struggles with authority figures, cultural oppression or abandonment, to name just a few. Yet to keep the survivor's reactions in perspective, it should be mentioned that adults who *weren't* traumatized as children often feel anxious, vulnerable, "not myself" in the same situations, even if the degree of intensity tends to be greater for the survivor.

Third, a person with PTSD lives with a "persistent avoidance of stimuli associated with the trauma or numbing of general responsiveness." The avoidance might include such details of daily life as eating, hygiene, working, going out of the house, or, in Amy's case, having someone in her bed, because it triggers memories and feelings belonging to an unresolved trauma. Survivors with PTSD may avoid any intimate connection, often resulting in "feelings of detachment or estrangement from others." Survivors often have highly developed social skills and may seem to be extremely extroverted, but their dealings with others may preclude vulnerability. They can talk about work or movies or the weather, but they have difficulty expressing their feelings. Or they may have "constricted feelings." They may be unable to identify and express a wide range of emotions, particularly the anger, fear and sadness so closely associated with the original traumatic events.

Finally, a survivor with PTSD would have at least two of the following symptoms persistently since suffering the trauma: hyperalertness or exaggerated startle response (as if one's radar were highly attuned or oversensitive to reminders of the trauma); sleep disturbance (insomnia to avoid nightmares or oversleeping to avoid events that might trigger the trauma in waking life); guilt about surviving when others haven't; memory impairment or difficulty in concentrating; "physiological reactivity upon exposure to events that symbolize or resemble an aspect of the traumatic event (e.g., a woman who was raped in an elevator breaks out in a sweat when entering any elevator)."

There are, of course, many degrees of PTSD. Amy's case was moderate until her mother's death. Under that stress and exacerbated by her thirtieth birthday, the disorder progressed and was diminishing her vitality until she began to talk about and resolve the trauma in therapy.

Certain circumstances can make the disorder longer lasting and more severe. If a trauma is repeated, for instance, as in chronic physical or sexual abuse, then the disorder might persist more than it would after only one incident. But this does not minimize the impact of a single rape or battering incident. For example, psychologist Lenore Terr's longitudinal research on the Chowchilla kidnapping case (where a school bus full of children was hijacked and buried underground) shows that a single traumatic incident can have a profound impact on survivors, resulting in diminished optimism and ability to plan for the future, memory loss and prolonged anxiety.[6] However, repetition does not seem to make one immune to the consequences of trauma. Rather, it has a cumulative effect, as unresolved trauma is layered upon unresolved trauma.

Traumatic events that are human in origin (violence, torture, bombings) seem to have more severe aftereffects than natural disasters (earthquakes, fires, tidal waves). Hurtful and frightening as it is to be raped or beaten by a stranger, or to be in the path of a natural disaster, the creation of a personal disaster by a loved one is vastly more bewildering and overwhelming.

The final circumstance that contributes to the persistence of PTSD is the victim's age. The younger the victim, the more vulnerable he is. The more developmental skills and life experiences uncontaminated by trauma a child has, the more resources she has to draw on in the face of trauma. When life goes well, and children are loved and protected, each day is like a deposit in a savings account. Neglect, repeated physical or sexual assault or other life-threatening events make huge withdrawals on the account. The more a child has in the bank when trauma strikes, the better the prognosis for a quick recovery. Small children who are repeatedly traumatized usually have few deposits and easily become emotionally bankrupt. However, it is not impossible to "make up the deficits" after the trauma, as Amy learned to do.

Integration of Trauma

As a child, Rita was befriended by a Native American medicine man, who told her to never forget the violence in her family: "He taught me to take a mental snapshot of it, frame it, and then put the frame facedown. He said it would always be there, and when I was ready, I would pick it up, look at it and begin dealing with it. I couldn't think clearly or feel fully about the abuse as a child. But now I can look squarely at the trauma."

When the survivor is ready to turn the picture over, memories and feelings begin to reconnect. He or she *remembers,* with the mind and heart, instead of *dis*membering through dissociation. When Jenny was seven years old, her father threw her across the kitchen for "adding too much salt to the gravy." A full forty years later she was heating up drippings for gravy. "I still wasn't used to using my stove from my wheelchair. [Two years before, Jenny had been in a serious car accident resulting in the amputation of her right leg.] I overheated the drippings and the grease splattered in my face. It was so painful. I told my husband, 'You're going to hear some strange noises, but please don't interrupt me.' I wheeled into my bedroom, took one of my crutches and pounded it on my bed, sobbing and screaming, 'I hate it, I hate it, I hate it.'" Later, Jenny understood that "it" was not so much her disability as it was the sharp and unpredictable pain to her face—both forty years ago and in the present.

The beginning of the process of reconnection is usually attributed to the fortuitous occurrence of a trigger—an event or circumstance obviously associated with or reminiscent of the original trauma, such as Jenny experienced. But, as a psychotherapist, I have noticed that there must always be the simultaneous occurrence of a "positive trigger" before reconnection can begin; for instance, the survivor may have found someone trustworthy to talk to (therapist, friend, partner, support group) and may finally feel safe and sane enough to explore and accept her feelings. Other positive triggers might include the death of an abuser, changes in life circumstances, such as getting a promotion or an inheritance, learning self-defense or becoming physically fit, or moving to a safer neighborhood. Even seemingly stressful events, such as admission to a psychiatric hospital or substance abuse treatment facility, can provide the safety and structure that finally allow the survivor to face the childhood trauma squarely, with both heart and mind. In Jenny's case the positive triggers were her relationship to her husband and a spiritual experience, which she discusses in Chapter Nine.

The pain and disorientation of reconnection can be balanced by focusing on the positive trigger. During this process I ask my clients, "Why now? Why didn't you remember or feel this six months ago, two years ago, five years ago?" They may speak of seeing a child who resembles themselves at the time of the trauma; reading an article about abuse or watching violent movies. Yet, often these circumstances have existed in the past and the question remains, "Why now?" The answer lies in the conjunction of this trigger with the positive trigger, which tells the survivor, You can afford to reconnect now—you have power, judgment, insight and support you truly did not have as a child. It is safe enough."

Dissociation and many of the coping strategies associated with PTSD eventually fall into something I call *healthy obsolescence* as survivors' adult lives become less traumatic. Rather than clinging to what had once been highly adaptive behaviors or dwelling on self-loathing because these behaviors had been discovered to be obsolete, the survivors I interviewed had gone about transforming what had once served them well. At a crafts fair many years ago, I bought an unsigned calligraphed saying that captured this process:

> And then the day came
> When the risk to remain tight
> In a bud was more painful
> Than the risk it took to blossom.

Walling off parts of the trauma was once the solution to an unbearable situation. Eventually, it causes problems in the body, mind, heart and spirit, in one's relationships with the child within and with others, and in one's work. In the following chapters, we will see how trauma— if left unresolved—is destined to be reenacted in one of these vital aspects of the self. We will also learn how, slowly but surely, with compassion and perseverance, survivors have taken down those walls, brick by brick.

CHAPTER THREE

Lies of the Mind

To recognize frankly that a mother
is exploiting you for her own ends,
or that a father is unjust and
tyrannical, or that neither parent
ever wanted you, is intensely painful.
Moreover it is very frightening.
Given any loophole, therefore, most
children will seek to see their
parents' behavior in some more
favorable light. This natural bias of
children is easy to exploit.

—JOHN BOWLBY
Separation

I f I were facing two doors, one marked 'heaven' and the other marked
'lecture about heaven,' I'd go to the lecture," Paul tells me with his
usual self-deprecating humor. No one can lecture on hell like Paul. He
spent the first seven years of his life there.

His mother gave birth to Paul after being raped by a stranger at the
age of nineteen. Patsy prosecuted the rapist—a gutsy move for a factory
worker in the mid-1940's—but his conviction and court-ordered child
support did not ease Patsy's pain. She loved Paul and tried to care for
him, but was overwhelmed by depression and instability. Paul's early
years were a ping-pong existence: a few months in a Catholic orphanage
where Patsy would leave him alternating with a few months with Patsy.

When Paul was four, Patsy met Hank, a foreman in the factory where
she worked. Three months later they married. Hank's mother, Millie,
and her six-year-old son, Jeb, moved in with them. Paul recalls, "Hank

was the meanest person I've ever been around. Patsy felt like she wasn't worth much. It didn't help that he kept on telling her she was lucky he married her. His mother would chime in about what a burden Patsy and I were to them. Hank didn't like the way I ate at the table. He put newspapers down in the corner of the kitchen, moved my dish to the corner and made me eat like a dog."

Paul remembers looking up at Hank from the floor and thinking, This guy is crazy. When Patsy was away, Hank would order Paul to stand against a wall, then sit in a chair across the room, point his rifle at Paul and repeatedly pull the trigger. Paul never knew beforehand if the rifle was loaded or not. To survive, he focused on Hank's craziness while denying his own fear. This worked: he did not give in to terror, and he took the abuse less personally. When Hank and Millie told Paul how bad he was, Paul fixed on what he saw: Hank was out of control.

"Once when I was five Hank sent me to the store to get him a bottle of pop. On the way home I accidentally broke the bottle. I remembered I had enough change from the quarter to get another bottle. When I got home, Hank wanted his change. It was a dime short and he started a prisoner-of-war interrogation. When I insisted I didn't know what had happened to the dime, he announced he was going down to beat up the shopkeeper for cheating him. I knew that would be wrong, so I confessed. Hank went up to the attic, where my bed and rug were. He folded the metal bed, put it away, rolled the rug up, took my clothes and teddy bear and put them in a basket. He threw me and the basket out the front door and locked the door. In the dark, I walked through downtown, trying to find my way back to the orphanage."

It took Patsy five months of pleading with Hank and Millie to bring Paul home. But nothing had changed. "It was the same old, same old. At Jeb's ninth birthday party, Hank didn't like something I did, so he stood me up on the kitchen counter, pulled down my pants and held a butcher knife to my penis, in front of the whole family." As always, Paul preempted his feelings and stayed focused on a thought: Why doesn't someone stop this guy?

In fact the castration gesture at Jeb's party got the family's attention. Millie had a second cousin, Anna, who desperately wanted children but had continual miscarriages. Word of Paul's unhappy situation was passed on to Anna and her husband, Walter, who were interested in adopting a child. Anna met Patsy one day after her factory shift. Patsy couldn't bear to think of losing Paul, who was the only joy in her life, but she realized that Anna and Walter might provide him with a safer childhood. They reached a compromise: Paul would go for an extended visit, and they would see how it went.

Paul remembers: "For the first three weeks I kept everything in my little basket. I didn't trust I would be staying—it was too good to be true. Then Walter came up and asked if he could help me unpack."

In the fall, Anna and Walter asked him if he would like to stay. When he said "Sure," they asked him to please call them Mom and Dad. They enrolled him in school, where for the first time he "felt and looked like a normal kid." But Paul never expected it to last: "I worried about how I could find my way back to the orphanage from all the way out in the country. I worried about when I'd have to go back to Hank. I was one worried little kid."

Not long after Paul's eighth birthday, Walter and Anna took him to the county courthouse. "The judge asked me: 'Do you want Walter and Anna Sorrel to be your parents?' I said 'Yes.' People say to me it's a shame I wasn't adopted at birth and spared Hank. But I say if I'd been adopted at birth, I would never know what it is like to choose your parents." Paul still saw Patsy on visits, but Anna was the only one he ever called Mom.

Yet Paul's story does not end there. Although his new home was relatively safe, it was not secure: "Walter was an alcoholic and they fought over it constantly. No one ever hit anyone, which was a relief." But Paul was again exposed to conflicts "too rich for my blood." When he was ten years old, Walter and Anna called Paul in to tell him Daddy might be leaving home for a while and asked how he felt about that. Anna took off her wedding ring, set it on the dining room table, and walked out of the house. "I thought to myself, They're not supposed to be doing this in front of a kid my age."

After this incident Walter traveled more to escape the conflict with Anna and to drink in peace. The more he pulled away, the more demanding Anna got. A few times, she moved out. "Compared to Hank and Millie, this was nothing," Paul said. "I had a high tolerance for problems. But I began to wonder, When is this merry-go-round going to end? I want off. And I did wonder what about me made people come and go in my life."

In high school Paul was an excellent student, but emotionally he was flat. "My highs weren't too high and my lows weren't too low. If I did feel anything, I kept it to myself. Mom and Dad taught me that as long as appearances were good—if no one knew you were having trouble— everything would work itself out."

Paul met Claire, a beautiful dance student, in their junior year of college. "We were the perfect couple—good-looking, funny, smart, real outgoing. I remember buying a pin for her, and later an engagement ring, and thinking to myself, I'm not ready to get married, but rationalizing away my doubts because it was all expected and it looked good. I never wanted to turn down anyone's expectations of me."

They married in Paul's first year of anthropology graduate school, where he studied the origins of aggression. Claire was unhappy from the beginning. She had affairs. "We broke up, got back together again, broke up again." Paul's ping-pong existence between living in the orphanage and with Patsy as well as his parents' on-again-off-again marriage had been re-created. "I wasn't particularly upset or angry. I just thought, This isn't working and analyzed why." Eventually the marriage became too irrational even for Paul's Herculean powers of detachment and rationalization. "Finally I woke up: We don't get along. You can't buy or fix this." This time Paul left and Claire pursued him. This last reconciliation resulted in the birth of their son, Kevin.

"After Kevin was born, Claire was even more restless. A marriage counselor told us that our relationship was destructive and that he saw little motivation to change. He said Kevin would suffer." Claire decided to leave for good, but she asked to live with Kevin and Paul for another six months, until she finished her college courses. Paul became a single father; Claire was his houseguest.

"One Saturday, Claire came in at seven-thirty in the morning after being out with someone all night. I was doing Kevin's morning feeding and said to her, 'I wouldn't do this to my worst enemy.' Then I thought, What am I—my worst enemy? I'm allowing this to happen to me!" They separated for the last time that day.

"My feelings were so intense, I just couldn't ignore them anymore. And I realized, if I'd been aware of my feelings and listened to them, I wouldn't have married her to begin with.

"One day a wall of rage hit me. I was standing outside my classroom, shaking. A colleague, who was also in my divorced men's group, came over and asked me what was wrong. I told him I felt like killing someone. He told me sometimes he'd felt that way too after his divorce. It was only a feeling, not an actual plan, and the rage would pass. That helped a lot."

At first, Paul felt inadequate in caring for Kevin. He calmed his fears by "taking parenting classes night and day and reading every book I could get my hands on. When Kevin would spill something or be obstinate, I'd remember how Hank and Millie used to punish me. And I'd think, They did *that* over something as inconsequential as this—that's terrible." With the help of his friends and therapy, Paul recovered and embraced his feelings. "It was my second birth."

When Kevin was five, Paul met Dianna. "You better believe we dated for a *very* long time." Paul was conscious of his feelings by now. "We became engaged and then Dianna broke the engagement. It was the merry-go-round again. I was despondent. I took Kevin to visit Anna and Walter. I just didn't think I could go on. Walter had been sober and in Alcoholics Anonymous for a year. I was telling him how sad I was. He gave me the AA pep talk—One day at a time, let go and let God, you know. It wasn't what I needed to hear. I went over, put my arms around him and broke down sobbing. Walter embraced me. It was one of my lowest days *and* the beginning of my road back."

Eventually Paul and Dianna married, and Dianna adopted Kevin, who now has a toddler brother and an infant sister. Today Paul is one of the most animated people I know. He has learned to keep the thinking that saw him through the worst of times from obliterating the feelings that are allowing him to experience the best of times. "You know, in my twenties, with all my accomplishments, it looked like I had the world by the tail. In my thirties, when it all caught up with me, it looked like the world had me by the tail and wasn't going to let go. Now I'm in my forties, and me and the world—we have a truce."

Learning to Think

It is not just the child's body that is abused or neglected. Troubled families mess with a child's mind. Like Paul, virtually all of the survivors I interviewed believed that their ability to think, to intellectually master the challenges in their lives, was one of their greatest strengths as children. Like other coping mechanisms, their *over* reliance on rationality fell into healthy obsolesence and became one of their greatest weaknesses. Joan told me, "I can get through anything as long as I understand what is happening and why it is happening. But sometimes I wish I could switch off all the thinking and analyzing. It gets in the way of my feeling."

Children struggle to make some sense of a loved one's abusive and neglectful treatment. "Why would someone who loves me want to do this to me?" "Does this mean this person will quit taking care of me?" "How will I take care of myself?" "Why me?" All good questions. If the child understood what abuse really was—a random and violent imposition of another's will onto a relatively helpless person—he would despair at such hopelessness and betrayal. Therefore, he uses every mental effort to make himself seem in greater control while transforming the abusive parent into the safe and loving caretaker he so desperately needs. Such lies of the mind require mental gymnastics.

Children don't do this thinking in a vacuum. In some situations they are told what to think. In most cases they are influenced by the abusers' faulty thinking and by the rationalization of adults who passively enable the abuse to go on. Children hear what those powerful adults say and don't say about the abuse.

That Never Happened

Denial in families is akin to having an elephant in the living room. No one mentions that the elephant is there, yet every morning someone bumps into the elephant or the animal steps on or rolls over on someone. Everyone just brushes himself off, goes about his business and pretends the elephant doesn't exist. Even if the child screamed at the top of his lungs, "Look out! Elephant!" everyone would stare at him and say, "What elephant? Are you crazy?"

Imagine that you are forced to deny the best thing that ever happened to you as a child. Your fondest memory may be of a baseball game at Fenway Park. What if you had to forget it totally, pretend it never happened, believe "there is no Fenway Park." At best, this would cause self-alienation, a tension between your stated belief and the gnawing feeling that it is not true. You'd use up a lot of time and energy denying this delightful aspect of your past. The same happens when a person denies the *worst* thing that ever happened to her. On top of the abuse and neglect themselves, denial heaps more hurt upon the child by requiring the child to alienate herself from reality and her own experience. Denial of the harm they are doing protects abusive adults from facing themselves and from having to make changes they believe they cannot make.

In troubled families, abuse and neglect are permitted; it's the talking about them that is prohibited.

Denial of violence or the harm done by violence is the best way to ensure that the violence is transmitted from one generation to the next and is often the crucial difference in how abuse affects siblings. Amy, for example, accepts the reality of the abuse, feels its full force and, acknowledging it as abuse, will not inflict it on another person. Her brother Chuck was similarly abused but denies the reality of family violence. Two six-packs of beer each day supports his denial. To prove to himself and others that physical violence is of no consequence, he constantly brawls in bars. He has been arrested for molesting children. Each time he protests, "That never happened"—something that never happened cannot hurt anyone.

The survivors I spoke with had learned to stop denying. Over the years they had found the courage to denounce the party line "It never happened." They understood that if they did not acknowledge the elephant in the living room, they would be forever stumbling over elephants in their own and other people's houses.

Refraining from denial is an act of courage for these survivors. They had to choose quite literally between being alienated from themselves and reality or being alienated from family members who still denied abuse. Each of them eventually chose reality and themselves, often at the cost of family ridicule or even ostracism. Several survivors told me that when they had tried to confront their families, they were told that they were crazy, that they were abusing their families, and that they were not welcome back until they apologized for making such hateful accusations.

It Couldn't Have Been That Bad

Elaine is one of the most severely physically abused survivors I interviewed. Her sisters have told her that their mother, in a psychotic state, would continue to punch and kick Elaine after she was unconscious. Yet, Elaine told me, "I don't consider myself 'severely physically abused.' I feel I've had enough of a taste of it that I can empathize with others who've been abused yet not so much of it that I was devastated." Moments later, she reflects, "You know, I'm grateful that I didn't have brain damage or paralysis, given all the blows to my head."

Minimization is a thinking error designed to protect the injured self, making one seem a little less injured. The need for it can lessen as the survivor can afford to embrace the full reality of the past. After all, there are costs in telling yourself "I have a sprained wrist" when you really have a broken arm.

Nancy jokes that "minimizing is a contagious disease." Her stepfather, Mark, sexually abused her and battered Nancy's mother and all five children throughout Nancy's teen years. After she adopted her daughter, Nancy confronted her mother and stepfather about the hell she'd endured in adolescence. She told them they would have no contact with her or their granddaughter if they didn't seek therapeutic help.

After six months of therapy, Nancy, Mark and their respective therapists met for a joint session. Nancy had recovered new memories in the past six months and she needed to confront Mark with them. His therapist thought he was ready to apologize to Nancy and begin a less exploitive, healthier relationship with her. "It took me forty-five minutes, talking nonstop, to get through the inventory, from when he killed my gerbils, to what it was like when he used cellophane as a condom to the secret abortion—of his child—he arranged when I was fifteen. By the end of it *his* therapist was in tears. When it was his turn to talk, Mark shrugged and said, 'So, is that all?' Within a month my mother was back supporting him, telling me it couldn't be as bad as I remember it, and they were both out of therapy." Nancy kept her relationship with her mother, but neither she nor her daughter has any contact with Mark.

Many survivors minimize their abuse by comparing their experience with others'. "At least it wasn't my father or mother who sexually abused me, it was only my brother or sister." Or "At least I was a teenager, and not a toddler." Nancy told me, "At least I grew up in a part of the country where it was sunny most of the time and I could be out of the house. It would have been much harder if I had had winter to contend with on top of everything else."

In the film *My Life as a Dog,* twelve-year-old Ingmar lives in a minefield of abandonment and severe neglect. His father leaves him at birth, his mother is dying, and he is passed back and forth among relatives without the comfort of his beloved dog. He is lonely, frightened and confused. He keeps himself going by telling himself things like, "At least I'm not the dog the Russians sent into space with only five months of dog food and no way to return to earth. At least I'm not that spectator at a bullfight who was gored by the bull. At least I am not one of those people at that soccer game who were killed by lightning. One has to take such things into consideration."

But does one? Empathy for others is healthy only when balanced with empathy for the self. How well can Ingmar understand other people's reality until he has accepted his own? The reality is that Ingmar is not a dog in outer space or a spectator at a bullfight or soccer match. He is a profoundly neglected little boy. He has lost every important relationship long before he was prepared to endure such losses. What good does it do him to try to feel another's feelings if he cannot feel his own?

Guilty and Responsible—But in Control

In troubled families, the thinking around who is responsible for whose behavior is convoluted at best. Abusive parents externalize, blaming other people, places and things for their behavior. The wife who burns the meat loaf "makes" her husband batter her, even though millions of people burn food and no one lays a hand on them. Obsessive care of one child "makes" a mother neglect her other children, even though she refuses all the help the community offers and chooses to live like a martyr. It is the alcohol that "causes" a father to sexually abuse his child, even though he has also molested the child when sober.

Life "just happens" to troubled parents. They compensate by controlling everyone around them. But in their heart of hearts, they feel out of control. They must blame others because it is too painful to take responsibility for their unhappiness. Children are easy targets because they cannot challenge their parents' thinking errors. Few children can argue when facing an enraged mother, her fists clenched and face twisted, who screams, "If it weren't for you, I'd still be sober." Hearing such accusations often enough, children come to believe that they are responsible for their parents' troubled behavior.

When Amy's brother Chuck was arrested for kidnapping and child molestation, her family agreed that "that slut Amy got him into this.

If she had stopped him when he was a teenager, he wouldn't be in this mess today." Amy was four years old when Chuck molested her.

Unfortunately, children receive an internal psychological payoff when they believe abuse is their fault—a false sense of power. The child can let the unfairness and danger of the violence shatter him, or he can tell himself, I'm not frightened or angry or sad or helpless or innocent. There is nothing wrong with this situation. This is happening to me for a good reason. This is happening to me because I deserve it, because I provoke it, because I was put here on earth to endure such things. There is really nothing out of the ordinary about this.

The child is doing the best he or she can to make sense out of the abuse or neglect, by feeling *guilty and responsible,* thereby holding on to the illusion that he or she is in control of what is truly out of control.[1] This illusion of power seems better than acknowledging that one has no power at all. Such pseudologic quells feelings of hurt, rage, terror, confusion or sadness, rationalizing them into a deep freeze.

The child's sense of guilt and responsibility is useful to the abusive parent, who believes he isn't abusive—that it is the child who forces him into being abusive. The nonprotective adults want the child to bear the guilt so they won't have to face the harm their neglect is causing. What begins as a face-saving illusion for the child—that he controls what in fact he does not—becomes a protection racket for the adults. They tell the child, "Yes, yes, you are right. You are bad and at fault. I am good and doing my best." So the dance of the violent family begins: children are responsible for adults' behavior; adults are responsible for nothing.

Faced with random, senseless abuse, a child begins to think of herself as inherently unlovable. Eight-year-old Esther's mother tied her to the water heater in the basement for refusing her offer to braid Esther's hair. "I assumed I must be bad or else my own mother wouldn't be doing this to me. The worst part of it was I felt I was an accomplice. If I raised my hand or struggled, I made it much worse for myself. Her view was that she needed to do this, like scratching an itch. It made her feel better, and if I resisted, I was evil—I was abusing her instead of the other way around."

Sometimes a child buckles under the accumulation of guilty feelings and in addition feels inadequate. Janet never thought she caused her father's alcoholism, gambling or physical abuse of her and her mother— he never touched her brother—but she did think: "I should be able to control it better, to stop it. I would think to myself, There must be something I could do to be more acceptable or lovable so he won't want to do this to me. If I were a boy, this wouldn't be happening to me. Then I'd be an athlete and he'd be proud."

Believing oneself to be guilty, responsible or in control of others' hurtful behavior can be a tenacious habit. Many survivors deal with any overwhelming experience—physical illness, abandonment by a friend or lover, academic or job demands—by "comforting" themselves with the illusion that they are in fact in control and to blame. An enormous amount of energy is sapped by this irrational guilt.

Rarely do they see themselves as so powerful over the good in their lives. Here, their parents' constant projection has left its mark. Many survivors, convinced of their inherent worthlessness and inadequacy, look to other people, places and things for salvation: only when they have the perfect intimate partner, their dream house, or public recognition for their work, will they be redeemed. Of course, anything so powerful to save their lives might also destroy their lives, which brings the survivor back full circle to his original feeling of powerlessness. Responsible for all the pain in the world, he is inept at enjoying his own happiness.

For Your Own Good

In some troubled families, abuse and neglect *are* talked about, but euphemistically, as if they were something "good" for the children. Rarely does a sex offender say, "Come on over here, I'm going to sexually abuse you." Instead, he says, "This is what people who love each other do."

No one would dare say, "Mommy's drunk again"; rather, one would say, "Mommy's happy" or "Mommy's tired."

Would anyone admit, "Dad is in the institution again"? More likely, the explanation would be "Daddy's on a business trip" or "Daddy's gone hunting."

Battling spouses will not acknowledge the fear in the faces of children watching helplessly, or affirm, "That's right—a person you love and depend on could be injured or killed." Instead the children are admonished, "Stay out of this—it has nothing to do with you."

Nor will a neglectful parent say to the child, "Look, what you need is perfectly legitimate and reasonable, but I'm sorry, I'm incompetent, I just can't meet it." If the need is acknowledged at all, the child might be told, "Look at how much you need. You need too much. If it weren't for your needs, I would be just fine. Your needs get me into trouble."

Never would a physically abusive parent say, "Now I'm going to dump my rage on you because you can't hit me back." Instead, the child is told, "This hurts me more than it hurts you."

Laura's parents, who were physically abusive, made her share a bedroom with her noticeably disturbed half brother, John, eight years older than she, who frequently sexually abused her. Her mother made no secret of how she raised her children. She had earned a bachelor's degree in psychology and worked briefly with handicapped children before quitting work to raise her children. She would lecture to the working-class mothers in the park: "I think of beatings as giving them medicine when they are sick. It's good for them." Abuse wasn't just good for you in Laura's family—a nobility surrounded it. "One Christmas Eve, right before my sixteenth birthday, both my parents got slobbering drunk. They began weeping: 'What selfish assholes, spoiled, shallow, worthless people you kids are. You've never suffered like we have. You have to suffer to be good. You'll never be as good as us.' I was like that kid in 'The Emperor's New Clothes.' I got up and said, 'You're both drunk and I'm not listening to this.' Now, my father had never hit me—he only hit John. That night, he hit me for saying that."

It is no wonder some survivors succumb to their parents' thinking errors. If they buy the propaganda, they can remain in the family, they buy a little safety and serenity for the time being.

The Escape Through Learning

Thelma comes from a large, chaotic and violent family who lived in an East Coast industrial slum in the 1920s. The local library was an oasis for her: "I started going to the library when I was six because it was warm and clean. I can still remember the librarians: they dressed nicely, spoke softly and always had flowers on their desks. I kept a diary in which I listed the books I read with a few words about what I thought about each. I read every single book in the children's library."

Rob would escape to the attic and write poetry: "little eight-year-old rhymes about what a great guy Abe Lincoln was. Then I'd hide them in the attic, afraid someone would find them and make fun of them. I think about going back to see if they are still there."

Rita could more easily understand existentialism than her parents' alcoholism and violence and her mother's self-hatred as a Native American. At ten years old, Rita wrote an essay, "Man Against Himself: The Battle He Cannot Win." She won statewide honors at thirteen with another essay, "Franz Kafka: Blind Man or Prophet?"

In their intellectual pursuits, many found safety, respect, recognition, even affection. Affirmation from teachers and occasionally from parents, who could take the child's good grades as a reflection of their outstanding parenting, encouraged these survivors to live in their minds, to find power and self-esteem in the realm of thinking.

For some the mind was a more immediate ally. Elaine says, "My mind saved my life. When my mother was towering over me, punching and slapping me, my mind kept on repeating, 'Cover your face, stay on your feet,' over and over again until I was knocked out. All I had was the coaching my brain gave me."

The brain can still be a coach. Survivors have applied their skill in thinking to the intellectual mastery of their childhood trauma. Stefan lay awake nights as a kid trying to figure out how they built the pyramids or how rocket fuel works: "Now I lie awake nights figuring out how my family worked."

Stefan and other survivors understand that they learn best with other people's help. Neglected and abused children learn faulty thinking from adults. A survivor can *un*learn faulty thinking from other adults who either know more or have unlearned it themselves. It is difficult, if not impossible, to correct thinking errors in isolation. The majority of the survivors I interviewed believed their recovery had been enhanced—if not begun—by reading books, watching films and listening to lectures.

Gathering information is essential to healing, but is not an end in itself. Psychotherapists Jane Middleton-Moz and Lorie Dwinell offer workshops where they encourage survivors to build what they call a "cognitive life raft." As they wrote in *After the Tears:*

Participants who were abused physically or sexually begin to make intellectual sense out of their pervasive fear of normal conflict, their fear of trusting, and the patterns of repetitive abuse in their adult lives. Even though the "cognitive life raft" does not ease the pain or the fear of trust, participants report a lessening of pervasive shame. They begin to realize, if only intellectually, that with work their lives can change and that perhaps someday that rigid control they feel as such a prison can lessen and they can feel and enjoy the spontaneity that others seem to have achieved.[2]

In his study of invulnerable children of chronically mentally ill parents, psychiatrist E. James Anthony found that children of mentally ill parents who suffered less debilitating harm than was predicted "had a stubborn resistance to the process of being engulfed by the illness; a curiosity in studying the etiology, diagnosis and symptoms and treatment of the illness . . . a capacity to develop an objective, realistic, somewhat distant and yet distinctly compassionate approach to the parental illness, neither retreating from it not being intimidated by it."[3]

The potential for intellectual mastery should not be equated with high intelligence quotients, love of school or learning ability. Four of the survivors I interviewed were diagnosed later in life as having severe forms of dyslexia. Esther and Stefan spoke a foreign language until they entered elementary school. They reported being mistreated in school, called lazy or stupid. Vinnie had difficulty in school because of severe stuttering. Christina's deafness was initially misdiagnosed as mental retardation. Still, they persisted in their quest to learn and eventually made sense out of senseless violence. They overcame disadvantages and disabilities to gain intellectual mastery over their lives.

Daryl's experience as a college freshman reflects the tenacity of so many survivors. "I didn't do so well in high school and I knew the only way out of the draft as a young black man was to go to college. This small fundamentalist college accepted me. They assigned me to a tutor for remedial English composition. He was a Southern Christian who felt I was one of God's children so he *had* to help me, but he didn't expect much. His favorite phrase was 'Now, Daryl, you are far too ambitious.'

"This was in the early 1960s and I had just woken up to how black people had been treated. He wanted me to write about 'Bobby and Alice went to pick apples,' and I wanted to write about slavery, Malcolm X and lynch mobs. He always admonished me, 'Some things are better left unsaid.' Still, I took his advice about my writing—he really did teach me some things—and I wrote about what I wanted to. After a couple of years he started giving me higher grades, and once or twice even admitted I had a point."

And, like Daryl, many of the survivors interviewed "woke up" to unfairness and abuse in the greater world before they recognized it within their own families.

Fantasy

Abused or not, we tend to use fantasy to entertain ourselves, boost our spirits or to express feelings that would be inappropriate to express in reality. When someone cuts you off on the expressway, you may fantasize running him off the road and then find you are done with feeling so angry. Do you fantasize about making love or being famous when you are bored? When anxious about a meeting, do you fantasize about all the possible outcomes, especially the most favorable ones? We all have a little Walter Mitty in us.

Current psychological theory holds that traumatized children have a diminished capacity to fantasize. For many, intrusive recollections of traumatic events preempt budding fantasies. But the survivors I interviewed had fantasized frequently as children.

Sometimes their fantasies acknowledged the trauma as real yet provided a more desirable ending. Esther recalled: "I would play with my dolls and imagine that I was a model or movie star. Even back then, I was short and wide, so I knew I couldn't be that, so I'd switch to fantasizing about being a prostitute or pornography star. Then I was wanted, desired, loved, and that was all I cared about."

Laura fantasized that she would be sent to live with Dale Evans and Roy Rogers. Almost every day when she was five years old, she dressed up in her cowgirl outfit, leaned over her bed, pulled her pants down and spanked herself. She had not yet unlearned the lie of the mind that love equals abuse, so she figured that if Dale and Roy loved her, they'd have to spank her. What she played out was infinitely milder than the choking and kicking, the sexual abuse and name-calling she endured in real life. She was Dale and Roy's favorite daughter.

Glen was "the original latchkey kid," left alone to care for himself at seven years old and was regularly called "the little shit." He lost himself in television, especially shows like *Perry Mason* and *87th Precinct*. Glen imagined that someday he would murder someone and thereby gain the full attention of those "good guys." In prison he would be safe from his father, and others would be safe from him. Through fantasy, he vented his rage about being constantly humiliated.

Like Glen, some survivors occasionally have revenge fantasies, which they find "cleansing." But there are important differences between their fantasies and those that propel actual crimes. The survivors' fantasy target is invariably the abuser himself, and they balance their vengeful fantasies with other types. They also understand that to translate revenge fantasies into real behavior would be harmful and would ultimately result in a loss of self-esteem. In short, their fantasies are not real to them.

Others used fantasy to soothe and comfort themselves while acknowledging the trauma. Joan's assaultive stepmother put her out to work cleaning wealthy white families' homes when Joan was thirteen years old. "I liked the break from Dominique, but most of all, I liked pretending that I lived in those houses. Since the *real* cleaning girl was sick that day, I would be a gem and pitch in with the cleaning."

Christina "created a guardian angel. I could feel her tap me on the shoulder, letting me know she was there. She'd reassure me, 'It's going to be all right. Someday you'll be out of here, taking care of yourself.'"

Hans Christian Andersen transformed his traumatic childhood into fairy tales. Again, from E. James Anthony:

People were aware of Hans' combination of extreme vulnerability with resilience. He was described as a 'sensitive plant but able to unfold and withstand the most inclement weather.' From very early on, his extraordinary competence showed itself in his gift for creative fantasy, his high intelligence, his eagerness, his enthusiasm, and his extraordinary persistence in the face of setbacks. . . . He himself thought that he thrived for various reasons: because he had an extraordinary capacity for withdrawing into fantasy and escaping from brutal reality; because he knew how to abreact his intense feelings by pouring out details of his "case" in endless representations, metaphors and self-knowledge; and because he was able to transform "horrible" situations into fairy tales and achieve a few glorious moments of relief during the act of creation. . . . The high degree of competence he demonstrated was related to the disturbing chunk of reality, reshaping it imaginatively in accordance with wish fulfillments, and then, creatively, retelling the idiosyncratic fantasy as a universal story or fairy tale. In the process (to use Andersen's most famous metaphor) the "ugly duckling" of reality was changed into a beautiful swan.[4]

Finally, most survivors "took vacations" from the reality of their trauma by fantasizing about the future. Recalling his childhood, Rob says: "I listened to my crystal radio and looked at the lights across the bay from our tenement. I'd listen and know there was a better life. I didn't know where it was—the radio was my only link with it. I didn't know what a good life might be, but I knew, 'This ain't it—these people are crazy.' The radio and lights kept me looking forward and up." Rob's metaphor is apt for many of the survivors: their minds were like crystal radios, constantly receiving messages from beyond the troubled family.

Vinnie had no role models in his impoverished neighborhood, so he fantasized: "From the time I was a little kid, I fantasized about being a wealthy businessman with a gorgeous secretary, and wearing only white shirts and expensive suits—having the best of everything." Putting himself through law school, Vinnie eventually achieved his dream.

As with many coping strategies, the ability to fantasize can also be a weakness. During childhood Esther's imagination was her only friend, the only reliable, consistent and helpful thing in her life: "And so much of what I fantasized about work or travel has come true. But relationships don't work like that. Too often my fantasies become more real to me than the relationships. And I fantasize a lot about what other people think or feel about me, assuming my fantasies are true. It takes a lot to convince me that they aren't."

Christina's rich fantasy life "convinced me the rest of the world was wonderful and only my family was a threat to me. As an adult, I've had to mourn the loss of the ideal world. For a while, I was scared out of my mind because I didn't know whom to trust. What a rude awakening after I'd expected to trust anyone and everyone and found that wasn't realistic. That was painful, but I wouldn't have made it through without those fantasies."

Some researchers believe that trauma causes survivors to be preoccupied with the past, often in the form of intrusive recollections of the trauma, at the expense of thinking about the present or future. But the survivors I interviewed tended, if anything, to concentrate too much on the future. After all, in childhood, the future had represented hope to them.

Many survivors find they must make a conscious effort to remain more in the present. Esther continues, "I am constantly looking around myself and commenting on what is here right now, like a beautiful sky, a house I've never noticed that I must drive by every day, the color of a car that I like. It helps with the 'mind-wandering time.' In the past, I used to have flashbacks or quickly sink into the depths of despair because I was only noticing things that reminded me of the horror of my childhood. Then I'd fantasize about traveling with Martina Navratilova. I wasn't paying attention to my real life."

Balanced Thinking

Trauma influences our ways of organizing in our minds what goes on in our world. Survivors who have not fared so well in life tend to think in sweeping generalities—people or situations are either good or bad, with no gray area in between. Everything is "always" or "never," with no room for "sometimes" or "hardly ever." Everything is "life or death," with little room for "doesn't matter much."

In contrast, several survivors told me that their thinking is highly compartmentalized. Christina described her mind as a chessboard with many squares: "I can jump from one square to the next. I'll allow myself to cry, then, through willpower, focus on something else because I'm afraid I've cried too much."

As a child, Glen categorized people as either like his parents or not like his parents: "I'm so thankful I recognized early on not all adults were abusive. Somehow, in research terms, I felt the group of subjects, the 'n' of two people, was too small to generalize from and I stayed open to adults who could be helpful."

Esther's thinking accommodates both the reality of her mother's abusiveness and her love for her mother: "When she was hurting me, I thought of her as Ilena and when she was kind to me, I thought of her as Mom. You know, good people can have bad behavior."

Survivors also tended to make a strong distinction between the past and the present. "That was then, this is now." Yet, some had difficulty when compartments overlapped, when "now" is too reminiscent of "then." When Joan was ten years old, she had a fight with her mother and wished her dead. The next day her mother died. For thirty years Joan believed she had killed her mother, until she *learned* differently in a graduate school course on hospice counseling. Although she has made great progress in her healing, if she receives mixed messages from a man she loves and depends on, "my mind takes over and writes a story about abandonment. I've killed another one off, and I fall apart."

However helpful compartmentalization has been to survivors, it's clear it takes a toll on their images of themselves as whole and integrated people. Joan continues, "When my father married my stepmother, Dominique—a crude fishwife, one of his drinking buddies—she saw my role in the family as 'the little mother and wife' and set out to destroy it. Worse than her frequent beatings were the voodoo curses she put on me, telling me my dead mother's ghost was coming back for revenge that evening. It was difficult to be the evil person she saw me as. When I looked in the mirror, I was afraid I would see the devil looking back at me. But then I would go to school and be the person teachers liked and respected. Even today, there is one part of me who knows I can do anything and another part of me who feels dreadfully insecure and worthless. At times, I feel like two totally different people."

Children simply do not have the cognitive development or life experience for clear thinking in the face of trauma. Their thinking errors reflect their best attempt to comprehend the incomprehensible when the truth wasn't offered or allowed. A first step to recovery, then, is to examine, challenge and change these old ways of thinking about trauma.

Janet says, "I understood real early in my life that what I tell my brain tends to come true. If I tell myself, I'm a victim, I'm helpless, life is awful, then those things keep on happening. Instead, I tell myself, I'm a survivor, the worst is behind me, I'm strong, healthy and deserve love and safety. And, for the most part, good people and situations come into my life."

Like Janet, Rob has learned to "flip the metaphor": "I can't control what has happened to me, but I can control how I think about it and what impact it will have. When I have events in my obsessive little boxes of doomsday—like something is my 'last chance'—I can look at the same event from a different angle. Perhaps there is a 'first' or an opportunity in this challenge. Then I can be more hopeful."

For other survivors the problem is in thinking so much. During her freshman year at college Esther experienced panic attacks. "Paralyzed with fear, I couldn't go to classes. I went to the campus counseling center for help." At the end of Esther's first session with a therapist, "he told me I was intellectually overdeveloped and emotionally under-developed. Those words still burn in my mind." What an insulting thing to say! The therapist could have said, "I admire your capacity to think and your powers to intellectualize your experiences—I wonder if you would be here to talk to me today if you had not developed your intellectual side. There is no reason not to believe that someday you will be just as comfortable with your emotional side."

A "cognitive life raft"—realistic and empowering ways to think about the trauma—is absolutely necessary before a survivor dives deeply into feelings. One plank is learning the facts about trauma; another is expanding one's capacity to fantasize about power or hope; another is adding more compartments to the mind to provide for more possibilities. Esther says she has a "cognitive life raft that could float an oil tanker." Yet her capacity to think is not the problem and should not be derided. At age forty-two she has an emotional life that is as healthy and vibrant as her thinking.

The goal of sorting through the lies of the mind is to learn to take the abuse less personally, and thereby to feel safer. By looking back, the powerful adult mind can more objectively measure the powerlessness of the traumatized child: "I was not to blame after all."

Thinking clearly may not be the entire answer, but it is an excellent and necessary beginning. Emerson said, "It is the wounded oyster who mends its shell with pearls." But, unlike oysters, we are not solitary creatures. We mend one another as well as ourselves. Pearls of wisdom help us to take the next step, to heal in the company of other people, feeling the effects of the trauma while we hold on to our life rafts.

CHAPTER FOUR

Looking Good on the Outside, Feeling Bad on the Inside

We can endure much more than we think we can; all human experience testifies to that. All we need to do is learn not to be afraid of pain. Grit your teeth and let it hurt. Don't deny it, don't be overwhelmed by it. It will not last forever. One day, the pain will be gone and you will still be there.

—HAROLD KUSHNER
When All You've Ever Wanted Isn't Enough

Ask Beth how she feels and she'll tell you what she thinks. She has unlearned the lies of the mind and thinks very clearly. She has never forgotten a detail of the battering she witnessed or the neglect she endured as a child. She amazes her therapist with her ability to give a blow-by-blow account of it, almost as if she were describing a rather unexciting basketball game. When the therapist asks her, "Where are the feelings?" she takes the question literally and looks down at her body. She feels no pain, she says, no pounding of the heart, no wrenching in the stomach, no dizziness, which is to say she feels no fear, no sadness, no anger. She feels the way she's always felt. Telling someone about the abuse does not make a difference.

Beth is well liked, but no one is especially close to her. She tends to keep the conversation focused on others. To show that she cares, Beth offers advice. If her friends want someone to listen quietly, they don't go to Beth. But if they want analysis and solutions, they make a beeline for her.

Beth is a therapist at a residential treatment center for severely abused children who have been removed from their homes. In Beth's mind, these children are deserving of a sympathetic listener. She lives through their therapy vicariously but believes her own "time for such things has long passed." Her intellect keeps "self-pity" firmly in check.

Beth's family "looked good on the outside." Her father was a hard-working, upwardly mobile Ward Cleaver type and her mother was a housewife who appeared to dote on her family. "But it was really more like *Who's Afraid of Virginia Woolf?* They hated each other with a passion." Many of their fights were about an unsatisfactory sex life. Alice would accuse Tony of being impotent or a homosexual. Tony would counter that no man in his right mind would be turned on by Alice. Yet their battles usually ended in the bedroom. Looking back, Beth believes "the fighting was foreplay for them."

One fight stands out as Beth's worst childhood memory: "I was only six years old. They'd been at it all night, then suddenly, I heard this bloodcurdling scream. Susan and I ran down the stairs. My mother had poured the percolator of hot coffee over my father's head. The grounds were in a heap on the top of his head. The coffee drenched his shirt. What I remember most was his sobbing—it was the *only* time I saw him cry—the tears running off the end of his nose. My mother quite coolly ordered us back to bed. She said, 'This doesn't concern you girls.' "

Both parents used their daughters as confidantes. Alice would pour her heart out to Susan, who, like herself, was "full of piss and vinegar." Tony, feeling more comfortable with the demure Beth, would sit with her, stare out the window and sigh a lot. "I always thought of my parents as two halves of a brittle, chipped teacup patched together with glue. If the teacup broke again, neither half would be any good."

From early on, Beth and Susan, one year younger, dealt with their parents' violence very differently. Beth, the "good daughter," would numb out, "playing music or writing stories in my head until it got so noisy, I couldn't concentrate. That's how I knew it was getting dangerous, time to break it up." Susan, the "troublemaker," was hyperalert, listening to every word. Her anxiety would build until she had to take action, move her body to be free of the tension, banging her head, rocking or bouncing on her bed.

The differences carried over to school. In the second grade Susan was identified as "hyperactive" and given medication. Beth believes "it was her first lesson in 'better living through chemistry.' No one asked us if anything at home might make her anxious. They just treated the symptom without knowing the disease." Susan's difficulties in school reinforced the "bad" label she was getting at home.

Beth retreated into her mind at school, her "only safe haven." She was an excellent student, well liked by teachers but isolated from other children. "I thought if I got to know other kids well, I would end up screaming at them, so I avoided it." Her teachers assumed that Beth was "shy, mature beyond her years," and thought little of her social isolation. Following in her family tradition, "I looked as normal as I could, even supernormal academically. No one knew I felt like a freak on the inside."

Once during the sixth grade Beth suddenly began sobbing in class and couldn't stop. Her teacher was appropriately concerned and asked if anything was wrong. "I had to think on my feet. I made up a story about my hamster dying the night before. We weren't allowed to have pets, but it was the best I could do. He believed it." She renewed her resolve to "keep my mind busy and not think about home while I was at school. I'm safe here—no need to bother myself."

Susan's anxiety became harder to control with medication once she reached puberty. Like Alice, she vented her anger and restlessness on those around her and used food to stuff excesses of emotions. Alice and Susan dieted and took amphetamines. Unable to wall off trauma as effectively as Beth, Susan became bulimic and her behavior became more aggressive. Sometimes, in frustration, she'd punch Beth. "If it weren't for Susan," everyone would lament, "this family would be fine."

The wounds between Susan and Beth have never healed. The few times Beth has talked with friends about her family, she will joke about Susan: "She got all the drama and angst and I got all the brains." Susan does in fact have enough anger, sadness and fear for at least two people, which she self-medicates with cocaine. Under the influence or not, Susan has a hard time distinguishing "what was" from "what is." She does not remember as well as Beth does what they endured. She can't recall being left alone for long periods of time, as Beth can. But if a friend stands her up, she assumes that she has been cast off for good. Susan has never kept a job for more than three months because she experiences the slightest criticism as an all-out attack on her worth. Susan's feelings could not be more real to her, and they are continually on display to the world.

Beth's emotions make her "feel like that stupid toy, the jack-in-the-box. I'm going along, minding my own business, getting through a normal day. But I'm getting too wound up, not letting my feelings out as they happen. Then, maybe every month or two, I'll lose it over nothing. One day I asked the secretary to type up a discharge report as soon as possible. She was backed up with work and said no, very nicely. I went into my office and sobbed. Last Saturday, after months of being jerked around, I was finally supposed to receive my new washer-dryer. I wasted the whole day waiting, and around four o'clock made absolutely rageful phone calls to the department store, threatening them."

Unlike Susan, Beth has bursts of emotion that are not always tied into "what was." Sometimes the sheer accumulation of unexpressed emotions causes "the clown to pop out. I scare people and look like a fool." But it is not just the clown Beth fears she resembles: she worries she is "unstable, a raving lunatic, like my sister and mother." More determined than ever, Beth gathers her composure, and "stuffs those feelings back into the metal box."

The adult Beth's "safe haven" is work, where the kids she counsels "do the feeling" for her. But at a seminar on stress management the speaker hit a nerve when she defined burnout as "driving eighty miles an hour with your emergency brake on."[1] Beth sees that she is doing just that by keeping the "emergency brake" on her own feelings while she works with abused children. "I'm not just objective," she realizes, "I'm dead from the neck down."

Susan just received her ninety-day chip from Narcotics Anonymous. Her sponsor reminds her daily of one of the twelve-step slogans: "Feelings aren't facts." She's beginning to realize that just because someone has one or two characteristics that remind her of her parents, his intentions toward her are probably not the same and, certainly, the consequences of interacting with him will not be the same. She is learning to talk herself down when she begins to panic and to stop seeing other people as "psychic stand-ins" for her parents. Both Beth and Susan are learning that they can express rage at other people, but they will not feel better until they connect their feelings to "what was."

Beth is learning to rechannel precious psychic energy from "looking good on the outside" into grieving the losses of her childhood. Through a good therapist and a group for survivors, she has been able first to feel more and then to feel better. "I try to have compassion for myself, to accept the depths of my feelings. You know, if I'd been able to let *any* of my rage or tears out when I was a child, it wouldn't be popping out today. I try to make constructive choices about how I express my feelings, but I finally know my feelings are not my enemy." Beth feels less like a jack-in-the-box and is beginning to feel as good on the inside as she looks on the outside.

Thinking and Feeling

Feelings begin in the body, not in the mind. Consider some of the many body-based phrases used to describe our feelings: weak in the knees, heart in my throat, pain in the neck, jumping for joy, hair standing on end, swept off my feet. We have a physiological response to something or someone in our environment. The brain receives the sensation and labels it correctly: "I am nervous . . . scared . . . annoyed . . . happy . . . surprised . . . or ecstatic."

In his workshops on emotional healing, psychotherapist Terry Hunt has a slogan: "A thought for every feeling and a feeling for every thought."[2] Thinking helps us to identify our feelings accurately, to put them into perspective and to make healthy choices about what to do with them. Talk them out? Act them out? Work them out? Let them be? Feelings, in turn, supply the brain with authentic information about who or what is around us (or has been around us in the past and now is reemerging). Thus intuition and rationality enhance each other.

Culturally, we tend to split the head from the heart and to encourage the head to reign. Given the choice, we tend to prefer survivors like Beth who can think well but are numb to the real pain they've experienced. We are put off by those like Susan, who have lost conscious memory of the abuse but "act out" with the full force of their feelings, reminding us of the agony of family violence. Beth's professional success and compartmentalized feelings—notwithstanding their high and unnecessary personal costs—lull us into believing that violence against children can't be so bad.

Yolanda speaks for many of the other survivors interviewed when she says, "One of the residues of my childhood is that I live with a dichotomy between what my head comprehends and what my heart feels. I *know* I am smart, semiattractive, and have many skills and gifts. Rarely do I *feel* that. I *know* what happened was not my fault, but I still feel somewhat unlovable and damaged. My self-worth is measured by how other people see me. My head knows that is wrong but my gut feels differently."

Seventeen of the survivors I interviewed had full recall of their abuse but identified awareness and expression of their feelings as a problem area: "Thinking comes much more easily to me—it's still a big risk for me to feel." Their pattern as children was to avoid *outward* expression of feelings about the trauma, to "stuff" their feelings. As psychiatrist Henry Paul said on a television interview program, "feelings are not like the keys of a piano. You cannot push one down and expect all the others to stay up." Survivors are sometimes afraid of the intensity of such a backlog of feelings. Laura used to worry, "If I ever started to cry, I'd cry a river. If I ever got angry, I'd blow up a building. If I ever felt the terror of it all, I'd disintegrate into nothingness."

Like steam knocking around, trapped in an old radiator, feelings need to be safely let out, little by little. Perhaps the survivor cannot remember, but there was a time when he or she instinctively knew how to do this and did not fear the feelings getting the best of them or being bigger than they were.

Have you ever watched an infant rage against being bathed? Red in the face, body stiff, her clenched fists flailing, she screams at the top of her lungs. A short time later, someone special enters the room. Her eyes widen, she smiles, her arms and legs flap with the joy of recognition and the anticipation of loving caresses. A while later she wants to sleep instead of being fed and is frustrated with her parents, who can't figure her out. She rejects the bottle, closes her eyes, moves her head back and forth, and squirms—all to express her feelings.

If all goes well, if her parents are sensitive and receptive to her feelings, she will relax and fall asleep. When she wakes up, she will be ready for more feelings. She will not fear or judge them or keep them to herself. She learns that each feeling has a beginning, a middle and an end, and when it passes, she and her parents will still exist.

This natural ease, this instinctive expression of feelings, can be stifled and distorted by abusive or neglectful caretakers.

Frozen Feelings

Many therapists would refer to Beth as having "frozen feelings." Beth has had this problem since childhood, just as Susan has had problems thinking clearly. How does a troubled family put the chill on a small child's natural responses in the first place?

In her book *It Will Never Happen to Me* psychotherapist Claudia Black, a pioneer in the treatment of adult children of alcoholics, identifies the three ironclad rules of the alcoholic family: "Don't talk, Don't trust, Don't feel."[3] Abusive and neglectful families have the same rules. To break any of them means risking rejection or punishment.

Children don't innately know how to repress their spontaneous responses. They have to be taught, and troubled parents are perhaps the best teachers of all.

In the "good enough" family, toddlers learn to match words with the music of emotions. The toddler cries, and his parent, reading the expression on his face and attempting to empathize, will comfort him and ask, "Are you sad?" The child thinks, "Tears equals sad, I get it." Perhaps the parent notices crying, wide eyes and a cowering posture and asks, "What are you scared of?" The child learns: "Pounding in my chest equals scared. I get it." Hopefully, the parent explains to and protects the child from what frightens him. When the toddler goes red in the face and her body makes aggressive motions, the parent says "You're mad." The child learns: "Burning equals mad, I get it." Hopefully, the parent helps the child express anger safely and constructively.

If such experiences are consistent, the child learns to say "I am sad" or "I am scared" or "I am mad" and to ask for comfort and protection when he needs it. If he consistently gets recognition ("I understand how you feel") and affirmation ("That is OK with me,"), he learns "Talk, trust, feel." He keeps on expressing feelings because his needs are being met.

In families where there is neglect or abuse, a child's crying might be

met with indifference ("I can't be bothered with your feelings"), intimi-
dation ("Keep that up and I'll really give you something to cry about")
or denial ("You don't really feel that way" or "You have nothing to cry
about"). Or the child's crying triggers the parent's own sadness, and the
parent may smother the child with a blatant play for comfort. The child
soon forgets about his own sadness and gets on with the "more important" business of making his parent feel better. At the very least, he
buries those pesky feelings, keeping them from the eyes of others. At
worst, the child may be struck for crying, and the awful physical threat
of annihilation will overpower the physical sensation of sadness.

One of the few predictable aspects of a violent family is the unpredict-
ability of the parent's responses. Every time the child cries, he gets a
different response. Soon he realizes that it is unsafe to cry. He will not
learn what to call his feelings, what tears genuinely mean or how to talk
about them. After a while he keeps his feelings to himself and perhaps
loathes spontaneity because it causes so much trouble.

Young children offer their feelings to adults as gifts, as their currency
of exchange in intimacy. All they can do to be close to adults is to offer
their feelings. When their feelings are ignored or rejected as wrong, bad,
troublesome, sick, crazy or stupid, they feel rejected. The young mind
reasons, "Since my feelings are unacceptable, I must be unacceptable
too."[4]

Feelings and Behavior

Beyond teaching children to recognize and articulate their feelings,
"good enough" parents help children to contain and express feelings
constructively. Ideally, feelings are translated into life-affirming
thoughts and behavior. Parents have to convey that there is nothing
wrong with feeling angry, but that hitting or name-calling is prohibited.
Other messages "good enough" parents transmit are: "You can be mad
at me and still listen to me"; "It is all right to be scared as long as you
tell someone about it and don't think less of yourself for it"; "You can
cry in my lap and I will hold you, but I will not let you become
hysterical." When children do not learn how to express their feelings
constructively they may be overwhelmed by them, experiencing them
as floods, like Susan. They come to fear or loathe their feelings.

Children do not have the cognitive capacity to understand why a parent would beat them up, get drunk and frighten them, pass out and look dead, leave their children alone or rape them. From the child's point of view, these are spontaneous actions, not so different from the child's impulse to cry, squeal or throw a tantrum. The child may conclude, "It is my parent's feelings that make him or her behave this way." It is a small leap from "My feelings cause me trouble" to "*Their* feelings cause trouble." Who in his right mind would want anything to do with feelings? The child has not learned that a feeling is very different from a behavior and that it is not the feeling but the parent's choice of behavior that is problematic.

Whether they are aware of it or not, parents model feeling styles for their children, thereby offering "coming attractions" of the emotional life of adulthood. And as adults are physically larger and more powerful than children, their feelings seem larger and more powerful to children than their own feelings. Therefore, when a child has adult feeling, as Beth describes it, "shoved down my throat," her own spontaneous feelings are overshadowed and eventually can be snuffed out altogether.

In almost every interview, survivors recounted some variation of this scenario: A man's boss yells at him, threatens to fire him if he makes another mistake. The man feels very frustrated and angry, but he knows better than to yell back at his boss. He doesn't know how to have a constructive and calm discussion with the boss, however, and since he can't or won't express his anger and frustration to his boss, he looks to dump it.

When he gets home, he attacks his wife for making him "live in a pigpen" and for "sitting on your fat ass all day." Now she too feels angry and confused and frustrated by this unpredictable and unprovoked attack. But she's afraid of escalating this into a fight, so she goes after the oldest child, who has forgotten to take out the garbage, calling him a "good-for-nothing little shit."

The oldest son in turn takes out his anger and frustration on the next child, who takes it out on the youngest child, who takes it out on the family dog, who takes it out on the family cat, who goes out and kills a mouse as a finale to a Rube Goldberg emotional contraption set in motion hours earlier.

Whatever any family member had been feeling before the angry man came home—boredom, affection, sadness—has been flooded by his more dominant feelings. Each family member's anger and frustration are genuine, but only in response to a contrived situation.

Such a dynamic has a synergistic effect. Whenever a child is compelled to take on his parent's feeling instead of or in addition to his own, that feeling will be twice as intense.[5]

A parent's regurgitated anger added to the child's anger at being attacked equals rage.

A parent's sadness imposed upon the child's sadness can cause despair.

A parent's false euphoria loaded on the child's need to be happy can take both dangerously out of touch with reality.

A parent's fears injected into the child's own natural fears can become terror.

Laura's mother was widowed during World War II. Later, she married again, had Laura and her two brothers, and became a prescription-pill addict. "No one could make it up to her for the loss of her husband. She never let me get close to anything because she was afraid I would love and lose like she did. So, she'd let all my pets go, or give them away. I really loved those animals and she was doing to me exactly what she feared so much. Later, when I had a boyfriend, she'd make up wild stories about him so I wouldn't like him. I was her therapist for years, listening to how terrible her marriage to my father was and what a saint her dead husband had been. She convinced me: Love means someone dies. Love hurts. Love is terrifying. I'm thirty-seven years old and every time I want to get close to a man, I panic and let him go, like one of my pets. Today I am trying to sort out what was her fear and what is mine. If my partner died, I would be deeply sad, but not devastated."

As Laura knows, often it is not permissible for the child to feel something *different* from what the parent feels. The child can either feel the parent's feelings or feel nothing at all. If he chooses the latter, the child loses the connection to the parent and learns to be numb. The seeds for depression have been planted.

No one likes to be alone with her feelings. A toddler has tantrums not just because she wants to get her way but because subconsciously she wants those around her just as frustrated, overwrought, angry and out of control as she feels—through the intensity of their similar feelings, she will feel less alone. In pursuit of such closeness, a child may take on his parent's emotional style, sacrificing his own feelings, as

Vinnie did: "Early on, I learned the 'look' from my father and the nuns. I wore my anger, rejecting people before they could reject me, just like he did."

Others rebelled against their parents by covering up their feelings, perhaps acting the opposite of what was expected of them. Christina said, "I was scared all the time. The worst thing was the fear that I would lose my mind and no one would care, and I'd be lost forever. But you'd never know it because I had this tough veneer. I was so defensive. If anyone tried to tell me something, I'd turn it around and attack them."

Ironically, Laura has received many community service awards, most for her courage in children's rights work. "I am the most frightened person on the face of the earth—if they only knew! It is much easier for me to say 'I'm angry' or 'I love you' than 'I am scared.' Yet, lately I've had a few situations where I chose to express my fear. People were terrific—really took care of me. I see now the work of healing for me is to accept my fear as a natural and healthy part of me. It is not all of me—you know, I have been genuinely courageous too—but it is a part of me."

Many could identify with Paul, the hero in Frank Herbert's novel *Dune*. Paul is subjected to trial by ordeal. To prevail, he recalls the "Litany against Fear" his mother taught him: "Fear is the mind-killer, fear is the little-death that brings total obliteration. I will face my fear. I will permit it to pass over me and through me. And when it has gone past I will turn the inner eye to see its path. Where fear has gone there will be nothing. Only I will remain."[6]

Shame on You

Shame is the feeling of having a deficit of the self that all can see yet one is helpless to correct. Worse yet, as psychologist Gershen Kaufman puts it, "the eyes are turned inward."[7] There is no escape—twenty-four hours a day, seven days a week, the shamed person lives with a sense of his fatal flaws and unrelieved worthlessness.

Troubled parents shame their children for having feelings or needs. Shame differs from guilt, which tends to be more based in behavior ("I feel guilty that I did this—it hurt other people or it hurt me and I'll try not to do it again, but good people can have bad behavior—I still have worth as a person") or embarrassment ("This circumstance or situation causes me to feel foolish or vulnerable, but it will not last forever: before long I will be back to my old self"). Shame amounts to an all-out attack on the child's worth: "If you were a good or worthy person, you wouldn't be this way."

Shame causes a rupture in what Kaufman calls "the interpersonal bridge":

> An *interpersonal bridge* forms out of reciprocal interest and shared experiences of trust. Trusting must be matched by the parent behaving in a trustworthy fashion. Consistency (not perfection) and predictability (not rigidity) are crucial to building an interpersonal bridge, whether with a child, friend, or client.[8]

Ideally, this bridge has been under construction since infancy. Each time a parent accepts, affirms and responds to his child's needs and feelings, trust and unconditional love bridge the healthy gap inherent in their separateness. Gentle and loving hands across the river make both parent and child feel less alone in the world. Moreover, children learn that occasionally they will feel emotionally vulnerable or helpless but it is not the end of the world. They accept these feelings as part of life and cope with them by sharing them with a trusted person. In "good enough" families, the interpersonal bridge is strengthened by the open expression of vulnerabilities.

In troubled families the bridge collapses anytime the parent disapproves of the child's needs or feelings. Or it operates like a drawbridge: down when the child pleases the parent and up when the child displeases the parent. The parent's behavior tends to be untrustworthy, inconsistent and unpredictable. Desperate and alone, the child reasons, "If I don't need, if I don't feel, then maybe the bridge will be put back together again."

The child's shame is always an extension of the troubled parent's shame. Troubled parents abhor their own feelings of helplessness, powerlessness, emptiness and intense vulnerability. They believe these feelings will "get the best of them," so they escape them through drinking, drugs, ridicule, abandonment, physical punishment and sexual abuse.

When their children demonstrate vulnerability, helplessness or neediness, no matter how appropriate to their age and circumstances, the abusive adult sees a shameful and intolerable aspect of the self being mirrored. How can a parent accept vulnerability, dependency, helplessness in a child when she rejects those aspects of herself? Her impulse will be to "smash the mirror," shaming her child for reflecting the intolerable back to her.

The shaming of young Laura happened to involve a real mirror: "My mother would get into these rages. By six years old, I could tell when it was coming because I learned to notice her running her tongue across her upper dentures. She had lost all her teeth when she was pregnant with me and it became my fault. She would grab my hair and pound my head against the wall until I couldn't see. Then she'd slap and scratch my face. As I was going down, she'd pummel my back with her fists and kick me. She weighed twice as much as I did. Each time, I thought I was going to die. But the worst part was, if I was still conscious, she would drag me before a mirror and say, 'Look at yourself, look how ugly you are. You disgust me. You look like a monster.' My face was contorted with absolute terror. I was sobbing because the physical pain and emotional humiliation were devastating. Now I can see that it was she who looked unnatural. It was her face that was contorted and ugly with rage. All I was doing was showing her the reality of her ugliness, and she hated me for it. But at the time, and for a long time afterwards, I believed I was ugly."

Faced with disownment or exile from the abusive family, the child learns to disown her own feelings instead. Shame fills the vacuum created by this abandonment of the self.

Until recently, whenever Laura felt frightened or overwhelmed, shame was reactivated and flooded her feelings. "I'd feel exposed, unworthy and totally helpless to redeem myself." Her mother and the mirror were gone, but Laura had learned to shame herself.

The message "You are a horrible person, of no worth," if consistent enough, is sufficient for the child to develop the pattern of feeling shame *instead* of actually feeling or needing. Add to that message physical abuse or the invasion of sexual abuse, and the propensity toward shame becomes stronger.

No wonder so many adult survivors feel and need in isolation. "If my parents blow up the bridge when I am like this, why would anyone else keep it intact, let alone cross it to be with me when I am vulnerable and needy?" For them the interpersonal bridge is still a drawbridge. It remains down in situations that evoke little need or feeling in them. They may even be willing to cross it to comfort others, just as they cared for their parents. But when their own needs and feelings arise, the bridge goes up and no one can cross it.

Children who have been shamed often grow up to be adults who shame others. Most of the survivors I interviewed were aware of this propensity and had overcome it. As a child, Rob was shamed by an alcoholic mother and a father who sexually abused him. Any longing for closeness or reaction to their violence was ridiculed as not being "like a marine." Recently, Rob's wife, Judith, went away on a weekend camping trip, leaving Rob to care for his two daughters, Megan, four, and Heather, two. It was their first extended separation from their mother, and they asked continually, "When is Mommy coming back? Is Mommy gone for good?" Megan had recently "seen a squirrel run over on the road and was curious about the concept of death. On the second day, she incessantly asked, 'Is she dead? Is she dead? Mommy's dead, right?' I was so tired of it and felt so helpless with their vulnerability. Intellectually, I knew that Megan's talking about her was her way of keeping her mother alive in her mind. But eventually, I just felt like screaming, *'That's right. She's dead. She's never coming back!!! Now shut up!!!'* We got out pictures of Judith instead. When she called in, I told her to call back more often. I put stickers where the hands of the clock would be when she was coming home so Megan and Heather could watch it get closer and closer. I think I did a good job of reassuring them, but it was a struggle."

In therapy, Rob has learned to accept and resolve his shame, ending its tyranny. "I had to 'fess up, telling my therapist how defective and empty I felt. He didn't try to talk me out of it. He didn't tell me not to feel that way. He didn't tell me how wonderful I was. He just told me that I was 'good enough' and just stayed with me as I exposed my flaws. But his acceptance of me gave shame less power over me."

Rob's daughters had made him acutely aware of his inadequacy as a parent and of his own yearning for his wife. He could have expressed his vulnerability by shaming them, rupturing the interpersonal bridge between himself and them. Instead, he fantasized this behavior and was done with it, then chose rational and empathetic responses.

Survivors tend to rely on a limited repertoire of behaviors that are intended to deny their capacity to feel and need and, thus, to avoid shame. The three most common behavior styles of this sort are self-medication and pain-avoidant and counterphobic behavior.

Self-medication

Have you ever gone away on vacation, bought too many souvenirs and ended up with an overpacked suitcase? Rushing to make your flight home, you sit on your suitcase, struggling to get it shut. You might ask someone else to sit on it with you to push it into shape, or perhaps you pile heavy things on top, but however you manipulate the suitcase, for the time being you have a one-track mind: Get that sucker shut.

Most survivors of abuse and neglect carry into adulthood suitcases overstuffed with repressed emotions and shame. When they exhaust their own psychic resources trying to keep them shut, they turn to the outside for help. They "pile on" a regular dose of alcohol, drugs, work, sex, food, others' approval, romance, shopping, television or gambling, as needed to distract themselves from their internal reality.

Despite their different styles, Beth and Susan were remarkably similar in this respect. Susan was no dunce: she knew her intense feelings got her into trouble. She used cocaine to "take the edge off," not understanding that it gave her even less control over her outbursts. Beth used work to keep her backlog of feelings in deep freeze, lest she become someone like Susan. She submerged herself in "her" children's feelings to medicate her own.

Vinnie started drinking in his teen years. "But I'd cry when I was drunk and I hated that. In college, I started smoking marijuana, which mellowed me out. I continued to be a daily pot smoker for the next fifteen years. I couldn't leave home without it and I took crazy risks, like smoking in airplane lavatories and in my government car."

He was always clear why he self-medicated: "to keep my feelings down. I just wanted to be numb. There were so many things I was ashamed of: my father's alcoholism and violence; being jealous of the attention my brother got, even though he was dying and in a wheelchair; my stuttering; our poverty; not being able to get my mother to give me more attention. My brother begged me to stop. Finally, I recognized I was controlled by marijuana. I went to Pot Smokers Anonymous and have been sober for seven years. Sometimes when I drive along, the tears will just come. It feels healthy. I'm not as overwhelmed with feelings as I was afraid I would be." Vinnie reflects for a moment, then adds, "My sensitivity is the best part of me. What a waste—all those years I was trying to get away from it."

Pain-Avoidant Behavior

Adults from abusive homes can also become what psychotherapists Karen Paine-Gernee and Terry Hunt term "pain-avoidant."[9] Survivors attempt to control the people and events around them so that they will never feel pain again. As Simon and Garfunkel sang, "a rock feels no pain and an island never cries."

There is nothing wrong with avoiding hurtful people and dangerous situations. The problem lies in the lengths to which one will go to avoid pain. Choosing friends is one thing, but selecting only those whom you can keep beholden to you, so that they will never dare reject or criticize you, is being pain-avoidant. Taking romance one step at a time is taking care of oneself; shunning any romantic involvement, never risking the first few platonic dates is being pain-avoidant. Keeping the relationship platonic when the urge to be sexually intimate joins trust and caring is also being pain-avoidant.

What is most tragic about pain-avoidant behavior is that it is a defense against something that has already happened and that cannot be undone. The survivor has been hurt, but he has prevailed and has lived to tell the tale. Yet he behaves as if the worst is not behind him but just around the corner. Terry Hunt describes this as "trying to drive your car down the street while looking in your rearview mirror the whole time."[10] A survivor cannot live fully in the present until he or she has the past in perspective. Sometimes being preoccupied and defensive about the pain waiting in the future is just a distraction from addressing the real pain of the past.

To be intimate is to risk pain. There are no guarantees. To miss years of loving to avoid the pain of loss is too high a price to pay for safety.

Counterphobia

Some survivors take a different path entirely. In an attempt to master the trauma, they re-create it over and over again. The impulse is a healthy one, best carried out in therapy, where faulty thinking can be examined and feelings expressed and affirmed. Counterphobic behavior, however, seeks to re-create the trauma *as if* the survivor had no feelings about it. A female incest survivor spots a sexually dangerous man a mile away and pursues a relationship with him, all the time telling herself, I'm not scared, I'm not angry, I'm not worried about being exploited. I'm in charge here. Or an adult male survivor of physical abuse starts a barroom brawl, telling himself, This is fun—I'm too tough to feel pain and I like to win, even though he is often injured and sometimes loses.

The underlying thrust of counterphobic behavior is the thought "I'm going to keep on doing this until I get it right." Each time the survivor hopes the trauma will turn out differently: he will not be helpless or hurt. Each time he is.

Society prefers the overly controlled, pain-avoidant survivor, who isolates and hurts no one but himself, to the counterphobic survivor who directs each new production of his trauma, drawing others into playing parts. Some survivors told me of dangerous behavior in their youth, like Rob who "rode with bikers while tripping on LSD and drunk on Johnnie Walker."

Yet others found socially redeeming ways to be counterphobic. Stefan, whose parents were imprisoned in Nazi work camps during World War II, remembers: "Fear ruled our lives. Although we were European immigrants and my parents were very Old World, our family reminded me of the Wild West: Put the wagons in a circle and keep the hostile invaders out."

As a boy, Stefan was not allowed to express fear openly. Between the violence in his home and the bigots who attacked his ethnic origins, there was much for him to be afraid of. Instead, he "cultivated fearlessness in the face of fear." Beginning with martial arts training at twelve, he adopted a stance of "combat preparedness." Not surprisingly, he is comfortable working with violent people. The day before his interview with me, a belligerent teenager brought a knife into the family therapy session, intending to kill his father: "I wrestled it away from him and restrained him until two police officers got there. In the momentary distraction of their arrival, he got the knife back again. Now it was the police officers' turn to take it away. I noticed the younger cop's hands trembling slightly afterwards. I thought to myself, I think I've been in this situation more often than he has."

There is nothing wrong with Stefan's ability to cope with danger. Yet, over the long haul, who will have less to repress: the young cop, who allows himself to feel the reality of a life-threatening situation, or the stoic Stefan?

The counterphobic survivor is being a good little boy or girl, doing exactly as the abusive parent would wish: repeatedly enduring trauma and acting as if it were no big deal.

Grief: The Road Back to Feeling

These patterns of emotionally denying behavior are not mutually exclusive. A survivor may be counterphobic at work and pain-avoidant in her relationships, and self-medicate in her leisure time. There are many potential combinations, but behind them all is an attempt to flee from feelings about having been abused, from normal reactions to an abnormal situation. Because that situation was life-threatening, some survivors mistakenly believe that to experience those feelings today would also be life-threatening, would bring on an emotional breakdown, a falling apart akin to death. They do not understand that the breakdown had already happened, when their feelings became frozen or were preempted by shame. Psychiatrist D. W. Winnicott refers to this as a "death that happened but was not experienced."[11]

A survivor can afford to look that "death" squarely in the face when he has people who will stand by him as well as the insight and power he did not have as a child. When it is finally safe enough, the survivor will remember the memories and feel the feelings about the trauma. Such a "thawing out" is a second chance, an emotional reincarnation. Still, the first sensations of emotions that have been repressed or avoided all of one's life can feel like a tidal wave.

References to grieving were common among those survivors who no longer found feelings to be problematic: they understand and accept their more intense, trauma-related feelings as part of a grieving process. They could articulate the many losses inherent in trauma:

The nurturing and protective parent the child needs in order to survive has been lost to a neglectful or violent adult.

When that trust is repeatedly betrayed, the child eventually loses faith in the goodwill of others. The child comes to expect the worst of people and loses innocence. A child who has a violent parent knows how cruel people can be. For him, the disbelief that keeps many people detached from the horror of this world has been obliterated by a daily dose of the unbelievable.

If the child has had to parent her own needy and controlling parents, then she has lost her childhood.

Every time a child is hit or molested, he loses control over his body. If chronically violated, he loses a sense of his very self.

Abuse and neglect rob children of their spontaneity, of the uncensored expression of their feelings.

All of these losses need to be mourned.

According to psychiatrist Elisabeth Kübler-Ross, in *On Death and Dying*, the first stage of grief is denial. Disbelief allows a person to get through the first few days or years of a loss. When it is safe for the denial to wear off, he may feel profound anger: anger at the gods, anger at himself for all he believes he should have done to prevent the loss, or anger at the deceased for abandoning him.

To soften the anger or to repair any alleged transgression, the bereaved may bargain with his gods: he will worship faithfully forever, if only what was lost is returned to him. Or he rationalizes the loss away as not so important, or laden with supernatural meaning. He looks for a way to lessen the loss a bit, to strike a deal that will make the loss more acceptable and, more important, will make him feel less helpless in its aftermath.

When all such defensive avenues are exhausted, he experiences the depth of his sadness. Yes, it is a loss; it feels terrible. He cries and cries until he is cried out. Eventually, he reaches resolution. He is angry and sad, but he has made peace with his loss. If the loss is a death, he can remember his loved one fondly, but he realizes he does not need to bury aspects of himself to feel close to the deceased. He can go on with his life.[12]

Grieving over a trauma is much the same process. The first stage is dissociation, the repression of the memory, the feeling, or both. The survivor goes on with life as if nothing had happened. When he is ready, the thoughts and feelings return. In response to what has been uncovered, he often feels great anger at the betrayal itself and the injustice and randomness of the violence. Underneath that anger is a terror and helplessness that is more difficult to experience than the anger. Bargaining can offer relief from imposing anger: "Maybe it wasn't so bad—I'm just exaggerating." This can go on for a long time, but with the help of others the survivor will eventually accept that the trauma was as bad as he knows and feels it was. Profound sadness follows. This compassionate acceptance of "poor me" and the mourning of the losses that the trauma created eventually lead to resolution. Completing the grieving process means divorcing the trauma from one's sense of identity and self-worth. Abuse is something that happens to you, it is not who you are.

In her helpful book *Necessary Losses* Judith Viorst describes the process and payoff of grieving:

> In our own different ways, we will have to pass through the terror and tears, the anger and guilt, the anxiety and despair. And in our own different ways, having managed somehow to work our way through our confrontations with unacceptable losses, we can begin to come to the end of mourning. . . . Starting with shock and making our way through this phase of acute psychic pain, we move toward what is called the "completion" of mourning. And although there still will be times when we weep for, long for, miss our dead, completion means some important degree of recovery and acceptance and adaptation. *We recover our stability, our energy, our hopefulness, our capacity to enjoy and invest in life* [emphasis added].[13]

When the losses engendered by trauma are fully mourned, the trauma loses its power over the survivor. Instead of the emotional breakdown they feared, survivors experience an emotional breakthrough.

On Being Seen

True recovery involves the risks of vulnerability. The dictionary definition of *vulnerability* is "capability of or susceptibility to being wounded or hurt." Emotional vulnerability is characterized by feeling out of control ("I do not want to be feeling this way right now but I am") and in need of support or protection ("Please accept me as I am—do not take advantage of how I am feeling"). To make themselves less vulnerable, survivors may first grieve on their own, in isolation, like Joan, who went to her mother's grave to tell her she wished she had died with her. She allowed herself to feel as long as no one could see. It is often a fine line between feeling in isolation (feeling when one is alone) and loneliness (feeling alone).

As a child, Esther rebelled by feeling in isolation: "I think they wanted to see me cry. They didn't punish me for falling apart—they seemed satiated, calmer when I was hysterical. Then they looked good next to this shattered little girl. So, I was determined not to give them the satisfaction of seeing me cry. No matter what they did, I would do math problems or recite state capitals in my head. My lack of response made it worse—they would escalate—but I was fighting for my dignity and I was determined not to give them the power to break me. I held it in until I was alone, in the middle of the night. I could sob into my pillow and not wake up my brother in the next bed." Even now, Esther struggles to tell someone she is hurt or angry. "I feel like an oozing blob of pain—who would want to be close to me?" She tends to feel shame in the moment, delaying her tears until she is alone. The first time she cried in her partner Emily's arms was a turning point.

Rob explained, "It's relatively easy for me to say 'I love you' to my wife or 'I'm glad you're my friend' to someone else. But for me to be angry with someone, own it and express it without running away from my anger or running them over with my anger, now, *that's* intimacy. For me to be seen and not rejected in my anger is health." Fearing they would "fall apart" in the throes of exposed feelings, survivors find instead that they "fall together" as they tolerate and share their feelings with others.

All of the survivors who had learned to be comfortable with feelings had restored the interpersonal bridge. Not only did they allow others to see them in their vulnerability, but they allowed friends to cross the bridge to provide comfort. Eventually, grieving in isolation wasn't enough. Using feelings to scare people away no longer worked. Either option eventually became more painful than the pain they were trying to avoid.

Like Rob, many in therapy " 'fessed up" to shame. Or, like Paul, others found solace in family, friends and partners. As we will see in Chapter Seven, when they allowed others to accept their vulnerability, to comfort them in their grief, they could begin to trust again.

When Esther began to tell her psychotherapy group about the sadism she endured in her family, she lost her voice: "I felt so ashamed. I was afraid someone might criticize me for wimping out—bringing up the topic, then not coming through with the details. I wanted them to ignore me and go on to someone else. Then the group leader said, 'Everyone move in real close so we can hear.' And they did. It was a miracle."

CHAPTER FIVE

The Scene of the Crime: The Body

The great majority of us are required to live a life of constant, systematic duplicity. Your health is bound to be affected if, day after day, you say the opposite of what you feel, if you grovel before what you dislike and rejoice at what brings you nothing but misfortune. Our nervous system isn't just a fiction, it's a part of our physical body, and our soul exists in space and is inside us, like the teeth in our mouth. It can't be forever violated with impunity.

—BORIS PASTERNAK
Doctor Zhivago

Jake is proof you can't judge a book by its cover. Raised in a slum, Jake put himself through school, started a computer software company, and now is a community leader, tutoring teenagers in math and science at his local high school. He is the picture of success—tall, handsome and muscular. People see Jake's fitness mania—he works out two hours each day—as an indication of how self-disciplined and "together" he is.

But as a child, Jake was severely abused by his father, Howard. Howard was psychotic and believed that the devil lived in Jake's body and he could only be exorcised through beatings, burnings and being bound up. He'd wrap a rope through the slats of Jake's crib, over his son and under the mattress board and around and around again. Jake's mother was too afraid of Howard to protect Jake or his three younger sisters. She labored as a hotel maid because Howard was too disturbed to work. Jake remembers his mother being "exhausted most of the time."

Jake excelled at sports, particularly basketball. Older kids coached him, and he spent many happy hours playing. But Howard stalked Jake at the court, cursing the devil, wetting his pants and talking gibberish. Finally, Jake quit playing, but his best memories are of those times. "I felt on top of the world. Sports today feel like getting back to the best part of me."

When Jake was six years old, Howard broke his arm during a routine beating. After this Jake steeled himself against his father's assaults. "I wouldn't let him or my sisters or Mom see me cry. It was the only pride I had left. I'd count the blows, trying to set my own record on how much I could take. You know, like a triple double in basketball. My highest score was twenty-seven punches." Unlike many other survivors, Jake never lost consciousness during a beating. "My physical self was all I had—I wouldn't let him take that away from me. I knew from all the fighting in the neighborhood—as long as you stay on your feet you'll be OK."

His mother compensated for her husband's abuse by smothering Jake: she bathed with him until he was nine years old, and she brought him into her bed until he was ten, on nights when her husband wandered the streets. She rationalized that her behavior would let Jake "be close to someone." In reality, it satisfied her own needs to feel comforted and be less alone.

Jake grew up in a crazy-making world of being intrusively touched and violently abused. By adulthood, he did not feel his body was his own. Being the focus of his parents' twisted needs, he felt his body had caused him endless trouble. The rapid changes of puberty brought further confusion. "I couldn't control my body anymore. When I was twelve, after I quit basketball, I started to wet the bed. By sixteen, I weighed 240 blubbery pounds." Every night, his mother brought food home from the hotels where she worked. Jake and his sisters gathered around to "feed, like sharks in a frenzy. Food was the only thing we had enough of. And we ate to make my mother feel like a good mother." Subconsciously Jake was also trying to make himself a less attractive paramour to his mother and literally to give himself a buffer against his crazed father's fists.

When Jake was twenty-five, Howard was stabbed to death while passed out in an alley. With Howard gone, Jake no longer needed his "cushion," so he quickly dropped eighty pounds. Ten months later his mother died suddenly of a heart attack. Feeling contempt for his body and believing "less is better," he continued with a harsh regime of dieting and relentless exercise.

"If someone cuts me off on the freeway, watch out! I want to kill." Jake realizes he feels more than normal annoyance. His heart pounds, adrenaline surges through his blood, and his fists immediately clench. "I force myself to think about the distinct possibility of a lifetime in prison and the grief of the victim's loved ones to keep my homicidal rage in check."

Jake dreads the times when he is alone and his mind wanders. Suddenly his eyes flinch and his head involuntarily jerks to the left, then to the right, just as they did when Howard slapped him. Before he can figure out what is going on, his arms cover his face. A minute or two passes before he realizes he is "in that goddamn position again." It can take fifteen minutes for him to get his arms down. He hates his body most of all at these moments.

Three years ago Jake's wife, Barbara, nearly divorced him. After nine years of marriage, she was sick of Jake's dietary regimen and impatient with the time his exercising took from family life. She loved Jake dearly, but they rarely made love. Jake usually "has an out-of-body experience during sex," and he reaches orgasm infrequently. One day, during a heated argument, Barbara screamed at Jake, "Your father tried to exorcise your demons away and now you're trying to exercise them away." Barbara had made the connections between the "what was" and "what is" that had eluded Jake, and she got his attention.

Shortly after this fight, Jake was lifting free weights. His childhood habit of "numbing out" when stressed beyond his limits caused Jake to injure his back by lifting too much weight. His sports medicine physician referred him to a pain management group to learn relaxation techniques. "I was a terrible patient, never doing any of the assignments." For several weeks after the injury, Jake was flat on his back. He was haunted by flashbacks, overwhelmed by memories of physical pain from his childhood as well as from his current injury. Although his right arm had not been injured in the accident, the excruciating pain of the break he'd sustained over thirty years before came back now, in full force.

Jake tried hard to repress his thoughts and feelings, and refused to share them with Barbara. Within six months he had developed an ulcer and high blood pressure. "I decided maybe I ought to take those relaxation exercises seriously, so I went back to the pain clinic. I had nothing to lose, so I told the lady there about the emotional hell I was going through. She took me back into the group and sent me to a therapist."

Over the next three years Jake learned to let go of his absolute control over his body. Instead of imposing his will on his body, as his father had done, Jake began to accept his body as a partner in both his survival and his continued well-being. After a while Jake actually looked different. His square shoulders, which had carried the weight of the world, became more rounded and relaxed. He became less wiry and gained a healthy protective layer, not of flab but of softness. Jake no longer fears the "out of control" feeling of orgasm. He is becoming more spontaneous in his lovemaking with Barbara. He still watches how he eats, but he's become less "fearful of the wrong foods. My rigidity around food was a lot like my father's superstitions." Now, once in a great while, he'll enjoy ice cream sundaes with his sons or a hot dog at a ball game. Jake no longer lifts weights or jogs. Today, he plays basketball with his sons.

The Body Keeps Score

The aftermath of violence is not "all in the head." What blows the mind or breaks the heart the body knows; it becomes a museum, filled with artifacts from childhood. Trauma is stored in the tissue of the body until the day it is expressed and resolved.

Consider the phenomenon of anniversary reactions. Often on the anniversary of a trauma—the death of a loved one, surgery, being victimized, sudden loss of employment—a person feels "different," even if he is not conscious that one year ago or three years ago something painful happened to him. Throughout the day he feels anxious, short of breath, tearful, depressed, sad, listless, "for no good reason." If the original trauma involved the invasion of the body, the person may feel distinct physical pain in the injured area. His sleep may be disrupted by "bad dreams" during the week before the anniversary. He may feel he's "going crazy" because he cannot account for his discomfort. His body knows something very important.

Many children die from the kind of abuse Jake endured. Most people understand that the body manifests the aches and pains of, say, a car accident for months. For Jake, and others like him, growing up was like being in a car accident every day, every week or every month. And the aches and pains may persist for many years.

During the trauma Jake dissociated, attempting to ignore the impact of violence. His mind and spirit went to a safer place and left the body there to endure the abuse. Alone and overwhelmed, his body became a receptacle of violence.

A survivor may leave his hometown, leave his family, never see the abuser again. But he cannot leave his body forever; dissociation offers brief respite from the constant reminder of abuse. Eventually, awareness of the body returns, and with it awareness of the pain and humiliation of the past.

Body Integrity

From infancy on, children explore their bodies, playing with their feet, hugging themselves, touching their genitals. If parents respect their privacy, children become familiar with their bodies without feeling shame, learn to associate their bodies with pleasure and to feel connected to their physical selves. They learn to trust their physical reactions to what goes on around them, and from their parents' example they learn how to take good care of their own bodies.

A sense of safety and comfort with one's body and a sense of one's physical self as separate from others is called *body integrity*. Body integrity is like the borders between sovereign nations. Under the best of circumstances, children have an uphill struggle to maintain body integrity because of the size of people around them.

Adults are anywhere from two to twenty times bigger than most children. If an adult is not sensitive to and respectful of the child's body integrity, the adult can unintentionally violate the child—for instance, when he insists on hugging a toddler who resists cuddling. Later in life, body integrity enhances the integration of the physical self with all other aspects of the self—rationality, feelings, spirituality.

Many troubled parents treat their children's bodies as extensions of their own. Like Jake, the child may be brought into a parent's bed to comfort a distraught or lonely parent. She may be shamed for touching her genitals, although others are allowed to touch her genitals without her permission. She is ignored or overpowered when she wants privacy.

She learns that her body is not her own, that other people's wishes for her body—that they hold it, that she not touch it—are more important than her own. She has little opportunity to learn about her body in a safe and pleasurable manner; she becomes alienated from her body because it causes her so much trouble. An important aspect of her self becomes off-limits to her; it belongs to the bigger people around her. Alienation from the body leads to an alienation from the self.

Most abusers are likewise alienated from their bodies. If they could feel the pain the child feels from their abuse, they would probably stop, but they have silenced their own bodies, and try to silence their children's bodies as well. And many abusers, to feel aroused or powerful, purposely want to cause the child pain.

If body integrity is violated frequently enough, the child feels annihilated. Elaine was beaten often by her mother: "When you are beaten, you aren't a person, you have no mind of your own, no heart. You are nothing but an inert physical thing absorbing this awful pain. You are an *it.*" Ignoring the child's physical needs is dehumanizing as well. The message "You do not count, you do not exist, you are not worth bothering with" registers just as loudly as assault does. When Paul interviewed Hank's and Patsy's relatives about his first years of life, he learned that they had disliked him because his mother was so depressed she didn't take care of him: "I'd cry for hours. They were annoyed by the noise—but never came to comfort or change me. If Patsy picked me up when Hank was home, he insisted that she 'stop babying' me."

Paying too much attention to a child's body even "for the child's own good" also violates body integrity. Psychotherapist James Ritchie terms such intrusiveness "pathological nurturance."[1]

Sam's mother, Loretta, was a nurse and thought her four sons' bodies were her domain. "She was like a drill sergeant. It was always the same routine. 'Assume the position. Drop your pants. Bend over. If you cry or move, I'll make it a hundred times worse for you.'" Even when they complied perfectly, Loretta beat the boys with a belt until they welted or bled.

But more pervasive than Loretta's physical assaults was her "pathological nurturance" of her sons. She was especially focused on Sam because he was "the wrong sex." Sam was her third son and she had decided he would be a girl. "Before I was born, she wanted a girl so much, she tried to adopt this thirteen-year-old girl, Delores. But Delores stole from her and ran away. My mother was still reeling from that experience when I came along. Whenever she was angry with me—which was frequent—she'd call me Delores. When I was twelve, she decided my testicles weren't descending fast enough, so she gave me shots of hormones in the buttocks every day. Then a year later, when my voice wasn't deepening quickly enough, she talked a doctor into prescribing these huge horse pills of testosterone. She'd say, 'I love you,' but never once hugged or held any of us. There was lots of inspecting, poking and prodding, though."

Many survivors I interviewed told of similar experiences. Their parents examined their genitalia well into their childhood, intruded on their bathroom privacy, insisted that they shower, bathe or sleep together and constantly commented on their physical development.

Most male sex offenders rely on their authority ("Do it or else"), or they try to pass off sexual abuse as a relationship ("This is what daddies who love their daughters do," or "This is how people show that they love each other"). In contrast, female sex offenders tend to cloak abuse in intrusiveness about hygiene and caretaking by saying, "This is how I clean you," or "I'll masturbate you until you go to sleep so you won't have nightmares," or "The doctor told me to do this to you."

Such pervasive breaking down of boundaries around the body later aids an offender in actually committing specific offenses. Jake reflects, "If I don't even rate privacy while I am on the toilet, how is it that I could be entitled enough to tell someone they can't touch my penis?" Amy remembers: "My mother cleaned my vagina out with a Q-tip every day until I was about six years old. Eventually it became clear that she enjoyed doing it. When I was seven, my older brother started penetrating me. They made me feel creepy. There was nothing I could do about any of it."

In some troubled families, body ailments and functions are the center of family life. Inspecting and fussing over one another's bodies is the way for family members to be close. As Elaine remembers, "I knew for sure I wouldn't be beaten if I was sick, so I pretended to be sick a lot. But my mother insisted I sleep next to her so she could hear me breathing, and she was constantly undressing me, looking at my chest, and insisting that I show her what I had put in the toilet. When relatives came over, all they ever talked about was illnesses, diseases and doctors.

We never discussed ideas in my house. We never discussed feelings. Everything revolved around the body."

Elaine rebelled by becoming a "bookworm," living in her mind to distance herself from her mother's consuming interest in her body. Elaine also became a hypochondriac in her twenties: "I had so much I wanted to tell people, but the only way I knew to say it was through my aches and pains. Of course it turns people off, especially when you discuss it with as much detail and zest as I could."

Before rationality and emotions are developed, toddlers are preoccupied with the functions of eating and elimination—taking in and letting go. If independence is not encouraged, and separateness in the physical realm not respected, a child can become preoccupied with these functions, as did Jake. Indeed, his lifelong obsession with his body makes perfect sense as a way to protect himself and, at the same time, fight back against a father who intended to obliterate him. He controlled his body to the same degree that his father had tried to take his body away from him.

Emergency Response

Beyond the acute injuries it can cause, chronic violence affects how the body functions. Experience influences physiology. If an infant is held in a tender and reassuring manner, fed and changed as needed, gets enough sleep and grows up in a calm environment, his body develops and functions in a normal way. If, however, home life is violent or unpredictable, even an infant will become vigilant and anxious, and have difficulty sleeping and digesting food.

As discussed in Chapter Four, children in troubled families are often not taught the appropriate words, let alone constructive behaviors, to express their physiological experiences or feelings. They are bombarded with powerful stimuli that cannot be digested at a reasonable pace and manner.

When children are first abused, their bodies respond spontaneously and completely to the threat, like a burglar alarm registering a break-in. They scream in terror, become red-faced with rage, gag and spit up, wet their pants or collapse in helplessness and inconsolable sobbing. Such spontaneous reactions enrage the abuser, who wishes not to see himself or herself as "bad," or monstrous. The child's reaction propels the abuser deeper into those feelings. Or if, like Jake's father, the abuser actually desires to cause and see pain, the child's responses fuel the abuser's pursuit of gratification. Either way, his natural reactions place him at greater risk. What is a child to do?

When faced with potential annihilation, human beings are physiologically prepared with two instincts that are "hard-wired" into our bodies: taking flight or fighting.[2] These "emergency responses" ensured the survival of our caveman forebears and they continue to serve us well today when we encounter the occasional immediate threat. Most of us have heard of the mother who, thanks to the adrenaline surge of the "fight" response, picks up the car to free her trapped child. Or perhaps you have been threatened by a mugger, and were astonished at how fast you were able to run.

Although most abusers prevent their children from running away, Justin believes that the wings on his feet saved his life: "When my father would get drunk and started beating us, my mother would yell at me to 'go get John.' John was a huge, mildly retarded man in our neighborhood—the only person my father was afraid of, and one of the few people in town who didn't work for my father's company. John would come over and tell my father to leave the house for the evening or he'd 'teach him a lesson.' It worked. When I got older, I'd run to Marjorie, our neighbor, who would welcome me in her arms."

Christina remembers a screen over her crib. "I pushed my head through it and got out. As a youngster, I was always running out of our yard. My dad put up a barbed-wire fence in the back. I *still* climbed out. I just had to see what was beyond our family. I kept on running away from them and toward the rest of the world."

Although the child is physiologically prepared to fight, he cannot realistically hold his own against an adult. Physiology does not take into account the politics of children's lives. It would not be safe to hit someone two, three, ten times bigger than himself, especially when he depends on that person for survival. The rush of hormones, dilation of the pupils, increase in heart rate and other physiological changes preparing us for fight or flight are the "alarm reaction," the first stage in what physiologist Hans Selye calls the general adaptation syndrome to stress or threat.[3] Once a crisis is over, the alarm reaction should cease and allow us to return to a more relaxed physiological state.

In a violent family, however, the threat is never over; the child lives in a state of waiting or preparedness. This leads to resistance, the second stage of the syndrome. Selye describes this as the body "getting stuck in a groove"—that is, never fully relaxing.

The child's body can become stuck in the groove of numbness, as if to quiet the constant ringing of the alarm. Numbness stifles crying, gagging, struggling, screaming and so on. The child may in fact be "weak in the knees" or have "his heart in the throat," but the transmission of that information from the body to the brain is blocked; the child has no *conscious* awareness of pain *at that moment.*

Jenny believes: "I have my own supply of anesthesia in my body from when I had to submit to my father's beatings. A few years ago, my dog bit hard into the palm of my hand. I needed several stitches. I didn't feel a thing."

Jenny is right. The body manufactures endorphins, which help us bear the unbearable by blocking our perception of excruciating pain. This mechanism allows us to survive trauma, just as it allows us to survive surgery.

Anxiety is another groove the body can become stuck in. Some child victims and adult survivors appear perpetually "hyperactive," nervous, irritable, driven, or unable to concentrate. Reality has been overwhelming; staying focused on it has only brought pain. The mind protects itself from overwhelming stimuli by frequently changing focus.

Others can concentrate but not relax. They may channel their "high energy" into work or, like Jake, into exercise, but have trouble knowing when to stop. It seems the constant anxiety around survival in childhood has "set the timing high" in their bodies, just as the idle on a car can be "revved up."

"I am so jealous of people who can relax," Glen told me. "I literally can't. You know how sometimes if you drink too much coffee and you get anxious, you start looking around in your life for reasons why you are so anxious? You start attributing how you feel to those things instead of to the simple fact that you drank too much coffee. You start overreacting or trying to fix things that are not the problem. That is how my life is. I've always been anxious; even as a toddler I used to rub the border on my blanket threadbare. I would rock and rock for hours just to be rid of the anxiety. I had good reason to be anxious. But, today, I tend to blame my anxiety on other things and I forget that instead of getting mother's milk as a baby, symbolically I got caffeine."

The third stage of the syndrome is exhaustion. The body tires of the demand to be on emergency alert, which prevents it from gaining respite in a more relaxed physiological state. The alarm will not stop ringing. The survivors I interviewed who had attempted suicide all said that they were "bone-tired," or "absolutely exhausted" at the time of the attempt.

Later in life, when encountering an event or circumstance that is not threatening but is reminiscent of the original trauma, the body may involuntarily switch into fight or flight. As psychiatrist Bessel van der Kolk describes it:

> Victims of trauma respond to contemporary stimuli as if the trauma had returned, without conscious awareness that the past injury rather than the current stress is the basis of their physiological emergency responses. The hyperarousal interferes with their ability to make calm and rational assessments and prevents resolution and integration of the trauma. They respond to threats as emergencies requiring action rather than thought.[4]

Such a survivor may be easily startled by events reminiscent of the trauma. For instance, some Vietnam veterans involuntarily drop to the ground and scramble for cover when they hear a car backfire. For the survivor of childhood violence, an unexpected touch on the shoulder, a smell associated with the offender, or being crowded too closely against others, brings about the same kind of extreme involuntary startle response.

Beth remembers that of all the different happenings in the chaos, the worst was being awakened from deep sleep by her parents' brutal fights. She'd go downstairs to break it up, and they'd turn on her: "Don't ever come between us again!" She would "slither back to bed and lie awake all night. The next morning, it was as if nothing had happened." She had no way of discharging the terror and rage she felt, or even the physical stress of breaking up a brawl between two adults twice her size. She could not even talk out the way her body felt. Her eyes stayed wide open, her heart raced, her muscles remained tight, ready for action, until dawn.

Today, when Beth is awakened, particularly by loud parties or drunken brawling, her body reacts with the same fight response, ready for battle. She could kill the people who wake her up, yet she is afraid to ask them to quiet down. She cannot get back to sleep. Her response is so extreme that others think she is overreacting.

Elaborate fantasies of doing harm to those who woke her were Beth's only relief until she made the connection to the experience of being awakened by her parents' fights. Now she talks to herself the way she would calm a startled little girl, and she also focuses on deep breathing and relaxation techniques to help her to fall asleep again. The next day she calls her good friend Angela. Having acknowledged the traumas for what they were and having someone to listen to her, Beth can let go of her fear and anger and return to a state of relaxation.

Beth normally found herself stuck in numbness, as she described herself in Chapter Four. But intrusive stimuli sometimes caused her to become stuck in a different groove: she would become anxious, hyperaroused, ready for a fight. This vacillation between high anxiety and numbness felt "like a never-ending roller coaster" and is not at all unusual among survivors.

Beginning when Sam was six years old, his older brother Claude would put a pillow over Sam's face while he roughly grabbed and squeezed Sam's genitals or rubbed his penis against Sam's struggling body. Other times he forced his erect penis into Sam's mouth, causing him to gag, and called him sexually derogatory names. Each time Sam's body went into alarm reaction: his heart pounded, he gasped for breath, his body surged dizzyingly with adrenaline. Claude derided Sam for "loving it," then threatened him with castration if he told anyone.

The abuse finally ended five years later when Claude left home to join the Army. Several years later nineteen-year-old Sam was vacationing near an Army base when he encountered a soldier who resembled Claude: "He was much bigger than me, looked rough, crude, muscled up, dark-complexioned and had black hair. My body started to tremble, my heart pounded, I felt dizzy and short of breath. I thought I was sexually attracted to him. I approached him and had sex with him."

For the next ten years Sam's conditioned response to a unique constellation of stimuli closely associated with his brother persisted. When Claude was discharged from the Army, he worked as a mechanic, and Sam would experience the same "sexual frenzy" around dangerous-looking mechanics. Later, when Claude rode with motorcycle gangs, bikers would trigger it. Finally, when Claude was arrested and incarcerated for sex offenses against local teenagers, Sam found that his frenzied response was stimulated by "criminal types. It's a wonder I wasn't killed. Somehow I could control these dangerous characters, outsmart them. I told them I was a photographer, flattered them by telling them they should be models. I'd get them to pose in various states of undress, then seduce them. I rarely felt sexually satisfied afterwards—mostly just disgusted with myself. I felt myself in the grip of something bigger than I was. Relief came only in tricking these guys, conquering them with my cleverness." During this time, Sam maintained a committed relationship, and his lover never knew of the "sexual frenzies." "I felt tormented, like I was living two lives. I even used another name in these encounters. I went into therapy because I was afraid I was becoming schizophrenic."

With the help of his therapist, Sam now recognizes his physiological "frenzy" as an abreaction of "the terror I felt when Claude sexually abused me. It has nothing to do with sexual arousal or attraction." Sam's behavior was also counterphobic. As the powerful initiator who was able to manipulate and control "rough characters" like Claude, he was attempting to gain emotional mastery of his trauma while denying his fear.

Escape Through Athletics

Some children are lucky enough to find physiological release through play or sports, which gives them both flight from a troubled household and a safe way to fight out pent-up energy.

As Jake found on the basketball court, sports offered a place to belong: "As long as I tried, the older kids accepted me, even made a fuss over me." Stefan found "a second father" in his karate teacher. "Karate is very health-oriented and anti-alcohol. It saved me from becoming a teenage addict, like my younger brother Peter." Most important, "It gave me a place to battle my demons. Our family was afraid of English-speaking people, afraid of outsiders, afraid of everything. I felt like I was always fighting, but I couldn't say who or what I was fighting. In karate, we do routines, like dances, where we fight an imaginary foe. Finally, I had a place to put the fight, contain it, finish it each time."

Glen grew up breaking up fistfights between his parents, who battled each other for his loyalty. It was no wonder that he grew up fascinated by the Alsatian Province, "where the nationality switched back and forth from Germany to France with each invasion." To his parents Glen was an ally, the spoils of battle, not a child. His mother plied him with food and secrets about his father. Craig, a frustrated athlete, bribed his artistically inclined son with the latest sports equipment and with the time they spent together while he coached the teams he ordered Glen to join.

"During World War II, my father was a Navy officer, an underwater demolitions specialist. In photos he looked like he just walked out of *Muscle and Fitness* magazine. But something happened, because ever since I can remember he weighed almost three hundred pounds and smoked three packs of cigarettes a day." Baseball was the sport Craig loved the most, so it had to be Glen's sport as well; the son's body had to do what Craig's body could no longer do. But Glen found a way to express the rage he felt at "being torn in two, cut off from noncompetitive contact with other kids and just plain used."

"Sports saved me because it kept me in control, ironically, by giving me a place to be out of control and leave it there. My idol was Cleveland Indian baseball player Jimmy Piersall. Just like him, I'd break bats when I struck out, scream obscenities at umpires, climb halfway up the net and shake it violently. My dad defended me—'The kid's a genius, what can I tell you.' I wasn't a genius, but I thought as long as I was forced to play a game I hated, I was at least going to use it to vent."

Although his baseball behavior alienated and frightened his teammates, it allowed Glen to express his rage. As an adult, Glen knows that "it was not a foul ball or somebody's missed catch that really caused my rage. It was my parents' battle over me." But having had the opportunity for pure bodily expression as a child, he's had less repressed rage to overcome than many survivors.

Of course, participation in organized sports is not the only way children gain knowledge of and comfort with their bodies. In healthy families, children are encouraged to play, alone and with other children, thereby learning how to interact with others and to express their creativity. Play also helps the child experience pleasure in the body without sex.

Generally, children who have been abused have missed these vital experiences. Play is thought to be a distraction from a child's "proper" role—caring for the family. Sexual abuse of children in particular contaminates the sensation of bodily pleasure, so that one of the most common and highly valued adult forms of play—sexual contact—becomes contaminated as well. The survivor of physical abuse knows more about the miracle of the body's ability to absorb pain than to experience pleasure. Glen reflected, "I learned not to give in to any kind of pain—physical, emotional, spiritual. I think I would have left a terrible marriage earlier if I'd paid attention to my pain. Today, I resent that 'Buck up and go on' attitude. It isn't good."

The Body Speaks

Trauma is stored in the body's tissues. For survivors who have no conscious memory of abuse, or who have conscious memory but little access to their feelings about it, medical problems sometimes signal trauma waiting for resolution. In my clinical practice I have seen many survivors with chronic dental problems or throat infections that do not respond to routine medical treatments who were strangled or forced into oral sex as children.

As he described being choked by Howard, and in general when he feels vulnerable or overwhelmed, Jake often gently strokes his neck. Esther lost her voice—her ability to tell the secrets—as she told me about her worst childhood memories.

The week before his long-scheduled interview with me, Justin's leg started to ache, which only happens when he talks about his father. When he was seven, his father threw him against a fireplace poker, and he still has scar tissue and nerve damage in his leg from the trauma. He could barely tolerate the pain during our time together.

Trauma also lives on in the carriage of the body. Some survivors appear to be literally "scared stiff." Their eyes are wide, their color is pale, their shoulders look as if they were forever "backed against the wall," and their joints are inflexible and strained.

Another common body type is Jake's: "armored," highly developed muscles, protruding defiant jaw, clenched fists, watchful eyes always on the lookout, battle-ready stance.

Children who have been taught that their worth does not extend beyond the use of their bodies for other people's pleasure sometimes become sexually stylized, since their survival has depended upon over-emphasis on their sexual aspects. They sometimes appear to be older and more sophisticated than they actually are.

Christina grew up "in a house of hands—hands everywhere." She recalled: "My mother was always inspecting and touching my genitals. My schizophrenic brother thought nothing of walking up and fondling my breasts. Recently, I'm recovering memories of my father sexually abusing me. I'd tell them, 'Stop touching me,' but they wouldn't. The only compliments I got were for having a 'sexy body.' I felt empty inside, I thought sex was all I was good for. After I left home at seventeen, I was very promiscuous."

Other survivors of sexual abuse seek salvation in asexuality, mistakenly believing that their physical attractiveness caused their abuse. They may overeat to achieve obesity, which would hide secondary sexual characteristics such as developing breasts or descending testicles, or starve themselves in an attempt to slow the development of their genitalia, pubic hair or breasts.

Nancy was approximately sixty pounds overweight at the time of our interview. "I think my body is pretty ugly. I've set it up to be a test of a relationship. Clearly, if someone is interested in me, it isn't for my body. People have to be *so* attracted to what I think and who I am that they can ignore my body." Recently, after Nancy confronted her stepfather about his sexual abuse of her, she and her husband, Ed, went into couples therapy to work on communication and sexual issues. "Ed told the couples counselor that his greatest anger at my stepfather was about my overeating. He said I was eating myself into the grave over the sexual abuse and he felt helpless to stop me."

Many survivors I interviewed were physically scarred by their abuse. Elaine showed me several facial scars and had difficulty believing that I hadn't noticed them before. She not only felt like damaged goods; she believed she looked like damaged goods.

If It Weren't for My Body . . .

A survivor tends to think of his body as "my enemy" or "not mine," especially when it reminds him of or releases the trauma he suffered as a child. Jake speaks of "having a terrorist live inside of me." Body hatred or body distortion is common among survivors of childhood violence, who have internalized the family's attitudes.

The body offers a dumping ground for feelings about the abuse that are harder to articulate and perhaps overwhelming. It may seem easier to say "If it weren't for my body, it might be OK" than "I can't exactly remember what happened, and I don't want to feel the pain, fear and rage within me, but something is wrong and I don't know how to make it right again."

Some survivors believe their body betrayed them in the face of trauma. Particularly in sexual abuse, any physiological response on the victim's part may exacerbate feelings of guilt, responsibility and complicity. In cases of physical abuse, such as Laura's, where the beating is the offender's way of discharging sexual energy, children are sensitive to the eroticized atmosphere. "It was like watching a dirty movie—except I was in it. I didn't fully understand my mother's sexual arousal, but I knew there was something very different, very titillating going on for her. It was like picking up a static shock in the air."

Psychotherapist John Prebble has a wonderful analogy he uses when working with male victims who experienced erections or other signs of physiological arousal during abuse and worry that they were complicitous or desirous of it. "You know how you laugh when you are being tickled?" he reminds them. "It's not because you think it is funny, or because you are enjoying it or because you want the person to keep on tickling you. You laugh because you can't help it. Your body does it for you, regardless how you think or feel about it. Having an erection while being abused is like laughing when you're tickled. It sometimes happens, but it doesn't mean you wanted or caused the abuse."[5]

Each of us has a picture of our physical selves in our mind's eye. Trauma dramatically distorts this. Between beatings by his stepfather, lighter-skinned peers and gang fights, Daryl did not see himself as the physically strong youth he really was. "The worst thing about the violence is that they psyched me out of my own body and prevented me from seeing myself as I really am."

By anyone's standards, Janet is beautiful. Although she is frequently complimented on her "come-hither" good looks, she visualizes herself as "a brick—husky, unattractive and plain." Bricks are durable, invincible—they can withstand the punishment Janet has suffered.

Rob is an ex-marine in good shape, six two and two hundred pounds. "I feel like I'm five four and weigh a hundred pounds. I have no awareness of looking down on most people. I feel most of them look down on me. When I weighed forty pounds more, I overate to feel stronger, to gain a critical mass to protect me."

The roots of these distortions can be found in the abuser's own body hatred, projected onto the child. Once-limber Craig, who'd let himself become morbidly obese, commonly referred to Glen as "bushel-butt," but Glen says, "I've studied pictures of myself as a kid and I'm finally convinced I never had a fat ass."

Sheila hissed at eight-year-old Laura, "You have a double chin." When Laura was in high school, she told her, "You should always wear slacks—your legs are so skinny they repulse people." Laura too has studied photographs and realizes now: "I had and have long model-type legs. She was losing her figure and dumped her disgust on me. It's taken me a long time to unlearn those lies."

Several survivors showed me family albums during our interviews. I was struck by how *old* many of them looked as children and by the false personas they projected. Jenny looked like a harried housewife at ten. At eight years old, Beth was already frail and elderly in appearance, someone whom she hoped no one would dare hurt. At seventeen Stefan looked like a hardened criminal. Each persona served a vital purpose for the youngsters—they appeared frenzied or fragile or foreboding to ward off any more pain.

As they learned to care for the physical self the survivors began to look younger and more relaxed. The protective shells dissolved, giving way to a more natural and inviting appearance. To look at them today, you would never know they grew up with the threat of annihilation.

Giving Thanks to the Body

In *Love, Medicine and Miracles,* physician Bernie Siegel reminds us that our attitudes about our bodies influence health and healing:

> We don't yet understand all the ways in which brain chemicals are related to emotions and thoughts, but the salient point is that our state of mind has an immediate and direct effect on our state of body. We can change the body by dealing with how we feel. If we ignore our despair, the body receives a "die" message. If we deal with our pain and seek help, then the message is "Living is difficult but desirable." . . .[6]

Healing the body begins with forgiving it for its inevitable vulnerabilities, for having been abandoned, powerless and overwhelmed in the face of trauma. The body did the best it could under abnormal circumstances. Instead of judging it for what it could not do—protect itself from injury, defend the self, become immune to trauma—the body must be appreciated for what it did do. After all, many children's bodies are annihilated or permanently damaged by trauma. Jenny believes: "If it weren't for the tenacity of my body, if I hadn't been born of sturdy peasant stock, I don't think I'd be here today to tell you my story."

Fortunately, the circumstances of survivors' adult lives no longer demand the chronic or extreme responses of childhood. It is finally not only safe but necessary to return to a state of relaxation. Many survivors I interviewed felt that when they neglect their bodies, they are more vulnerable to flashbacks, overwhelming feelings, faulty thinking and existential despair. Recovery is a "team effort"; the body must be cared for in order to work effectively with the mind and heart.

Food is an obvious way to nurture the body. Laura says, "I shudder to remember my early twenties, when I lived literally for years on frozen pot pies and Coke. And then I wondered why I was always so run-down. Today, I love to cook and to eat, mostly healthy foods and an occasional rich French recipe, as both a hobby and a celebration of the fact that I am alive."

Many survivors who grew up in violent families describe feeling chronically exhausted as children. Resting each day, getting enough sleep, not working or exercising the body beyond its limits are other forms of nurturing the body. This includes taking vacations as needed, having leisure time that is refreshing, and scheduling one's days to minimize stress. The body should be given every possible advantage rather than being pushed to see how much it can take before giving out.

Exercise is a daily part of life for the majority of the survivors I interviewed. For many, like Jake, the initial motivation was a need to keep the "offending" body in line, but later this evolved into a desire to help the body relax, discharge stress and express feelings.

Several survivors also practiced meditation, to help alleviate numbness, to calm the "emergency response," or to quiet intrusive recollections of trauma. Meditation also helps reconnect the mind, heart and body in a state of serenity. Jake says, "My body used to speak for me—getting sick, lashing out, running down—but now with meditation I can use my thoughts and feelings to express what is going on with me. Only after I began daily meditation was I able to have all three working together."

Soothing touch in the form of massage can often heal the body from the injury done by violence or the yearnings unfulfilled by neglect, although survivors will require a sturdy "cognitive life raft" first and, above all, trust in the person providing the touch.

Eight of the twenty survivors I interviewed had once self-medicated; all have been abstinent for at least seven years. Vinnie and Laura had used marijuana to "numb out" from free-floating anxiety or other undesired feelings. For a few, the physical release and euphoria of orgasm was for a time their only relief from pervasive numbness or despair. They now believe that self-medication and other addictive behavior prevent the body from fully releasing and resolving trauma. Each came to realize that he was taking on the role of his abusers by numbing or overstimulating his body, by continuing to stress himself beyond his limits. Many had availed themselves of the various "Anonymous" groups.

Survivors see nurturing the body as a healthy form of control. Jake says, "All of my childhood, my body was other people's property, to do with as they wished. It was beaten, groped, starved, overfed, run ragged, neglected, rejected and at times, broken. Today, I've liberated it. I've claimed it as my own. With everything I eat, each hour that I rest, the fun that I have, I intend to treat my body in the tender and loving way it *should* have been treated when I was a kid."

What was shattered can be put back together again. The body is neither the survivor's sole hope for salvation nor the cause of all that went wrong. It gave the mind, heart and spirit the gift of survival; now it deserves rest from battle or an awakening from numbness.

CHAPTER SIX

The Child Within, the Parent Within

We shall not cease from exploration
And at the end of all our exploring
Will be to arrive where we started
And know the place for the first time.

—T. S. ELIOT
"Little Gidding," *Four Quartets*

Like most children, George loved to play outdoors with friends, sleep late, eat junk food, be messy and constantly ask questions. This enraged his mother, Evelyn, who was usually on the edge anyway. When she was just getting drunk, George could get away with being a kid, but when she crashed or was hung over, she'd beat him with a belt.

Once, when George was eight years old, he and two friends were playing in a soggy construction site. George came home covered in mud. Evelyn—coming off a week-long bender—beat him until he had welts, then gave him an enema with boiling water, just "so you never forget to stay clean, you disgusting pig." At that moment George stopped being a kid and became a "little man." More precisely, he became Evelyn's nursemaid, staying by her side constantly, taking care of her. He was an "ear to bitch to" and he cleaned up her vomit and elimination when she was too drunk to make it to the bathroom. George's new persona worked; there were fewer beatings and they seemed less random. Although she still beat him whenever she thought he didn't take good enough care of her, at least now, in George's mind, there was a "good reason." He clung to the illusion that he could prevent the next beating by "trying harder, being more of a man."

George's father was a traveling salesman. Feeling trapped in his marriage by George's unplanned birth and repulsed by Evelyn's behavior, he spent as much time away from home as he could. Divorce was out of the question, he knew, because they were Catholics. Maybe he didn't know how badly abused George was, maybe he did. But he took little interest in his son. To protect himself, George took care of his father too, commiserated with him and entertained him in an attempt to keep him at home. He became a "little father and little husband" to his parents.

Well prepared for the job by his mother's illness, George worked as a hospital orderly in high school and college. Nurses loved him because he was so reliable, a good listener and not squeamish about the job. Work got him out of the house and gave him enough money to send himself to college.

In George's junior year of college, Evelyn killed herself by drinking wood alcohol for a week. The medical examiner pronounced it cirrhosis so that her insurance money could be collected. Evelyn had named George sole beneficiary; he took the insurance money and went to veterinary school.

Today, George is a veterinary surgeon and the department head at a large teaching hospital. He is still a hard worker, and his colleagues and clients hold him in high esteem. He's a good listener, compassionate, extraordinarily diplomatic, and nurses, as always, love him. He continues to care for his ailing father, who is now in a nursing home.

But when anyone gets close to George, they meet "little Georgie." Male friends are appalled when he storms out of a racquetball game because a point didn't go his way. He'll entertain friends at his house but is uncomfortable visiting them, and usually cancels at the last minute. George sweeps women off their feet and into bed. But when they wake up the next morning, they face a needy tyrant who lectures them on cleanliness, whines when they don't pay attention to him and rages when their fantasies about the relationship do not match his. George feels as if he were two people stuffed into one body: the "thousand-year-old man" and "an overgrown toddler."

George had an uncanny knack for dating women with chemical dependencies or eating disorders. His relationships always ended badly.

Recently he met Sandy, who is newly sober and has a seven-year-old son named Will. George and Will get along wonderfully. They play with Will's dog, build elaborate sand castles at the beach and read science fiction and riddle books together. But Sandy and George's relationship is rocky, especially when Sandy needs time alone or with Will. Then George feels unappreciated, abandoned, frightened. He throws tantrums, accusing Sandy of not really loving him.

Finally, Sandy issued an ultimatum: either George got into therapy, or the relationship was over. George went, but he told himself that he was "helping Sandy with her sobriety problem." He was sure that his earnest young therapist, who specializes in treating adult children of alcoholics, would be no match for him. But the therapist wouldn't speak to the "too good to be true" adult George. Instead, he appealed to the "too bad to be true" little Georgie. He reminded George that at one time he too had been just as innocent and loving as Will, and he encouraged George to draw, paint and work with clay to express his feelings rather than to rely on the usual talking therapy. George humored him, knowing that no therapy would mean no Sandy.

One night, as Sandy was undressing for bed, George commented, "Don't you think you need some new bras? Yours are always so frayed and dirty." That did it for Sandy. She told him to leave. George slept alone that night, afraid he would never see Sandy again. He had a nightmare: "I dreamed I was at a picnic with friends and I left them to walk alone in the woods. Suddenly, I was surrounded by acres and acres of burnt trees." George desperately wanted to get back to the picnic, but he couldn't find his way out. "I started to run in circles. Suddenly, I fell down. As I lay on the ground, full of despair and terror, I heard a faint cry. I got up and followed the sound." Coming to a deep hole, he looked down and saw little Georgie crying for help, whimpering, scared out of his mind. "I yelled at him: 'Climb! . . . Jump! . . . Stop crying! . . . Try harder!'" Little Georgie tried hard, but the more he did what George told him to do, the more he flailed and the deeper he got stuck. Just when he was about to disappear into the center of the earth, George woke up, shaking.

At his next session, George told his therapist about the dream. He started to sob, although he didn't know "why a little dream should scare me—I should know better." His therapist suggested that George close his eyes and remember the last scene. Then he could try to finish the dream right there. The terrifying image of little Georgie being buried alive came back. This time, though, George jumped into the hole with little Georgie, took him in his arms and carried him to safety.

After weeks of analyzing his dream, George made a few changes in his life. He began to garden, a suitably adult way to play in mud. Recently, his panic has subsided enough that he can go over to his friends' houses "to play"; he realizes he won't be punished. He still hasn't stopped fighting with male friends over lost points in racquetball, but he is learning to give Sandy the space she needs.

George describes his life now as being like opening a gift. "You know that joke where you start out with a real little package, put it in a bigger box and then you put that box into an even bigger box, and then you put that box into an even bigger box, and on and on forever? Now I'm unwrapping the bigger boxes, one at a time. I keep my adult boxes around in case I need them. But, most important, I am getting down to the gift, the littlest box."

The Child Within

Many survivors described to me the severe abuse they suffered in excruciating detail but with absolutely no show of emotion. Yet, when asked about their strengths and weaknesses today, they often cried for the first and only time. Yolanda speaks for many of the others when she talks about her greatest weakness: "I just can't believe I'm lovable or worthy. Why would anybody want me?"

This profound loneliness often flourishes in the midst of love and admiration from many people. These survivors are experiencing the loneliness of alienation from the child within, who is dying to be loved. They may have genuinely high self-esteem as adults, but they often have nothing but contempt for the child within who is still so needy, so emotional, so traumatized. Psychoanalyst Alice Miller describes this phenomenon in *Prisoners of Childhood*:

They recount their earliest memories without any sympathy for the child they once were, and this is more striking since these patients not only have a pronounced introspective ability, but are also able to empathize well with other people. The relationship to their own childhood emotional world, however, is characterized by lack of respect, compulsion to control, manipulation and a demand for achievement.[1]

Some survivors may feel "at war" with that child within, and they may speak of themselves as children in the third person:

"How could he have been so sick?"

"Why was she so solicitous, trying to get blood out of a stone?"

"Why was he in trouble so much of the time?"

"What's she *still* so afraid of?"

Most of us had winter coats when we were growing up. Remember when you were six, seven, eight years old, how you could outgrow a coat in a season? Styles of coping are like psychological winter coats. The child probably tried on a hundred—getting sick, rescuing, people-pleasing, troublemaking or becoming invisible in the face of violence— before she settled on the one that best kept her warm and protected in the family storm. Fortunately, the world she lives in as an adult doesn't behave like her family, and she has outgrown her coat.

George was a terrorized child and his "winter coat" was, to mix a metaphor, to "whistle in the dark," deny his fear and get busy taking care of other people. He hates little Georgie's panic when invited to dinner; he despises little Georgie's clinging to a lover to prevent her from leaving; he abhors little Georgie's raging at all of this.

George's professional success and friendships (on his terms) provided "bigger and better boxes" to stuff little Georgie in. Only when he began to have compassion for little Georgie and allowed him to rage in draw-ings and finger paintings was there a reunion.

For those who doubt the existence of a child within an adult personal-ity, proof is not hard to come by. A friend of mine describes her visits home: "I get on the plane here in Boston, and I'm still my forty-two-year-old successful and mature self. The plane lands in Nebraska, and I'm in my early twenties, unsure of myself, but excited about the world nonetheless. The cab takes me from the airport to my elderly parents' home and I go through my adolescence: let them just try to tell me what to do; I'm going to show them—I know more than they do. They open the door and greet me and I'm seven years old. I think they are the greatest thing since sliced bread and I've got the coolest parents in the world. By the end of the second day I'm saying *"No!"* to everything, just to let them know they can't push me around. I get on the plane back to Boston sucking my thumb." If we could hear from her parents, they might confess to interfering in ways they swore they never would, desiring to cook and care for their adult daughter in exactly the way they did when she was little and, worst of all, treating her "the same idiotic ways" their parents treated them when they went home for visits.

Suicide for Love

Several years ago psychotherapist Nicholas D. Etcheverry was driving along the highway when he saw a billboard of "a little girl, a victim of child abuse, with a single tear running down her wide-eyed face. The caption read: 'Mommy, if I die, then will you love me?' " The image haunted him. From it, he developed the concept of "suicide for love."[2] Many survivors—more than we will ever know—actually do kill themselves. Others just kill off a part of themselves, the child part, hoping that this sacrifice will win their parents' love.

A few years ago I witnessed an example of a "suicide for love," while cross-country skiing in New Hampshire. It was a crowded Sunday on the trails and our beginners' class came upon a steep hill. At the bottom a woman and a seven-year-old boy were standing next to an enraged man who was berating a four-year-old boy, who was still at the top. "Get your ass down that hill right now or I'm coming up there after you," he bellowed. Very tentatively, the sobbing preschooler made his way down the hill, miraculously without falling once. He collapsed at the abusive man's feet, exhausted and frightened, his face in the snow. His father loomed over him, his voice echoing through the mountains, *"Stop acting like a child."* The little boy immediately stopped crying and stood up, and the four of them skied off.

Children in "bad enough" families sense they will never be loved for being who they are, so they hope to be loved for being someone else. In the face of chronic trauma, "acting like a child" puts them at greater risk to be abused and neglected. They learn quickly that they had better become an adult to keep the child within safe. They find a role—

caretaker, warrior, invalid, rebel, prodigy, diplomat, superachiever, scapegoat, entertainer—and their own true character and healthy strivings are silenced for the time being.

Traditional psychiatric thought holds that chronic trauma, such as George endured, causes a psychic explosion that shatters the ego of the child. For some that is true. However, among the survivors I interviewed, there seemed to have been more of an *implosion*. Like a clenched fist, the child's ego had contracted and around it had evolved a rigid, protective pseudoadult ego.

Yet the child within cannot be destroyed. Even buried deep inside the survivor's psyche, she makes herself known. The strivings in the child within that were the most repugnant or enraging to the abusive parent persist and express themselves into adulthood. George's attachments to playmates outside his family threatened his mother. In adulthood the child within both yearned for those attachments and feared their abusive consequences, so he wouldn't allow himself to "go out to play" with others or to stay close to them for long.

Elaine's mother resented her intelligence. When Elaine came home with straight A's, her mother said, "You think you're too smart, too good for us," and beat her viciously. Elaine has dropped in and out of college for the past ten years, unable to complete her undergraduate degree, yet she earns high grades, praise from her professors and occasional scholarships based on merit. "I can't stand being the smartest in a class or having people look up to me. It makes me feel like it's a crazy world, filled with incompetent people."

When a child's healthy strivings for love, nurturance, pleasure, mastery or autonomy are consistently punished by parents, children come to believe, according to psychiatrist Adras Angyal, " 'What I want is forbidden.' It is not a very big step to believe, 'The forbidden is what I want.' "[3] So otherwise healthy and competent adults relentlessly pursue the "forbidden" in some area of their lives: George pursued love; Elaine pursued academic competence. To want was life; to have was death.

Upside-down Families

Repeated violence—experiencing, witnessing or living with the threat of it—ruins childhood. All the psychological resources of the child become organized around surviving the violence, leaving little energy for normal development.

In a "good enough" family, children wonder, What will I get for my birthday? Will there be something good to eat in my lunch box? or How can I get my parents to take me to Disney World? In a violent family, children are preoccupied with questions like How can I behave to avoid being raped again? Should I get this beating over with today so that by the field trip next week, my bruises will be fading? How can I protect my younger brothers and sisters? and Will we live to see tomorrow?

Childhood trauma can cause aspects of the child's ego to become stuck at certain developmental stages. When George began to walk, his mother couldn't tolerate the separation. What if the baby left her—just walked away—as her husband repeatedly did? Her beatings made George curtail the normal process toddlers go through, learning to run away and feel proud of it. The conflict persisted into adulthood, in George's uncertainty about how to be intimate with another and give her space at the same time.

After the child's ego implodes, the "little adult" he has become undertakes tasks meant for true grown-ups. With the developmental tasks of childhood thwarted or incompletely mastered, he must speed light-years ahead. A sexually abused child must learn to accommodate the feelings of surrender and invasion that the first sexual penetration creates. The child of troubled parents learns to sacrifice his own tender needs to his parents' desires, whether for a paramour or for a scapegoat. To survive, the child must master the illusion of self-reliance at an age when dependency is necessary and healthy; she is forced to become "self-sufficient in an insufficient way."[4] Many survivors must parent childlike parents and perhaps brothers and sisters as well, becoming "little husbands and little wives" and "little fathers and little mothers." This is an "upside-down family." In a family relatively free of chronic trauma, parents look after the children's emotional and physical well-being. In a family with chronic trauma, home is adult-centered or abuser-centered, not child-centered or safe.

This role reversal doubly destroys a healthy childhood. Many survivors I interviewed, like Jenny, grew up with burdensome household chores. "I can still remember feelings of dread as I watched the dust come up the road. That meant my father was coming home from watching my mother waitress at the truck stop. He was insanely jealous, convinced she would have affairs if he wasn't there. But that left me to do all the chores on a subsistence farm he stupidly planted on red clay, and to take care of my younger brother and sister. I had to tend to five hundred laying chickens, cleaning their cages, feeding them, collecting the eggs, and milk a dozen cows every morning before I got the three of us off to school. One day, I mistakenly left the door to the chicken hatch open and a cow wandered in and ate the chicken feed. Not only could we not afford to replace that volume of feed, but it exploded in the cow's stomach and she might have died. For that he beat me till I passed out. I was nine years old."

At ten, when Daryl's parents' fights over his father's drinking and fear of going outside had grown increasingly violent, Daryl, his mother and his younger sister Shirley fled in the middle of the night. Daryl recalls: "For the next five years I came home after school every day, sat down with my mother, and we discussed things—like disciplining Shirley, who was only a year younger than me, how we should spend the little bit of money we had, what did I think of the man she dated. I'm forty-seven years old and a confirmed bachelor. Marriage holds no romance or mystery for me—I already know what hard work it is."

Elaine's father had several heart attacks when she was a child. "At twelve I had to drive my mother to the hospital. I'd figured out how to operate the car—sort of. My biggest problem was trying to calm her down. She'd be screaming and wailing about how poor we would be if he died. She'd get hysterical and I was always afraid she'd grab the wheel away from me and cause us to crash."

For some, the call to parent their parents was inconsistent. The chaos was painful for Thelma. "One day I got chicken soup and lots of hugs because I was sick, and literally the next day I'm still sick but I'm running around the house pouring vodka down the drain. At five years old, I could dial the police—and often did. From day to day, I never knew where I stood."

No wonder so many survivors complain of feeling inauthentic. In one aspect of life, such as work or taking care of others, they may be wise beyond their years. At the same time, in another area—perhaps taking care of themselves emotionally or physically—they feel helpless and incompetent.

Amy describes feeling like an impostor, a "lifeguard on a crowded beach who doesn't know how to swim and is afraid to say anything for fear of causing a panic."

Jake sees himself as "a house of cards: you can build on and gently touch the top part, but get anywhere near the shaky foundation, and it will all come tumbling down."

As others come to know the survivor he feels shame about this developmental disorganization. Not wanting them to see his inauthenticity, he may keep them at arm's length, where they can admire the attractive packaging but remain unaware of the child clamoring to get out.

The Parent Within

Just as there is a child within, there is a parent within. We take our families with us everywhere we go, as this old story illustrates: A young woman was having a dinner party. Her friends, gathered in the kitchen, watched her carve the top off the ham before she put it in the oven to bake. "What are you doing?" they cried. "You'll ruin it! It'll dry out!" The young woman was confused. "What do you mean, what am I doing? This is how you cook a ham. It's what my mother taught me."

The next time she talked to her mother, she mentioned her friends' reaction. The mother didn't understand it any better. "What's their problem? That's how you cook a ham. Your grandmother has been doing it that way since I was a little girl." Her curiosity piqued, the next time she saw her own mother she asked why.

"Well," the grandmother answered, "we had one of the first electric ovens and it was very small. Most hams didn't fit inside, so we cut the top off to make it fit."

Each of us inevitably thinks, feels and behaves in some ways as our parents did, whether we admit it or not. The legacy ranges from how we cook a ham to what we do when we feel helpless to how much we trust other people. The awareness of that legacy in part determines which survivors fare well as adults and which unthinkingly transmit violence to the next generation.

Some are very quick to accuse others. "You act just like my rejecting mother," they say, or "You remind me so much of my derelict father," pointing the finger away from themselves to distract from ways in which they behave like their abusive parent. A Sufi story tells of a passerby who encounters a man groping around on his hands and knees underneath a street lamp and asks what he is doing. The man answers, "I locked my keys inside my house and I'm looking for them." "But if the keys are inside, why are you looking out here?" The man responds matter-of-factly, "There's more light out here."

Perhaps there is "more light" available when one looks outside oneself, but the house remains locked up and dark, and the key usually *is* inside. Many survivors told me that their first awareness of the parent within was excruciatingly painful. This is, in part, why many survivors "bottom out" in young adulthood. In the troubled home the "enemy" was clearly outside the self and might be avoided, confronted, manipulated or cajoled. When survivors move away from the family, they may, for the first time, become aware of the "enemy within." Thinking they will finally be free of abuse and neglect, they are shocked to find themselves drawn to abusive or cold people or behaving destructively toward themselves.

Their first impulse is to trot out their old "winter coats." But they notice that the coat no longer fits—being sick, ultracompetent, delinquent, passive or whatever does not keep them safe anymore. Why are people reacting so differently from the way their families did to these same behaviors? Failure. Defeat. What used to work no longer works, but they don't know what else to do.

Rob believes: "It is important for me to know what my parents' choices were and weren't—to stop drinking, get help, walk away from violence, not have so many children—because I know those will ultimately be some of my choices as well."

Glen would agree. When he was twenty-five years old, his mother finally walked out on his physically abusive father. "He broke into her apartment and unsuccessfully tried to kill her by filling the apartment with gas and attempting to light a match. She pressed charges of attempted murder. I was in the courtroom, day after day, trying to support both of them. After the pretrial motions were done, his attorney told him to prepare himself for some jail time. It didn't look good. That night he killed himself with a gun. That was the turning point in my life. I was a junior high teacher, having a hard time supporting my wife and daughter. Some of my friends were bookies, and I often placed bets with them. Back then, in Chicago, no one was ever arrested for bookmaking, so I was planning on quitting my job and going into business with them. I was thirty-five pounds overweight and gaining, and drinking every night. At my father's funeral, I said to myself, Glen, you've got it all—the compulsive behavior, crime, weight and booze—you're walking the same path he did and it's going to the same destination. All you need now is a gun." Glen stopped gambling and drinking, and began exercising. He also, like so many of the survivors I interviewed, went into therapy at this low point. Two years later he quit teaching and became a drug and alcohol counselor.

Vinnie's parent within can be found in his dreams. "Between reacting to my dad's drinking and violence, nursing my terminally ill brother, and counseling, feeding and clothing the entire neighborhood, my mother didn't have much left for the rest of us. We all had to compete for attention, affection, even a place to sleep. She often gave my bed to some street kid and I'd sleep on the couch. But her martyrdom always embarrassed me because I knew there was another side to it. She wanted a lot back for what she gave others. She had Scarsdale tastes on a Bowery budget and was often bitter that she didn't have more in life.

"This dream keeps on coming back to me. I'm a little kid, riding on my bike. I spy a bunch of dollar bills rolled up in a tin can. I stop to pick it up, and out of the corner of my eye I see this old, haggard witch. We look at each other. We both look at the can. We both have greed in our eyes. It goes on and on like this, back and forth, forever. I know I am my mother in that dream."

Many talked with relatives or with their parents themselves to better understand their parents' troubled behavior. There are no *excuses* for abusing or neglecting a child, but many survivors found *explanations* in their parents' history, which helped them not only to let go of their anger but also to avoid following in the same path.

Rita's father received a Purple Heart when wounded at the Battle of Anzio during World War II. "He lied about his age, joined the Army, mostly to get the paycheck for his widowed mom. When he would beat me, he'd be yelling at me, 'Be a good marine. Take it like a man.' I don't think he knew where he was or what he was doing. Understanding this made me more committed to getting treatment for my post-traumatic stress disorder."

Laura was raised "on horror stories of my grandfather's physical abuse of my mother. She often told one in particular: She was sixteen and returned home from a date. She had stayed on the porch talking to the young man. Moments later, while she was using the bathroom, my grandfather burst in and beat her with a belt because he thought she'd been making out with her date.

"Her beating of my genitals was almost a picture-perfect replication of that scene with my grandfather. Even though I understood the power dynamic—now she was the powerful offender instead of the helpless victim—I couldn't understand how she could obsess about her own history and then repeat it with me.

"Then, a few years ago, she was fondly remembering her grand-mother, whose home had been a safe haven each summer for her. With great animation and warmth, she told me of a time when she was thirteen and had taken her little cousin up to the hay loft in the barn to read. All of the kids were forbidden to go up there because the lice were so thick. Of course, my mother and her cousin came back loaded with lice. Her grandmother beat her with a belt while she was naked in the bathtub. She was laughing about this. I told her I found the story to be very sad, that no child should be beaten and certainly never in such a sexually humiliating way. My mother became very defensive, saying she deserved the beating and her grandmother loved her very much.

"For me, things became much more clear. My mother didn't think striking a child was bad. She thinks there are good reasons and bad reasons for beating a child. She thinks there are good people and bad people who beat children. She and her grandmother were good people with good reasons for beating children. Her own father was a bad person with bad reasons for beating her. She couldn't grasp the com-monality or the problem with the behavior. When I understood how screwed up her thinking was, I was less confused by her and less fright-ened of her. I saw her as a very sad, damaged person. And it makes me more conscientious about distorted thinking in myself."

Many survivors try in vain to change their parents, to make them loving, sober, sane, gentle or sorry for the harm they've done. Their efforts are almost always like trying to turn back the tide, or as my colleague Phil Oliver-Diaz calls it, "trying to turn a rabbit into a squir-rel." But opportunities abound to change the parent who counts—the parent within.

Of course, no real parent (or parent within) is all bad, any more than is any real child (or child within). And although some survivors are prone to all-or-nothing thinking, the survivors I interviewed had become aware of a legacy of positive qualities from their parents, of being like them, for the good, in some respects.

Janet's father ran a gambling operation in the basement of their home; Janet tended bar there as a little girl. "He was a very funny storyteller," she says, "and he loved to be the center of attention. I am like him in that way and it makes me a good public speaker."

George told me, "My father's passivity has served me well in that I can sit back and consider all sides of a situation while those around me feel compelled to react. The difference is, I eventually do make a decision and he didn't, but his gentleness was wonderful."

Glen reflects, "I think I've been less depressed than other people I've known from similar homes precisely because I did follow in my parents' footsteps of explosiveness. It used to get me into trouble and I've had to harness it, but it would never occur to me to withdraw or isolate myself from the person I'm angry at. I let them know I'm angry. I think I get more things worked through. Of course, it took me years to learn to express my anger constructively."

Right before her eighth Christmas, Janet was rummaging through closets, trying to find her presents. "I always thought of my father as someone who didn't like living things. Clearly he didn't like children, and we weren't allowed to have pets or plants. He was so violent—both at home and at his job as a prison guard. Then, in the closet, I found these sketchbooks—exquisite drawings he'd done in charcoal of wildlife and landscapes. They were beautiful, inspired—he had been so talented." Janet studied sculpture in college and later became a fund-raiser for the arts, "trying to help others realize their potential as he could not."

Janet identifies a turning point in her own recovery that resonates for many other healthy survivors: "You know, when I accepted that he was more than just a batterer, then I could accept that I am more than just a victim."

Reunions

A survivor who parented others and missed her own childhood may see the task of parenting yet another hurt person—the child within—as a terrible burden, the last thing she wants to do. George recalls, "When

Sandy started talking about this 'injured child,' I wanted to throw up. I found it insulting—I'm an adult. But through that dream, playing with my 'best buddy' Will and just allowing that traumatized child within me to speak, I have found a missing piece of myself. This time, caretaking is not a burden. I was a pretty neat kid to begin with and I am glad to meet me. No, this is different from taking care of my mom. It's a parent-and-child reunion, a celebration. Its the only way I know to make it right."

Every survivor has both the opportunity and responsibility to be a good parent to the child within. Psychotherapist Nicholas Etcheverry reminds us that such "single parenthood" does not preclude seeking help from other people. We can learn to be "good enough parents" to ourselves by allowing others both to help meet our adult needs and to nurture the child within.

Jake was groping for words, trying to explain to his friend Bill how hurt he was by a colleague's criticism of his work. Bill responded, "So, you've had a setback." The child within Jake heard the comment, too: "Not only did I know Bill understood what I was saying but he helped me out by giving me a new name for it!"

Beth allows her friends to make a fuss over her birthday. This is hard for her because she never had a birthday party when she was a child and she is not always sure how to behave. She "watched like a hawk" when she went to other people's birthday parties before she let them have one for her. Now she can tolerate and even enjoy being the center of attention one evening a year.

Maybe Tom Robbins was right when he said, "It's never too late to have a happy childhood."

Once the parent-child reunion has begun, each of the previous steps of healing must be embraced again—this time for the child within rather than for the adult. Healing can come from reading books about parenting, watching how "good enough" parents speak to their children and learning about what a child's needs are at various developmental stages. Often, at this point, a survivor seeks and finds solace in children's books. This is the most healthy of regressions, to a simpler truth.

Deeper levels of feeling and grief will arise as the child within remembers how awful the trauma really felt, rather than focusing on how unfair it was. Free of adult judgments, there is a purity and cleansing to this deeper level of mourning.

The parent-child reunion also awakens the body. Imagine, if you will, that you are the parent of an eight-year-old child who has recently been traumatized. Would you give him a cup of coffee first thing in the morning and a piece of leftover pizza at ten o'clock at night, and nothing in between? Encourage him to smoke half a pack of cigarettes, drink six Diet Cokes, and eat the equivalent of five meals a day? Sleep only four hours a night, then sit at a desk for twelve, with no breaks for fresh air or exercise? Would you offer him a few drinks or pills "to take the edge off a bad day?" Hopefully not. But these are some of the ways the parent within harms and neglects the body it shares with the child within. As the body is treated with more respect and care, the giggles that were stifled, the agility that was beaten down, the sexual energy that was exploited, the strength that was shamed may come back anew.

The focus of the internal parent-child reunion should be on integration rather than on perceiving the self as a patchwork of distinct or contradictory parts or people, which can cause identity problems. My colleague Terry Kellog has pointed out that some survivors use "child-within fanaticism" to rationalize irresponsible behavior: "Recently I was leading a workshop and people were saying, 'My child within took a tantrum' or 'My abusive parent chewed out the desk clerk at this hotel for screwing up my reservation' or 'My nonprotective parent really wimped out when someone cut in front of me in line.' And I'm saying to myself, Who are all of these people? Do they jump out of the survivor's pocket, do these things and jump back in again?"[5]

Other survivors transfer the contempt they once felt for the traumatized child within to the pseudoadult, blaming this persona for all their problems. If only they could be childlike at all times and could throw a tantrum, nap and eat ice cream at will, they would recover. They miss the point that the problem with being "pseudoadult" is the "pseudo" part, not the "adult." What was "pseudoadult" behavior at age five may be genuinely admirable and functional behavior at age thirty-five.

To George's reunion, little Georgie brought renewed spontaneity, natural feelings and a gregarious nature. George still cherishes his adult power of reason, hardworking nature and the ability to ask for help when he needs it. As he integrates all these elements into his view of himself, George has stopped feeling "like a fake."

In Arthur Miller's play *After the Fall,* Holga tells her lover Quentin of her internment in a Nazi concentration camp and the aftermath years later. He is in awe of her and asks, "How do you get so purposeful? You're so full of hope!" She replies:

> I think it's a mistake to ever look for hope outside oneself. . . . The same dream returned each night until I dared not go to sleep and grew quite ill. I dreamed I had a child, and even in the dream I saw it was my life, and it was an idiot, and I ran away. But it always crept back onto my lap again, clutched at my clothes. Until I thought, if I could kiss it, whatever in it was my own, perhaps I could sleep. And I bent to its broken face, and it was horrible . . . but I kissed it. I think one must finally take one's life in one's arms, Quentin.[6]

So many of us search for intimacy, to embrace another or to be embraced. In the relentless nature of our search, we too often overlook the genuine intimacy of taking "one's life in one's arms."

CHAPTER SEVEN

Second Chances: Friends, Lovers and Children

One chimpanzee is no chimpanzee.

—RICHARD LEAKEY

Rob reminds most people of a "gentle giant." It is not just his six two frame and round features they are talking about. He has a wide grin, an impressive wit, an extraordinary grasp of complex medical and psychological concepts and, in his job as a social worker, a depth of compassion for "hopeless cases" his colleagues marvel at. Only a chosen few know that Rob as a child was a victim of the five traumas we have discussed. Even fewer know of his extensive history as a juvenile delinquent. Back then, he was often judged to be a "hopeless case" himself. So much of Rob's largeness today is a transformation of his "littleness" in the face of unspeakable acts.

Rob's father, Douglas, met Mary Lou when he was an ex-marine returning from World War II. When they married three months later, they did not know each other well and were not aware that they shared a traumatic family background. In Douglas's family someone being thrown across the room was an everyday event. His mother killed herself when he was fifteen years old. Mary Lou was neglected, constantly ridiculed by her mother, sexually abused and then abandoned by her father. No one noticed that Mary Lou had bipolar manic depressive illness resulting from a biochemical imbalance. She was simply "different," "touched." Mary Lou felt lucky that Douglas would want to marry her. Douglas longed for a better kind of family than the one he came from. Neither asked a lot of questions.

At first, Douglas and Mary Lou seemed to have captured the normalcy they both yearned for. Their first child, Vicky, was born eight months after their wedding. Rob—"Bobby"—was born three years later. They lived near Mary Lou's mother and spent every Sunday with her. Douglas worked in a meat-packing plant and sang in the church choir on Sundays.

Then Douglas's payday drinking sessions with his buddies started lasting well into the weekend. He would come home looking for a fight. Somehow he always pulled it together in time to sing for the Sunday service. Rob remembers his father singing those hymns, often getting a baritone solo: "I was *so* proud of him. That was my dad!"

Trapped at home with Vicky and Rob, Mary Lou began drinking in secret, trying to "settle the nerves" with vodka. After an all-night fight with Douglas that kept Vicky and Rob awake, it wasn't unusual for Mary Lou to slap Vicky around Sunday morning for "taking too long to get ready for church."

Before long, Mary Lou was drinking to control her wild mood swings, not realizing that the more she drank, the faster the merry-go-round went. When she was in a manic phase, she'd either chatter constantly or leave Rob and Vicky alone for hours while she went on shopping sprees. Sometimes she'd stand naked by the living room window. In her depressed phases she couldn't get out of bed for days, couldn't eat or speak except to say, "I want to die." She slept so deeply, Rob and Vicky would panic and think she was dead. Three times, her mother had Mary Lou committed to the state mental institution. "She'd come home more disoriented than ever," Rob remembers.

Douglas left home from time to time also, sometimes after the police arrested him for beating Mary Lou. Rob recalls: "One of my worst memories is being maybe four years old at the most. I can still see the bunny feet on my pajamas. I'm looking down and at my feet is my mother, passed out cold. Blood is streaming from her ears and nose. I'd just watched my father break a vodka bottle over her head. He's standing behind me, looming over me. All he said was 'She's only fooling.' I was paralyzed between them."

Mary Lou was in and out of the home so much, Rob never felt close to her: "I worried about her, but I couldn't depend on her for much." Douglas was less predictable. "He'd make Vicky and me march to bed every night, like 'little marines.' Then the three of us would say our prayers together. When he was home, it was a ritual I looked forward to. Funny, I still say my prayers every night."

But there was another ritual Rob did not look forward to. "He'd lean me over the bathtub, inspect and fondle my anus, 'checking for buggies.' Even as a little kid, I thought it was creepy. Sometimes he'd give me enemas and that caused physical pain."

Douglas's drinking began to interfere with his job. With each firing, the more he drank and beat his wife. When Rob was six, Mary Lou gave birth to another son, Roy, named after her missing father. The strain of another child was too much for the failing marriage. Mary Lou was quickly losing her grasp on reality, but she still had enough awareness of her plight to take action. "One night, when my dad left for the VFW Hall to drink, my mother packed a few things and we all fled to her cousin's house. We never went back."

After six months of frequently changing locations to avoid Douglas, Mary Lou and the three children "moved into the most notorious housing project in the city. It was bad in the house, but now, there was a fight on every corner. I wasn't safe anywhere."

After his parents' divorce, Rob "was caught in the middle." His father "was withholding support payments, allegedly because my mother was drinking the money away. But his actions meant poverty for us kids. And then my mother would interrogate me after every visit, 'So what's new with the big spender?' Mostly, I was embarrassed by his deterioration from Huntington's. I remembered him as this ideal marine. Now he was in a brace and shaking constantly. I'd pray to God every night, 'Please take me instead. Please make my father all better.' And then I'd lie awake nights afraid God might take me up on the deal. After I was nine, I refused to see him—it was just too painful.

"My mother used to order her drinking buddies to beat me up. I did what any self-respecting eight-year-old would do: I jumped out of the second-story window. After I jumped, they'd lock me out, so I'd kick in neighbors' basement windows and sleep in their cellars at night."

Vicky was committed to the state psychiatric institute when she was eleven years old. She had been carving deep cuts into her forearms. No one working with Vicky noticed that Mary Lou was not capable of raising Rob and Roy.

"We only had two bedrooms in the project apartment. My mother used to sleep with Vicky, except for when she was having sex in exchange for liquor. She'd do that in the living room, in earshot of all of us. After Vicky left she moved Roy into the bed with her. On the one hand I was worried about him and what she was doing to him. On the other hand, I felt abandoned by him."

Rob cared for Roy as best he could. "I'd make him cracker and ketchup sandwiches every day. He'd wander out into the living room in the morning and find my mom and some strange guy passed out and in various states of undress. He'd come wake me up and ask me what was wrong with Mommy." Rob retreated to his crystal radio and poetry writing. "I used to pull my hair and bang my head, saying to myself over and over again, 'Make it stop.'"

Rob's fourth-grade teacher, Mr. Kaminsky, was "like an island" for him. "I love him and wish I could find him. One day, at ten-thirty a.m., I remembered it was garbage-collection day and I had forgotten to take out the garbage. I knew that would start my mother on a rampage. I jumped up, ran out of the classroom, got home, put the garbage out and ran back to the classroom. I was winded and crying—mostly in relief because the trucks hadn't done our street yet. Mr. Kaminsky came over, put his arm around me and said, "It will be OK, whatever it is, it will be OK."

Everyone called Rob "Bobby" in those days. "Not long after the garbage-day incident, Mr. Kaminsky looked over at me in the middle of class and said, 'Bobby, from now on your name is Rob. Yes, Rob, that's a much better name for you.' Being Rob helped me to leave behind some of the shame and terror of being Bobby until I was better able to deal with it as an adult."

In the meantime, Rob acted out the shame and terror of being Bobby. He began drinking daily at eleven years old and was arrested frequently for fighting and running away. "When I was sixteen, I punched a teacher who was trying to make an example of me. They said, 'No more probation.' I was in court, about to be sent away to an institution. One of my Dad's second cousins worked there and called Dad. Quite dramatically, he appeared in his wheelchair and asked for custody of me. He got it."

Douglas and his new wife lived "in a safer neighborhood. It was easier to go to school. I checked in on Roy once in a while. It was an OK year with them." Douglas thought Rob should join the marines, which he did. "Nothing was ever good enough for him. I graduated in the top two percent of my basic training class at Parris Island. After graduation the first thing he said to me was 'It was harder when I was here twenty-five years ago.' "

After his four years of military service, Rob "picked up where I left off as a kid. I loved Harley motorcycles and I rode with gangs. Even then, part of me knew I was drinking to be closer to my parents. Yet I knew it wasn't right. It is my nature to absolutely *exhaust* whatever I'm using to get by. I found the daily fifth of Scotch and drugs empty— they no longer worked. One day, I just stopped and enrolled in a community college."

There Rob met Judith, who at first glance seemed to be from the perfect family. "There was no physical or sexual abuse, no addictions or major mental illness. Those were my criteria of health back then. I was interested in marrying Judith's family more than I was interested in marrying Judith."

Rob soon discovered that the closeness in Judith's family was more like fusion. In the early days of bonding—with Judith and her family— the distinction did not matter. "For a long time, Judith and I were 'the kids' in the family and that was just fine with me. We did everything together, finished each other's sentences, even ate off each other's plates. We spent virtually all of our free time with her folks and brothers."

With the safety net of acceptance by Judith's family beneath him, Rob began to experience "overwhelming and seemingly ancient feelings of loneliness and emptiness. Judith just didn't understand it. Her solution was to go over to her parents' house for dinner. You know, 'Eat something, you'll feel better.' "

Then Judith got pregnant and Rob "wanted time alone with her, not to be at her parents' house every weekend, all weekend. During her pregnancy, she sought their comfort and advice more than mine." He went nuts over the lack of separation. " 'Declare your citizenship,' I used to demand. 'You can't be a citizen of two countries at the same time.' After Megan was born, we'd fight over Judith's reliance on her parents for daily advice on baby care. By the time our second daughter was born I was insisting that my emptiness, my profound sense of aloneness be acknowledged in our marriage. Judith didn't want to hear it. So I left and we both talked with divorce attorneys."

Once again, Rob couldn't stay and he couldn't get back in. "I couldn't stay in a conflict-ridden marriage just for the sake of my two daughters. What kind of message is that—'Love is hate'? But I couldn't leave and give them the message you can quit on love, just walk away. There were times I really wanted to hit her, but I knew I would kill myself before I did that. My parents had open warfare. Judith and I had a cold war."

This time around there were no neighbors' basements to escape to. Rob contemplated suicide. Then he decided to face the despair he felt. He found a therapist to share it with.

For her part, Judith came to understand that she "was divorcing the wrong person." She began to separate from her family, spending less time with them, and began including friends in her life and relying on her own judgment instead of her mother's. Couples therapy helped, and Rob and Judith reconciled—or, more to the point, achieved rapprochement. "It's only been the last two years that we've settled in, feel really happy with each other. There's plenty I don't like about Judith, and she about me. It is still so difficult when one of us needs something that the other can't give. I still don't entirely trust that my needs will be taken seriously. But we've both learned to reach out to others too. I do love Judith and have learned, with her, through her, an acceptance of myself and others I've never known before."

Rob reexperiences some of his childhood through his daughters: "I still don't know how I'm going to explain my parents to the girls. Megan, my four-year-old, asks me, 'Where's your daddy? Is he in heaven?' I say 'Yes.' Or she asks things like 'Did your daddy ever tell you about being afraid of wolves? What did he say?' I'll answer, 'Well, let me think,' stalling while I remember how he was always too drunk to talk to us, and then we left. While I pause she goes ahead and tells me what she thinks he should have said and I tell her, 'That's right, that's what he said.' But it's painful."

Rob's pain is in perspective. "I'll always have some residue of my childhood. Right now, I'm trying to be more sexually open to Judith. And I still don't feel entirely comfortable having friends over to the house. Just last week I became very anxious in the middle of a dinner party. I had to get up, move around. Our friends are safe, they aren't like my mother's friends, but I'm not as secure in those situations as I want to be. Still, I have a very good life. I keep on painting myself into corners of health. It gets harder and harder for me to deny I am OK. Maybe I'm not 'locked out' and all alone anymore."

Welcome to the Party

Being born into a family is like coming late to a party where everyone has been talking, dancing, joking, eating, smoking and drinking for hours. If the first year of life is welcoming, the child believes, "I should be at this party. It is all right that I exist. I do not have to prove my worth or justify my existence." If the first year of life is not welcoming, then the infant believes, "Something has gone very wrong. My being causes other people unhappiness. I should not exist. I must prove my worth. I must justify my existence."

Long before infants can understand the spoken word, they receive powerful messages from how they are held. A smothered child learns that he exists only as an extension of another but not in his own right. A child who is held in a tentative or unsure manner learns that she is a burden to others, so she is better off staying alone, out of the way. A child who is not held enough learns to abandon awareness of his own needs because there is not "enough" available to him. A child who is physically or sexually abused learns that she exists only as a receptacle of other people's needs and rage. A child who is held tenderly learns comfort and security in his own existence and safety in relationship to others.

A few of the survivors I interviewed had a "good enough" experience with the parent who was not yet so troubled. Joan knows that during her first year she "was the center of the universe for both my parents." Long after five other children were born, her father's drinking problem worsened and her mother died, the early experience of belonging lived on in Joan's heart. This made bonding with her own infant son much easier. "Even though I was nineteen years old and scared out of my mind, I just seemed to know how to hold and care for Robert. It was like a good memory."

Most were not so lucky. Many "made do" with the intermittent offering of nurturance and abuse or neglect. Esther reflects, "You know, when someone is beating the crap out of you and telling you that you are responsible for all misery in their life, you are a *very important person*. My mother told me she couldn't live without me, that I was the center of her universe. The next day, she'd tie me up and beat me for 'rejecting' her wishes. I always hoped to be back in her good graces, but even the negative attention seemed preferable to indifference."

Several formed attachments to other adults—baby-sitters, grandparents, older brothers and sisters, nurses and the like—because the troubled parent was not physically available. Rita's mother was devastated that Rita was born a girl: "She gave me to my father's brother on a nearby reservation and I lived with my uncle and aunt for my first year of life. My father fought with my mother for that first year to get me back. After she gave birth to my brother, my father went and got me. They tried to shut my aunt and uncle out of the family. I bet they took good care of me. I feel so warmly toward them even though I don't remember much about them."

Other survivors said that they had not bonded with their most troubled or destructive parent. Laura's reflections are typical: "Sometimes I think there might be something really wrong with me, because I never yearned for my mother's love. Perhaps that is because my grandmother was there two days a week and that was enough. My first conscious memory of my mother is one of fear. I didn't like her. I didn't want to be close to her. I know my pulling away from her felt like rejection to her and that fueled her physical abuse of me. To me, it was self-defense." The lack of bonding—the enormous loss that it represents notwithstanding—also helped survivors to internalize less of the troubled parent and freed them to seek other kinds of bonding or love.

Several survivors reported that they couldn't have survived without their pets. Animals are often a source of soothing touch, unconditional love and mirroring of a child's emotions. The bliss of bonding throughout a lifetime does not always come in human form.

Where I End and You Begin

Sooner or later the bliss of bonding gives way to adventure. By the fifth month or so of life a baby begins to understand that there is a "you," distinct and separate from "I." As long as "you" respond empathetically to his needs for food, warmth, cleanliness, sleep and cuddling, bliss persists.

Then biology takes over. As psychologist Louise Kaplan explains in *Oneness and Separateness:*

> No one had to tell us when to move out of the blissful kingdom of our mother's lap. The urges to separate were inside us—in our body-mind, in the liveliness of our own growth energies, in the vitality of our stiffening-away muscles, in our looking eyes, our listening ears, our reaching-out hands.[1]

By about nine months a baby can stand on her own, gaining a new perspective of the world. By fourteen months she can walk, then run, then conquer. This ability to conquer the world upright gives separation a new meaning. The baby no longer lies passively as the parent leaves; now the child does the leaving as she runs to see what awaits her around the corner.

Children fall in love with the world at this time. A bargain is struck. The grand notion that the world exists to serve them is given up; now they believe the equally grand notion that they can conquer that world.

When children say no, they are putting language into their urge toward separation. Parents teach children no as they set boundaries of safety ("Sharp!" "Hot!" "Don't touch"), boundaries of body integrity ("Don't fondle my penis—you can touch your own but this is mine and is off-limits to you"); boundaries that are life-giving ("No, you have to go to sleep now or you'll be miserable tomorrow—trust me on this one"); psychological boundaries between people ("This is my private time"). "No" helps the child understand and internalize limits that enhance his life. When, in turn, some of the toddler's "No!"s are respected, he experiences himself as authentically powerful and competent. A new dimension of pleasure is added: "Life feels good because I'm in charge."

There are two potential separation dysfunctions in troubled families. First, the parent may not have said "no" enough to teach the child the concept of separation. "Yes, you can touch anything you want—what does it matter if you are injured?" or "Yes, you can touch my penis," or "Yes, you can keep me up all night playing," undermines the development of the child. Sometimes "yes" is merely neglect and silence: "Do what you want, I can't be bothered." The child whose "No!"s are *never* respected will also have difficulty learning separation. A parent who fears being alone and unloved may take "no" as personal rejection, as the child's refusal to "fix" the parent's unhappiness, even if that task is clearly impossible. Sometimes a child's "no" reminds troubled parents of all the times their own parents rejected or punished them. Whatever the reason, when children are not allowed to separate from their parents, bonding becomes unhealthy fusion. "Stuck together with Krazy Glue" or "like flypaper" were common descriptions of "family togetherness" among the survivors I interviewed. "My dad got a headache and we all took the aspirin."

The rich and complex dance of bonding and separating becomes distorted when addiction or violence interferes in family life. Separation becomes synonymous with abandonment. Attachment or bonding in some families of trauma may mean simply the *absence of abandonment.* Especially in families where there has been a real abandonment, the fear of abandonment reigns supreme and all family members must "serve time," as Glen put it.

The Rapprochement Shuffle

Even in a "good enough" family, the headiness of being a child conquerer is not without its costs. At a beach a child of three runs from her father toward the water's edge. As the tide tickles her feet, she giggles and runs back to him. In this way she experiences herself as separate from her father, powerful and competent enough to explore the world, yet feels secure that she can return to the safety of her father's love when she wants to. This is called *rapprochement,* a gentle reunion. The conqueror is always welcomed home.

In families with trauma, reunions after separation are rarely gentle. Thelma played hide-and-seek (a game of rapprochement) with her father, and it is a worse memory to her than all the physical and sexual abuse she endured. "My father would tell me to cover my eyes, then he'd run and hide. Now, most parents are somewhat obvious and it doesn't take the child long to find the parent. My father *really* hid, far away. I'd run from tree to tree, frantic. After five minutes or so, I'd be hysterical, almost in convulsions, convinced that he had left me alone in the park. Then, he'd come out from behind some building and laugh and laugh at me."

Rapprochement brings together the "yes" of attachment and the "no" of separation. "Maybe" becomes tolerable, even desirable, as in "Maybe I'll try this on my own" or "Maybe I'll ask for help with it." The child does not get stuck in an "all yes" or an "all no" stance toward life. Repeated positive experiences of standing alone and being welcomed back into the fold, with no loss of self at either juncture, foster a sense of self that tolerates both closeness and separation. What seemed in the past to be fragmented pieces of life—we, you, I, me alone, you not there for me—begin to come together as complementary rather than contradictory aspects of the self. This integration is called *object constancy.* The child no longer needs to think and feel in black and white terms, as Judith Viorst explains,

> For the hated mother who leaves us, and the loved and loving mother who holds us tight, are understood to be one, not two different mothers. The bad, unworthy child and the good, deserving, lovable child are united into a single image of self. Instead of parts of people, we begin to see the whole—the merely but magnificently human. And we come to know a self in which feelings of hate can intermingle with feelings of love.[2]

Constancy is experienced by a child in a "good enough" family as a "picture" in his mind of a good parent, a "photo album" of times his needs were met. When he feels bad, he recalls the image and sensation of bonding, of feeling good, to get him through. He learns: "I can tolerate feeling angry and frustrated and still be a good and lovable child. My parent can disappoint and enrage me and still be good and lovable."

In families with trauma, there usually are not enough "pictures" of the good parent to offset the "pictures" of the parent as threatening or unavailable. Failure to integrate the good and bad—in the self or another—is called *splitting.* Psychologist Louise Kaplan distinguishes constancy from splitting:

Constancy is the force that creates unity out of the disparate and often contradictory images of the self and other. The part of the self that longs for merging oneness remains connected to the part of the self that stands alone and holds on to the right to possess one's own mind, body, thoughts, special treasures, fantasies and illusions. With splitting there is neither the ecstasy of oneness nor the exhilarated vitality of separateness that joins down-to-earth people in partnerships of devotion, loyalty, playfulness, camaraderie, angry disappointment and grief. Splitting precludes the possibilities of whole human beings.[3]

Psychotherapist James Ritchie believes, however, that the abusive parent's lack of constancy, like the impairment of bonding, can help the survivor. The image of a parent as consistently unavailable, threatening or neglectful will not offer enough sustenance to the child to give him or her influence over the child's life.[4] As relentlessly abused as Laura was, she says, "My mother did me a favor by never wavering from her unabashed hatred of me. I've never been confused about whether or not she cared. She didn't. It was crystal clear. The people who liked me clearly did and those who didn't really didn't. I have little confusion between love and hate. Of course, my task as an adult has been to accept both my loving and hating sides and to accept that people who love me will like me better at certain times than at others—and vice versa—and that the relationship need not end because we are in a 'low' time."

Nonetheless, children are physiologically and emotionally injured by inconsistent, abusive or neglectful treatment. It is a small step from "This feels bad" to "I am bad." Laura has hindsight as an adult, but as a child she blamed herself for her mother's violent behavior. Why? Laura could not *consistently* change or control her mother. All she could do was change herself: cry more or cry less; sleep more or sleep less; need more or need less; and so on. When these changes are extreme and betray the true self of the child (i.e., smiling when frightened instead of crying because smiling pleases the parent), the child learns that his true self is bad, the false self is good, and relating to other people is a charade.[5]

Much current literature harps on survivors' tendency to be perfectionist, unable to integrate the good and bad in their view of themselves or others. When absolute perfection was demanded of them as children, and less-than-perfection swiftly and mightily punished, how would they know to take the good and the bad in stride? Their "perfectionism" is more a reflection on the enormity of their task than a character deficit.

In a "good enough" family, children are able to integrate less-than-ideal aspects of the parent—"My mother's feet stink" or "My father gets depressed around the time of year that my grandmother died." The parents' imperfections may be annoying, but they are not life-threatening.

The "bad" aspects of abusive and nonprotective parents are more likely to cause real harm to the child: "She hits for no good reason"; "They lock me out of the house when they get mad"; "They keep me up all night telling me their problems"; or "He doesn't believe me when I tell him how I am being hurt." Is it any wonder the child has a difficult time putting it all together?

The Apprenticeship of Love

Around four years of age, children begin to watch how adults behave when they like and love other adults. In "good enough" families, they see that their parents are at ease with other people and can talk with others about the joys and problems in their lives. Conflicts are resolved satisfactorily and without violence.

In a "bad enough" family, a child might have an aloof father who offers little emotional sustenance to his family and a mother who is emotional enough for two people. With these kinds of behavior as a model the child might grow up either to overwhelm others or to avoid them. Or perhaps the parent feels depleted, resentful, martyred and unable to get his or her needs met. The child will have no example of how to reach out to people for support or companionship. Or perhaps the model is serial relationships: the parent changes friends or lovers frequently, before anyone has a chance to get hurt or to get close. The child may learn to keep moving, to be attracted to the rush of infatuation but have little staying power for the more mundane aspects of intimacy. Or perhaps the parent is depressed, withdrawn, even paranoid. The child learns to be self-reliant to a self-denying extreme, not being taught that one of the best ways to take care of oneself is to have healthy relationships with other people. Finally, if the parent is violent, the child learns that acquiescence or dominance is intimacy.

Normally, children observe their parents' relationships from *outside* the circle that encompasses the adults in intimacy. Being drawn into that circle destroys children. Most of the survivors I interviewed had been "triangulated" between their parents. They were cast as "little husbands" and "little wives" to their parents, or as the "other woman" or "other man."

In a "good enough" family, children usually become flirtatious with their opposite-sex parent around the age of four or five. This is the beginning of what is referred to as the Oedipal struggle. They talk of wanting to marry Mommy or Daddy. This is a normal part of development; children are imitating the adults in anticipation of adulthood, exploring the mysteries of attraction. Some psychologists suggest that this process has more to do with trying to win over the most powerful person in the family than with having sexual desire.[6] In any case, a child may try to cozy up to or try to vanquish the more powerful of his parents.

Ideally, the parent expresses compassion for the child's healthy strivings toward intimacy and at the same time sets clear limits, laying the cornerstone for later relationships. The child learns that marriage and sexual intimacy are for people the same size and not to be shared between big people and little people. Yet this does not threaten the child's image of the self as lovable, attractive and worthy of healthy sexual intimacy at a later date. "If you can't beat 'em, join 'em," he decides and begins to imitate characteristics that seem to make the parent special.

In families with trauma the parent does not articulate or enforce intergenerational boundaries. A needy adult sees the vulnerable and curious child as a "sure thing" for intimacy. At the very least, what ensues is emotional or covert incest. Such a pseudomarriage is likely to bring on the jealous wrath of the other parent or adult lover who ridicules the child's yearning for closeness and sometimes physically abuses the child. The child's "favored status" becomes a liability. The jealous spouse may use the child as a scapegoat, even covertly encourage the alliance, to avoid dealing with the problems in the marriage. The exploitive parent also has a vested interest in maintaining the triangle. Rarely would one parent say to the other, "It is things between us, what both of us do, that has ruined the marriage. It's not the child's fault."

Triangulation makes normal sexual development difficult. Being the brunt of a same-sex parent's jealous rage prevents the child from moving on to identifying with that parent. And being attracted to age-mates may seem like emotional adultery. Two years after his mother died, Vinnie became engaged to Gayle, whom he'd been dating for years. "Gayle and I were taking my mother's wedding ring to the jeweler's to have it sized for her. Outside the store, I broke down sobbing, was short of breath, weak in the knees. I felt like a terrible person, betraying my mother."

Triangulated children come to believe—falsely—that in the realm of attachments they are powerful beyond their years. They attempt to use their pseudopower to make family life better. When this fails, they end up feeling alternately responsible for others' happiness and powerless to make it happen. It is no wonder that as adults they often feel unworthy of love.

Boundaries: The Gateways to Intimacy

From the first five years of life in a "good enough" family, children move into relationships with other children and adults with confidence and security. They look for that "good enough" love they experienced early in life. They also know to protect themselves from "bad enough" treatment in relationships. One psychoanalyst refers to this as having a "built-in bullshit detector." By elementary school age, they have a sense of the personal boundaries necessary for healthy relationships. In *Emotional Healing,* psychotherapists Terry Hunt and Karen Paine-Gernee describe boundaries as being like the membrane surrounding an amoeba. The membrane can allow food in or become impenetrable to a "bad" particle.[7]

I think of healthy boundaries as being like green hedges, planted firmly in the ground. They are always growing and perhaps they even bear flowers. They are airy so that you can see through them but not so tall that you cannot talk to your neighbor over them, shake his hand or look him in the eye. Most important, they are flexible enough that you can part the branches to let your neighbor through without destroying the ability of the hedge to continue to grow and protect you.

Some survivors of childhood trauma lack boundaries, having learned only fusion from their families. They may have trouble saying "no" and hearing others' "no"s.

But most of the survivors I interviewed suffered from having created too-rigid boundaries, emotional brick walls. To the degree their families threatened and exploited their selfhood, they became autonomous and individuated with a vengeance. As Judith Viorst explains:

> Certainly a union that involves annihilation of the self can generate annihilation anxiety. To give oneself up, to surrender oneself—in love or any passion—may feel to us like loss instead of gain. How can we be so passive, so possessed, so out of control, so . . . won't we go crazy? And how will we ever find ourselves again? Consumed by such anxieties, we may establish barricades, not boundaries. Shutting ourselves away from any threat to our inflexible autonomy. Shutting ourselves away from any experience of emotional surrender.[8]

Laura speaks for many survivors of abuse and neglect when she describes herself as "having calluses on the heart" by the age of five.

As we reach out beyond our family, first for friends, later for lovers and perhaps eventually for children, it helps if we were "filled up" during the first five years of life. If we have been given enough love, and if the love we so innocently offered was accepted without shaming or exploitation, we are better equipped to approach relationships with optimism and ease.

In troubled families the parents' demands during the first five years of life caused the child to give away too much of the self. The child feels depleted, hopeless, despairing that there will ever be enough love to fill him up.

Yet this despair is not a terminal disease. Even though they identified faith in their lovability and trust in intimacy as being among their "Achilles heels" or within their "zone of vulnerability," every survivor I interviewed had established healthy relationships with friends; some with lovers; and those with children were "good enough" parents. After all, intimacy is often an "Achilles heel" for adults who were not traumatized as children. These survivors became adults able to love and be loved. They are healing from attachment exploitation by the abusive parent and abandonment by the nonprotective parent. To be sure, some had chosen to go it alone in the past, never to risk such heartache again. Others had had relationships that replicated the family drama. Eventually, with the help of other people, they learned to love and be loved in healthy and fulfilling ways. If their parents could not offer an interpersonal bridge, they found it elsewhere.

Many discovered that their capacity to heal through relationships as well as their injuries could be traced back to childhood. They had learned to pay as much attention to what helped them as to what hurt them. So many survivors lament, "But nobody helped me when I was a hurt child!" These survivors teach us that this is not possible. Unless there was help—even help that seemed minor or inadequate next to the horror of the abuse—there would not have been survival.

Rob's one year in Mr. Kaminsky's class was "good enough" to send him on his way. One teacher managed to make a whopping deposit in Rob's psychic savings account. It sat there, earning interest, and today, Rob draws on the substantial balance.

We build bridges with siblings, friends, adults outside our families, relatives, lovers and our own children. All of those bridges seem to lead to the same place: peace, serenity, self-esteem and intimacy.

Brothers and Sisters

In her book *Children in Recovery,* clinical psychologist Rosalie Cruise Jesse discusses her work with siblings of elementary school age in dysfunctional families:

> In most normal families where there are siblings of a latency age, these children will show a typical, natural tendency toward covert functioning at certain times. Secrets will be traded and shared. Attempts to keep the parents off guard will strengthen the sibling bond. However, young children from alcoholic and addictive families function as a secretive group of prisoners in the family war. They will give name, rank and serial number but they will not discuss the dreaded family secret.[9]

Remarkably, many children rise above the chaos to love one another. Thelma was the youngest of six: "We were like puppies in a basket." Her mother was frequently hospitalized with tuberculosis and her father was too drunk to take care of them. "She'd be carried out to the ambulance and her last words to the six of us would be 'Take care of each other—you're all you've got.'"

Rita realized "very young that there wasn't going to be anyone there for me but my brother Harold. One Christmas morning, when I was six and he was five, I woke up before him and ran downstairs to find both my parents passed out drunk under the tree. Presents hadn't been wrapped yet and a bike for me was half put together. Until that moment, I still believed in Santa Claus. My first concern was for Harold. I went upstairs, sat on the end of his bed, waiting for him to wake up. I told him, 'Mom and Dad are drunk again and there is no Santa Claus.' We hugged while he cried for a bit. Then we went downstairs and somehow, the two of us put that bike together. Harold tells people we raised each other and I think he's right."

Elaine was the middle child among four sisters. "The hardest thing for me was to keep my feelers out for when my mother was about to get violent and then redirect it to me so that my sisters wouldn't get it. I am much angrier at her for beating my sisters than I am for what she did to me." Today Elaine says: "I have excellent relationships with peers because of the camaraderie between me and my sisters. In contrast, I'm highly critical of authority figures."

Nine of the survivors I interviewed were the eldest children in their families. Another three were de facto eldest because an older sibling was disabled by psychiatric problems.

Jenny, the oldest of three children, all injured by their physically abusive father, told me, "Seeing my brother and sister beaten helped me to feel less like I deserved it. I could watch their beatings and clearly see my father as abusive and crazy. Eventually, I was able to see my beatings in the same way. I would comfort them as best I could. In doing that, I would experience myself as a sensitive and caring person. I also felt I could do something about their abuse when there was so little I could do about my own. My struggle has been to not always be rescuing wounded birds, to love others who are *not* traumatized."

In turn, younger siblings care, as best they can, for the older sibling. As Laura remembers: "Being the oldest, I felt responsible for my two younger brothers and guilty when they were hurt. And I felt overwhelmed by how much they needed me. I remember being five years old and giving Phil a bath with laundry soap. My mother was too out of it to wash him and I didn't know what I was doing. At the same time, some of my fondest memories are of dressing Phil up in my old clothes, like a live doll. He was so compliant and fun. All three of us used to hide under the table and bark like dogs to drown out our parents' hateful fights. You know, that was kind of fun too, all things being relative. However, when we all got to be teenagers, they rebelled against me, the caretaker. I was hurt and furious with them. I alternately clung to them and rejected them. It was a big mess for a long time. Only in my thirties have I recaptured and appreciated their caring for me when we were all little."

Some older siblings, however, find it difficult to love unconditionally precisely because they were not loved this way. And some survivors who were younger siblings report inconsistent nurturing—and occasional abuse—by older siblings. Again, from Rosalie Cruise Jesse:

> It is the quality of the marital relationship which actually provides the most influential model for sibling interactions. When the parents are at war, the siblings will take up weapons and begin to fight each other, often without knowing the full reason for their bellicose actions.[10]

In adulthood, several of the survivors had traded and shared secrets with siblings. For many, this has enhanced their recovery of memories and feelings and lessened their isolation. Laura offers one caution: "My youngest brother, Phil, is the only one in my family I feel any connection to. We've talked some about the past, particularly as it affects our brother Chris's children. However, I have to accept that some of our perceptions of our childhood differ. Our older half brother, John, resented my birth. He hated me, as the only girl and my father's alleged favorite, and was incredibly cruel to me. But he was nice to Phil, so Phil has different memories of him. Chris was an easy kid for me to take care of, but he was abusive to Phil, so Phil has more anger toward him than I do." Sociologist Robert Ackerman terms this phenomenon, "Same house, different homes."[11]

Friends

Preschoolers see their families as the center of the universe, the source of inexhaustible support and love. During the elementary school years, children reach beyond the family circle, to join a same-sex "party."

This venturing forth is a problem for children from fused families. Outsiders are seen as competitors for the child's scarce emotional resources. Children learn that the world is a cold, cruel unpredictable place over which you can exercise no control and are encouraged to shun human contact, especially if there is a family secret—alcoholism, incest, mental illness—to be kept. Still, children seek friendships. Esther remembers: "No matter what my parents told me about how rotten other people were, I figured they couldn't be any worse than what I was living with at home." One of her worst memories is of a field trip in first grade: "My mother was the only one who refused to sign the permission slip. So I sat all day in the kindergarten. I felt big and oafish and no one paid any attention to me. One of my classmates had a birthday party and they saved me some cake and my party favor. Instead of feeling grateful, I felt humiliated. I distinctly remember thinking, This wouldn't be happening to me unless there was something wrong with me."

Some parents invade the child's world of friendships. One of Janet's worst memories was of "being six years old, playing at a friend's house. My father assumed we'd gone down to the river, which was forbidden. We hadn't, but that didn't matter. He took his nightstick from his job as a prison guard and beat me with it in front of my friends. More than the physical pain and terror, I felt so protective of my friends. They stood there, absolutely horrified. I worried about them being upset."

In a different way, Janet's mother was just as intrusive: "My fondest memory of childhood is of eating out with my girlfriends and Mother in the sixth grade. She acted and talked just like us. All my girlfriends liked her. Later, when I was a teenager, her behavior embarrassed me."

Many survivors described their nonprotective parent as 'more like a buddy' or 'my best friend growing up.' Janet has had many opportunities for having girlfriends throughout her life, but she has only one mother. While her mother attempted to be Janet's best friend, she failed to protect her daughter from physical abuse and covert incest.

Several survivors took solace in filling an irreplaceable role for their peers. Sam, who had a learning disability, says, "I became the class clown, distracting everybody when I didn't understand the work. So other kids knew, if you want a good time, a lot of laughs, hang out with Sam. That helped me feel better about myself."

Being "popular" helped Janet restore her faith in herself as a lovable person: "Yet, despondent over the relentless physical abuse in my home, I slit my wrists three days after being voted 'Most Popular' in my high school class. I was bone-tired and couldn't go on." Janet did not have the psychological resources to accommodate the positive regard of her peers until her thirties, when she says, "I finally started listening to other people and taking in the 'facts' of my life."

Like Janet, some survivors were very active and well liked as teens. Others were not so popular but had at least one true friend. Their accomplishments at school were posters in their troubled families' front windows: "See, we are OK—how bad could it be if this kid can do well."

Daryl's best childhood memory is of his friend Josiah, who was half white and could pass for white: "He stood up for me when the other kids bullied me. Then one day I dumped on him the way the other kids dumped on me. I think I insulted his mother, maybe used a racial slur. He stopped talking to me. That was devastating. I remember going over to his house to apologize, crying hard. He forgave me. His acceptance made me feel better about myself. His friendship over the years kept the idea alive that maybe—just maybe—I was OK." Today Daryl has recaptured some of that depth and caring in his relationship with his best friend, business partner and roommate, Ron.

Sometimes Daryl hears of what has happened to the kids he grew up with in the projects: "If the peer group was on you, you could take it if your family loved you. If your family didn't love you, you could take it if you were popular with the peer group. But if you lost both of them, you were sunk."

Role Models

Consistent with other studies of abused children, most of the survivors I spoke with told me of attachments to a healthy adult outside the immediate family, often in the elementary school years, with teachers, coaches, youth group leaders and others. Often these adults had no awareness of the child's abusive home; they simply had affection for the child.

Caring adults provide role models for young children. Exploited or abandoned by their parents, survivors know more about what they don't want to be like (the abusive or nonprotective parent) than what they do want to be. But they can internalize the "picture" of an adult other than a parent. Rob reflects on his relationship with Mr. Kaminsky: "The feeling of safety, of being loved once, of someone offering me comfort instead of a blow to the head, I go back to that all of the time when I am with my two daughters."

Laura's ninth year of life was especially difficult. School had been a safe haven—until the fifth grade. "Looking back, I can see that the teacher was seriously mentally ill. She hated me and constantly called my mother, telling her lies about me. Of course, I was beaten every time. One day she pulled me aside and said, 'I hope you don't mind my lying about you, but I just hate you so much, I can't help myself.' Yet that same year I was blessed to have Wanda in my life. She was a young black woman who cleaned house once a week. Quickly my brothers and I learned to be 'sick' on the days Wanda came so we could be with her. When we tried to get around her rules, like taking too many cookies and trying to tell her we hadn't had any at all, Wanda would smile and say 'Hmm, mm, you think so, huh?' The 'hmm' sounded like a yes, and the "mm" sounded like a no. Wanda's habit was sort of the "walk/ don't walk" of human communication. She was gentle, beautiful, funny, smart—I adored her. After a year my mother fired her. She told us kids that Wanda was epileptic and had had a seizure with an iron in her hand, which was dangerous to us. Twenty-five years later I tracked her down. What a great reunion! She's not epileptic. My mother had told her, 'The kids are too close to you, so you must leave.' I still have the habit of saying to my foster kids, 'Hmm, mm, you think so, huh?' "

"Good enough" families serve as a protective membrane to keep dangerous people away from the child. Troubled families, like Laura's, often do the opposite. Her mother found an ally in her teacher and banished Wanda, the one safe person in Laura's life. Other parents are less direct: they become "sick" or manifest "hurt feelings" if the child's affection is shared with someone else.

Breaking Away

Separation and individuation from parents is recycled in the teen years as rebellion. With greater physical size, years of life experience and increased language and cognitive skills, adolescents have "bigger and better" ways of saying no to their parents. "I am of you but I am not you," declares the adolescent.

Teenage rebellion had been a turning point toward health for many of the survivors I interviewed. Becoming the opposite of their parents was to become fully human—tender, loving, compassionate. To differentiate themselves from a nonprotective parent's passivity, they became action-oriented, learned to take a stand and fight back. In the next chapter, we will see how this dynamic affects the choice of meaningful work for these survivors.

Of course, years would pass before rebellion could metamorphose into true healing. In the meantime, most had a difficult time leaving home. After almost two decades of some degree of traumatic bonding, separation became traumatic as well.

The adieu of a healthy family includes the potential for rapprochement. "You are welcome back here anytime." There is "good" in "goodbye." But many survivors were able to leave home only in the wake of trauma. They finally got out of the family because they got arrested, disowned, pregnant or married, or because they reported the abuse and were removed, attempted suicide or had an emotional breakdown. There was no preparation for the enormity or finality of this ending. Janet left home at 2:00 a.m. in the morning, in her senior year of high school; when her mother hit her for the first time: "I was pushing her about doing something about my father—his drunkenness, gambling operation in the basement, physical abuse of both of us. She started swinging and punching me and I had had it. There was no going back."

Some survivors said they had stayed longer than they should have in order to protect younger siblings from abuse, or because they succumbed to a troubled parent's pleas or recriminations when they attempted to say no to the "bad enough" family and yes to the rest of their lives.

The Drama of Love

A colleague of mine tells this story of two painters on their lunch break. One of them looks into his lunchpail and says, "Peanut butter, peanut butter, peanut butter! I can't take another day of it!"

His partner says, "Why don't you ask your wife to make you something else?"

"Oh, I'm not married," says the first. "I make my own lunch."

In our choices of friends and lovers, we make our own lunches, but we start by repeating in them dramas of our childhood—good and bad. We tend toward what is "familiar." Yolanda's stepgrandmother Isabelle used to beat Yolanda until she'd admit to doing something they both knew she hadn't done: "I'd hold out until I couldn't stand the physical pain anymore, then I'd admit it. I just left a committed relationship of seven years because I 'de-self' in response to my lover's controlling behavior. With my friends and colleagues, I am equal. I stay myself and I can hold my ground. But when I'm in love, still, deep inside, I don't feel worthy of love. So, I abandon my self in order to please my lover."

George's drama is about rapprochement. He yearns for closeness but is afraid that if he touches it, he will never be separate again. If he falls into his lover's arms, will he ever be able to leave? Will the powerful woman punish him for even wanting to leave? He presumes so and treats his lovers as if they were trying to possess him. They feel misunderstood and cling more tenaciously to prove their love. George finally breaks away and keeps on running.

Laura has borrowed some of the best of Wanda and the worst of her father. From Wanda she learned to be grateful for what she has, never to expect it to last, and to make a little go a long way. From Patrick she learned to yearn for unavailable men, particularly those obsessed with disturbed women (or obsessed with themselves). She has brief relationships with men who are characterized by frustration and dishonesty.

In Glen's family, "you were either enraged with each other or you were nothing to each other. I figured you get as much contact out of wrestling as you do out of making love, so until I learned differently, every relationship was a wrestling match for me." For Glen and his wife, breaking up wasn't so hard to do: "We'd break up to make up, you know, the encounter-session, emotionally exhausted high after big fights. And we burned ourselves out on it after seventeen years." Glen thought his "style" was passion until he was able to distinguish "what was" (his rage at his parents) from "what is" (his fear of needing closeness to women).

Amy used to scream at her brothers and father, "Leave me alone!" That was all she wanted—to be free of their abuse. Today, she has what she wants. She still longs for the caring attention of a man, but she fears the abusive consequences of that attachment. She gets into a relationship, becomes fearful that she can't protect herself and then desperately needs to be alone.

By mid-life every survivor I interviewed had learned to make new choices in relationships or improved their existing relationships. Each had helped to create a "bridge relationship" that had allowed them to leave behind angry, anxious, abusive or neglectful attachments. On the other side of the bridge they found "good enough" relationships and learned to love again.

Many turned to friendship as an arena to unlearn early lessons about love. Laura has mentioned that it is difficult for her to believe that someone can dislike her behavior without withdrawing their love from her. Not surprisingly, she had difficulty extending the same courtesy to her friends. "I have a close friend, Katie, whom I met when we worked together. After I went on to another job, she would constantly report all the stupid gossip about me from our workplace. I was really hurt but unable to tell her to stop. I thought, If she cared about me, she wouldn't be doing this.

"Finally, I decided to end the relationship. But no matter how much I tried to avoid her, she kept on coming back—with considerable caring, which I couldn't reconcile with the hurtful gossip bulletins. Finally, I told her I couldn't stay in the relationship because I had been so deeply hurt. She listened very patiently, then admitted she had made a mistake but had had no idea she was hurting me. She had thought I was interested—and I bet that *is* how I acted, given I was covering up my vulnerability. Then she told me that she understood if I wanted to break off the relationship but she wondered if there wasn't a way to repair it.

"Somehow, I was in the right frame of mind to hear her. It was as if a light bulb went on in my head. Of course, we all hurt each other. And if we make amends and try to learn from it, it doesn't have to be the end. Ever since then, my ability to speak up sooner, to prevent myself from quitting too soon and to take the good and the bad more in stride in my friendships, all of that changed dramatically. Katie gave me a tremendous gift and I'm so glad we are still friends."

All the survivors I interviewed had healthy, long-term supportive friendships. The seven who were currently single were remarkable in their ability to create what therapist Sharon Wegschieder-Cruse calls "a family of choice." This "family" gives them what a "good enough" family has to offer: a sense of belonging, shared history, a safe harbor, a place where they love and are loved and experience themselves as tender and compassionate people.

Several of the survivors had married young and had grown with their spouses, transforming the union into a more healthy relationship. Some described themselves as having married their spouse's family; the unconditional love of in-laws had helped the survivor to unlearn early lessons about love.

In other marriages the couple helped each other understand and recover from their respective dysfunctional families. Early in their relationship, Vinnie once grabbed Gayle and shook her, just to get her attention. He says, "She told me, 'That's abusive. Do it again and you'll never see me again.' I tried to explain to her, 'Hey, this is nothing compared to what I've seen and experienced.' Fortunately, she wasn't convinced. She would have left me, so I stopped." Years later Vinnie and Gayle went to couples counseling. "The therapist said we were the most verbally volatile couple he'd seen. We used words as weapons against each other. It seemed normal to us. Now we're trying to unlearn that, to be more respectful toward each other."

Not all relationships lend themselves to growth. Eight of the survivors had divorced or separated from significant others. But in those cases saying no to the "not good enough" relationship was a sign of health, enabling survivors to continue their bridgework through friendships and, for some, with new romantic partners.

Trauma often leaves a formidable split between intimacy and sexuality. As Esther put it, "I've always separated who I trusted from who I had sex with." Many survivors who do well in other aspects of committed relationships still have difficulties in this area.

Sexual intimacy is a challenging endeavor for any adult, traumatized or not. The fusion, the intense lack of physical and emotional boundaries during lovemaking, is a journey back to the first five years. For some survivors this is the only kind of attachment they know, so they pursue it regardless of whether they trust their partner. Others avoid sex, finding it too painful to be out of control once again. Sexual touch may even trigger flashbacks, placing the mind out of control too. If separation in the past meant annihilation, rejection or abandonment, the parting after lovemaking may feel threatening, and the survivor may either cling tightly or reject the bonding rather than endure the pain of separation.

Familiar with prevailing over exploitation and pain, survivors may have less confidence and experience in accommodating pleasure. Rob still finds himself dissociating during lovemaking with Judith. "The performance of sex is fine for me, but I don't experience the emotional closeness that others do. When I connect it to feelings, like 'She really does love me' or 'I feel wonderful,' then I zone out. I don't think I deserve it. I can't help it and it really bothers me."

Even for the survivors I interviewed who did not currently have sexual partners, sexual intimacy was something desirable, something to consciously work toward. Again, they see the comfort of being a friend as a necessary prelude to being a lover. Janet says: "My husband is a friend who I have sex with. I used to get into these relationships where I was madly in love with a person—or at least the idea of that person—but I did not like him. I used to offer only the 'I'll take care of you so I can control you' kind of love. My twenties were about learning to like and trust. My thirties are about learning to love."

Parenting

Eleven of the survivors I interviewed were parents. They each reported that they had had anxiety about raising children but found it more rewarding and manageable than they had anticipated.

Nancy is both an adoptive mother and a longtime foster mother to emotionally disturbed children: "I wasn't born into a healthy family, but I deserve one. As a young adult, I figured out it was up to me to create a healthy family." She started in college, working as an attendant to institutionalized physically handicapped children while studying early childhood development. "As a child, I had been my stepfather's mistress and I ran the household as well. When I left home, my mother wrote to me every day. I remember this one letter where she told me she had done the laundry and then lost it. Later that day she went to prepare dinner and found the folded laundry in the refrigerator. Can you imagine what kind of a fog you'd have to be in to put your laundry in the refrigerator? On a less honorable level, I was also out to prove that I could raise kids better than my parents had."

An exemplary mother, Nancy now teaches others how to foster-parent difficult children. However, "awareness of how I repeat my parents' mistakes was the first important step for me. Without it all the book learning in the world is meaningless. For instance, one night I was getting my six-year-old foster son ready for bed. He had a pullover on, so I said, 'Skin the rabbit!' My parents had always undressed me that way. But I saw the fear on that little boy's face and realized what a violent image it is. So, I stopped saying it."

Glen was an only child triangulated between warring parents. Now his seventeen-year-old daughter is experiencing the divorce of her parents: "It's too easy to repeat history. I'm careful not to drag her into this, but it's hard to know how much information is too much and feels like pressure to take sides, or when am I saying too little and having secrets. I have to talk it over with other people a lot."

Rob finds that the role of father has enabled him to separate, once and for all, from the parent within. "When the girls were learning about their private parts, they were testing just how private they were. So, they'd tug on their vaginas and say, "Daddy, kiss my touchie," or when I'd tuck them in, one of them would wrap her legs around my neck. It wasn't until they were in the throes of exploring their bodies that I was *really* tested. Through repeated interactions, I learned I'm not an offender. In each moment, first there was the realization that I could molest them—it would be so easy—and next the realization that I wouldn't molest them. It's not who I am."

The deposits healthy adults made in the psychic savings account of the traumatized child often come into awareness while parenting. Justin remembers his neighbor Marjorie, who repeatedly told him, "God has a plan for your life. Quitters never win and winners never quit." Today, Justin's seven-year-old son, Matthew, has a severe stutter. "I drive him to school every day and we have this ritual. He gets out of the car and comes over to my side. I roll my window down and say, 'Now, Matthew, what's important to remember?' It takes a while, but he'll say, 'I'm a winner,' then run off to school."

Joan says: "My son is my payback for all that happened after my mother died. He's a gem. He's been easy to raise—a real delight." Now he is twenty, graduating from college and seriously dating a young woman. "The best job I've ever done is parenting my son. He's leaving, and at first it felt like an abandonment, but I'm learning it is not. Our relationship will be different—a 'good' different, I hope."

Jenny is in her mid-fifties, with four grown children. With great candor she admits, "I didn't enjoy being a mother. It was like a child taking care of children. I have good relationships with them now, but I hurt them, especially through my perfectionism. I recognize I did a better job than my parents did—I never beat them, nor did I intrude on their sexual boundaries. But I was so caught up in being a provider—feeding, clothing and sheltering them—I had little left over emotionally. I've admitted this to them and tried to make amends to each of them. My son is unable or unwilling to talk about it with me and that is painful. I hope someday he will accept my apology." Growing up in abject poverty as she did, we can understand how concerns about physical sustenance overshadowed emotional nurturance. Today, she continues to mature as a parent, reaching out to her children with awareness of her imperfections.

Four of the survivors had made conscious choices not to become parents *solely* because of their histories as abused children. Yolanda's sentiments reflected those of the others: "I decided in my early twenties not to be a mother. I didn't know if I would behave toward that child in some of the abusive ways adults had behaved toward me. I was not going to figure that out at the expense of another human being."

It is impossible for any human being—traumatized or not—to be a "good enough" parent in total isolation. Conscientiousness, awareness of their "zones of vulnerability," and reaching out to others for support, information and help were hallmarks of these survivors as parents. They are living proof that not all abused children grow up to be abusive parents.

Taking Love, Giving Love

Childhood abuse and neglect teach children that their love is not worthy. "Who would want your love—it isn't good enough. If it was, I wouldn't be hurting you" is the message inherent in their parents' behavior. Some survivors try to overcome this shame by protesting too much, giving away their love indiscriminately in an attempt to prove it worthy. They rarely stop long enough to take in love from others.

Other survivors take hostages: "Give me love, goddamn it, right now! Make it all up to me. Love away my rotten childhood." There are many problems with this demand. There is no restitution for an abusive childhood: what is done is done. Those whose love is extorted are not responsible for the past. It is an approach toward love based on weakness and injury, not on strength and wisdom.

The survivors I spoke with had learned to approach love with an attitude of positive entitlement: "I have much to offer. Love me because you see who I am and appreciate me. Don't love me because you pity me or fear me." In offering love—not manipulation, control, exploitation or abuse—these survivors were breaking the cycle of violence. And they were creating a balance between accepting love and offering love. Although it was often far more difficult, learning to receive love comfortably was as necessary to their healing as having the love they offer accepted as worthy.

CHAPTER EIGHT

Human Doings: Survivors and Their Work

Now *here,* you see, it takes all the running you can do to keep in the same place. If you want to get somewhere else, you must run at least twice as fast as that!

—LEWIS CARROLL
Alice in Wonderland

Yolanda is the kind of teacher Hollywood loves: dedicated, creative, effective and absolutely beloved by her students. She is a special education teacher of her native Spanish language and art in an alternative high school for emotionally disturbed youth. Yolanda knows the roots of her connection to her students: "As bad as things have been for me, there was always someone there who cared, to see me through each leg of the journey. It hasn't been the same person all the way through—but that doesn't matter. I believe we can survive anything as long as someone cares about us." Today, Yolanda is that someone for her troubled students.

Her start in life was rough. "I weighed thirteen pounds, and the delivery almost killed my mother. While she was being admitted to the hospital an ambulance arrived with my father—his face sliced open in a knife fight with a prostitute."

Her parents' marriage was a "Romeo and Juliet affair." Her mother, Carmen, was the daughter of Puerto Rico's leading physician and a socialite. Yolanda's father grew up poor. Carmen married him on the rebound from an arranged early marriage that had ended in shameful divorce. Yolanda has seen her father only four or five times in her life.

"My mother's story is that when she came home from the hospital with me the first thing she did was pack up all his belongings. Then she waited for him to come home. She had a pistol concealed in the folds of her skirt. She says she pointed the gun at him and said, 'This is a gun. Those are your bags. Now get your butt out of here.' " Because Carmen was recuperating from the delivery, she could not care for Yolanda's three older brothers. Thirteen-year-old Jose—the product of her first marriage—went to live with his father. Hector, ten, was taken in by her mother-in-law. "He was supposed to come back when she was feeling better, but he never did," Yolanda said, "We got to know each other as adults."

That left Edward, eighteen months old, and baby Yolanda. Carmen's father saw to it that his daughter and her children lived in the lap of luxury. "My mother was the nannies' supervisor and that was it. She *never* hugged us or kissed us. From the beginning, I was a huge disappointment to her. After the three boys, I was the awaited child. But my timing was bad—here she was, a Latino Catholic socialite, getting her second divorce, stuck with four kids. My mother was the epitome of a high-society woman: petite, beautiful, educated in Switzerland with the potential to be an opera star. But the arranged marriage slowed her down and then the marriage to my father stopped her dead in her tracks. I was supposed to pick up where she left off and live out her dreams. But I preferred playing cowboys and Indians with the black kids. I am big-boned and handsome and, worst of all, I'm the spitting image of my father."

Carmen took "discipline" into her own hands. When Yolanda squirmed in her chair instead of listening to classical music, Carmen beat her with an electrical cord. She was quick-tempered and violent. "I thought of her as an 'ultrastrict' mom, but I didn't identify her as a child abuser until I was adult. Abuse wasn't talked about in Latino culture. The parent was always right. While she beat me she kept on saying, 'You're just like your father, just like your father.' "

Then, when Yolanda was seven, her grandfather divorced his wife of forty-five years to marry his mistress, Isabelle, who insisted that he stop supporting Carmen and her children. For the next three years they lived in a one-bedroom apartment and Carmen worked as a hotel clerk. The sudden change of life-style didn't improve her disposition. The physical abuse worsened. Eddie started to torture neighborhood animals while Yolanda retreated into religion.

In the sixth grade Yolanda came down with the mumps. "My mom couldn't stop working to take care of me. In desperation, she called my grandfather. Isabelle said I could come live with them until I was better." But as soon as Yolanda left, Carmen sent Edward to live with his father, and Yolanda did not see her mother for the next five years. "I think she thought I could realize her dreams if I had access to my grandfather's money."

Her grandparents enrolled Yolanda in a convent school and she visited them on weekends, when she was subjected to Isabelle's violence. Isabelle would strike her servants, and if one of them quit, Yolanda was beaten. "One day, she made me watch her empty her walk-in closet into the middle of the floor. She told me if I didn't have everything folded and back in within the hour, she'd beat me. Then she went horseback riding. Of course, it was impossible. The servants overheard this, so when she left, they came in and helped me. When she came back and found the closet in order, she was so mad at being thwarted that she beat me with her riding crop anyway." Isabelle would chant, "You're just like your mother, a whore, good-for-nothing, just like your mother."

"You know, her fists weren't the worst of it. It was the insidious emotional torture. Anytime she saw me happy, she'd destroy it. So I figured out that I should put on a sullen and detached mask when she was around, and be more happy-go-lucky when I was away from her."

Yolanda credits her mental health to the nuns at the convent school. "They protected me the best they could. I got migraine headaches—only on Fridays—beginning at twelve years old. They'd tell Isabelle I was too sick to come home for the weekend. But Isabelle often insisted I come home anyway. The nuns would tend to my welts and bruises and pray over me. They couldn't approach my grandfather—they thought it wasn't their place and, besides, he sponsored charity events for them. The nuns and I did our best. I'd slam the door to my room over and over again, to relieve my stress and feel terrific afterwards. They were overwhelmed by my intensity sometimes, but they understood and accepted it. As long as I didn't hurt myself or another person, they let me be."

When Yolanda was fifteen, Carmen married a civil servant, Alberto, and sent for her. Eddie had joined his father in petty crime and had been disowned. "I had loaded all my feelings about my mother's beatings onto Isabelle, so I still had this idealized view of my mother. I was excited to go home." Reality quickly set in. Carmen was still quick-tempered, and Alberto did not want to share Carmen's affection with Yolanda.

Once, when Eddie was out of jail, Yolanda met him on the sly. "I only let him walk me to the corner, but I guess she saw us anyway. When I came back in, a big fight started and she broke a ceramic platter over my head. Alberto intervened and got me to bed. When I woke up the next day, the bedsheets were covered with blood. I felt this huge knot on the back of my head where I was bleeding. From his room, Alberto heard me moaning. He stuck his head into my room and said, 'Quick, quick, clean that up before your mother sees it.' I hid the sheets under my bed. I wish I had said, 'Fuck you, let her see what she did' or 'No, she can clean it up herself.'"

Later that day Yolanda escaped and staggered back to the convent school. The nuns took her to the hospital. "I stayed for four days and had over thirty stitches. My mother never asked where I had been."

Yolanda left soon after to join a cloistered order of nuns in Europe. "I'll defy authority unless it makes perfect sense to me. I was an opposi-tional novitiate. I didn't make it." She returned to Puerto Rico and lived with a group of nuns, her old chums from the convent school. "They were doing hospital work in the slums. I've always had good girlfriends like that. It was a wonderful time in my life." Fun, but not stable. "I couldn't stay at a job for more than a few weeks. I was hyper all the time. A lay missionary in her early thirties, Maria, who visited often, one day looked at me and said, 'You look like someone who refuses to grow until you have a family to support you. Come home with me.'" At twenty-one years old, Yolanda found a "foster mom."

Yolanda moved in with Maria and her elderly mother. "The one condition was that I get a job—any job—and keep it for a year whether I liked it or not. I worked in a dry cleaner's." At the end of the first year, Maria told Yolanda it was time to move on to something bigger. With

Maria's support, Yolanda went on to art school. "We were like family. Those were the four most 'normal' years of my life." Yolanda was learning to use work and study as an organizing force in an otherwise chaotic life.

After she graduated, Maria insisted that Yolanda "leave the nest." "It was lonely and difficult and I called her a lot," Yolanda says, "but I did it—without falling apart." Then she heard of an opportunity to do lay missionary work in a Harlem shelter for battered women, so Yolanda came to America.

"I started teaching art to the women in the shelter, first just as recreation but then it seemed to be like therapy. I didn't know from nothing about therapy then. All I knew was I was good at it and it made everyone feel better, including me." She found this work so rewarding, she began to teach adult education classes in community centers and in a community college geared to adults of color who lack a high school diploma. "I loved teaching and went back to school to get my master's in education."

By this time, Yolanda had made a friend, Molly. But Molly was too much like Carmen and Isabelle. "She was very controlling and I would acquiesce—whatever she wanted. I was making new friends at this community college and she'd interfere, be critical—she wanted me all to herself. I was volunteering at the shelter, exhausted, overextended. The migraines started up again and I'd have anxiety attacks and leave the classroom. My boss was wonderful. He told me to take two weeks off, get some help and he'd hold my position open. I started working with a wonderful therapist. With my permission, she invited Molly in for some 'couples' counseling and helped me get out of the relationship."

The intensity of Yolanda's friendship with Molly was a preview of coming attractions: "I'd always been attracted to women and never consummated any of my relationships with men. I began to awaken to my sexuality. First I was angry at God for making me gay. Then I was worried He would reject me. My therapist understood and accepted my struggles."

While Yolanda was going through this "soul-wrenching" time, work continued to be important to her and to her belief in her worth as a person. Still, "working with adults, it almost seemed 'too late' to make a difference. I know how much the nuns in the convent school meant to me. So I took a job in an inner-city high school."

Most of Yolanda's students are court-involved, usually for violent crimes. "These kids are social-worked to death. They use emotional problems to get out of schoolwork. But I can tell when a kid is really upset and when they are just putting me on. Quick changes of masks are how I survived Isabelle. If they are really upset, I get them to people paid to do counseling. All I want to hear is that their homework is done. I tell them, 'I give a lot of thought to what I teach you and I care about you. You have two choices: stay here and struggle to learn *with* me or get out of my classroom.' They have a different kind of relationship with me. I've been close enough to their pain to know what they're talking about yet detached enough to know they can do the work—and the work is important."

One student stands out in Yolanda's mind. "Jean is a Native American girl, severely sexually abused by her stepfather, who ran away and was arrested for prostitution at age thirteen. She came to us from a locked psychiatric ward. The depth of her anger and fear were unbelievable. I'd say, 'Good morning, Jean,' and she'd spit back at me. I made a deal with her. If she could just say 'Good morning,' I'd find a special art project for her. If not, I'd take away privileges. Then I'd expand it. Five minutes of civilized conversation each day, then ten minutes. I told her, 'If nothing good happened for you to talk about, then make something up. That shows creativity.' She thought I was a riot. First I wore her down by not rejecting her and then I won her over."

Yolanda is very close to the other teachers she works with. Recently, she and her lover, Gisella, broke up after seven years of living together. "My colleagues moved me out. They were so supportive. That high school is like home for me."

Yolanda knows that learning and "finding work you are good at can change your life," but she has other interests as well. She belongs to a lesbian Catholic choir that sings at special liturgies. Meditation is a daily ritual. She showed me a collection of beautiful ceramic masks she'd created; in each, seemingly contradictory emotions were strikingly represented—just as they exist within Yolanda.

Human Doings

Sigmund Freud believed that there are two pillars of a healthy life: love and work. Wishing to escape the pain of attachment exploitation or believing they were not worthy of love, many survivors I interviewed turned to work for a sense of identity and fulfillment. They believed that when love hasn't worked out, work probably will, at least for a while.

As a result, some survivors become what psychologist Terry Kellog calls "human doings,"[1] people for whom being well in the world— evidenced by healthy relationships, relaxation and fun—is less of a priority than being productive and creative.

In a "good enough" family a child is encouraged to be happy as well as responsible and productive. The child has nothing to prove, no need to "earn" love. Troubled parents' attitude is more likely to be "You're not good enough as you are, so let's see what you can *do.*" Abused and neglected children "work" to earn love and to justify their existence. Given little time or right to play, they are required to *do*—usually for the abusive parent. Certainly there was plenty of work at home for the "little wives" or "little husbands," and as "little mothers" and "little fathers" to younger siblings. The conditional love they earned was better than no love at all.

Thelma was born in 1929 in a large industrial city, the youngest of eight children. Her immigrant parents were both alcoholic. Her father's alcoholism caused him to be chronically unemployed and he suffered from blackouts. Her mother's drinking fueled vicious beatings of all the children. At five, Thelma and her seven-year-old brother were sent out to work. "He pulled the newspapers in his wagon and I approached people, asking them if they wanted to buy one. We went into bars. We learned that if I tap-danced on the bar to 'When Irish Eyes Are Smiling' the bar guys would buy all the papers. I loved the attention and the money."

Today Thelma believes that work is love for her. "It's when people see me at my best." As a high-powered public relations specialist, she can promote anybody else, but says "I can't ask someone just to be my friend."

One stereotype of survivors of childhood trauma is that they are underachievers who drift through life without stable work, too depressed to excel or feeling too undeserving of success to complete education or training programs. None of the survivors I interviewed were underachievers. Nor would I characterize them as overachievers, if that implies having exceeded one's limitations to reach illusory success. Instead I found a group of talented and dedicated human beings whose accomplishments reflect their personalities, not their excesses.

Yet many of them were aware that they discounted their competence, had not yet fully integrated it into their sense of self-esteem. Laura is greatly admired for her work, yet she feels that "no matter how much I accomplish, it is never enough. If I'm good at something, it must not matter. *Anyone* could do it. If someone praises me, I tend not to listen. But if they criticize me, they have my undivided attention. I still measure my worth by how lovable I seem to be at any given moment."

Work—once the child's best attempt to belong to a family who didn't seem to want him—continues to be a way to belong. Glen describes work as his "admission ticket to the world—without it, they wouldn't let me in."

Psychotherapist Nicholas Etcheverry tells of his youth, when work was a search for love for him: "I believed that if I accomplished enough, I'd get a lot of people to respect me. And if I could get lots of people to respect me, I could get a few people to like me. If I could get a few people to like me, then I figured I could get just one person to love me."[2] His formula is a very common one among survivors I interviewed.

Survivors of childhood trauma often feel that their identity is irreparably marred and that they must compensate for being "less than" others by working extra hard, a belief that society often applauds. Work, more than any other endeavor, can be a manifestation of "looking good on the outside."

Choosing Work

Trauma or no trauma, childhood experiences often influence choices of work later in life. Sam found in work a meaningful eye in the storm of his childhood that still carries a strong sense of pleasure for him. "As part of my housework, I had to care for the few plants we had. They responded to me and grew, reflecting something good about myself. While other kids were selling lemonade at roadside stands, I was selling cuttings. There was no touch in our lives, only the bodily inspections, shots or whippings. My pets gave me love and soothing touch. I was attracted to growth. By junior high, I was breeding gerbils and hamsters and selling them to my friends, teaching them how to care for them. The mother of one of my friends managed an aquarium supply store and I worked for her for years." Today, Sam, a businessman, is still attracted to growth. He owns a franchise of stores specializing in "life for your home—plants, tropical fish, pets, birds—you know, creatures you can interact with."

For others, work is an attempt at mastery over what once threatened defeat. Now they are helpful instead of helpless. As a little boy, Paul tried to make sense of Hank's crazy behavior. As an anthropologist, Paul's work on the dynamics of aggression has practical application in negotiations in hostage situations.

Daryl, who grew up in the projects, bullied by lighter-skinned kids, knew that "on some level the kids who were beating on me were hurting too." Today, Daryl works with gangs, made up mostly of teenagers of color, using "drama and music to reduce the ethnic, class and race tensions. Creativity is a great equalizer—we all look alike when we are making music."

Light heavyweight world champion Donny Lalonde literally found a training ground for his career in his childhood. Repeatedly knocked unconscious by his stepfather, he went into boxing partially to prove that he was "a person of consequence" and to show that he could "take it like a man, even give a little back."[3] Lalonde said that when he began boxing in his late teens, it didn't really bother him to be hit because nobody ever hit him as hard as his stepfather, mainly because his opponents were his size. "I felt that pain was part of life. But I also *wanted* pain. I subconsciously felt I deserved it." Lalonde's long-lost father saw him box for the first time in his November 1987 match against Eddie Davis. "You know, I would have rather died in the ring with Davis than not have the respect of my father. Why should a kid have to do what I did—go into boxing and put his life on the line—to get respect?"

Lalonde now questions his career choice. "I don't think knocking people out is something you should be glorified for." Yet, he's transformed his childhood survival skill into a capacity to inspire, not injure: "There's another reason I have to win. As a champion, I have a voice. I can speak out about abuse. Without the title, I'm just another fighter."

Speak out he did in May of 1988 after defeating contender Leslie Stewart for the light heavyweight championship of the World Boxing Council. His victory speech was a direct message to "all the little kids out there who are having problems at home. Believe in yourself and keep on fighting. You can turn your life around. It's the people who are abusing you that are having the problems—not you. They're the ones who need help."

Laura only recently discovered the connection between her traumatic childhood and her work. Her mother would stay locked in her bedroom for days at a time. When her four young children knocked on her door, needing food or attention, she would rage at them. The family myth was that Sheila was "writing great literature, a novel." In reality, Sheila did no more than eat and sleep, and often did not shower for days. The variety of prescription pills she mixed and matched made her behavior erratic and dangerous. "During a beating, if I ever raised my hand to protect my face, she went over the edge. 'How dare you raise your hand to your mother!' Then she'd hit me harder."

"I hate writing, yet I've always felt compelled to write. I was thirty-two years old and writing my third book on children's rights before I realized that writing was my way of hitting back at my mother. Of course, she'd never written anything, but she takes credit for my success as an author—it was her influence that made me who I am. In a perverse sense it did. I beat her at her own delusion."

Pioneering child psychologist Jean Piaget, who developed innovative theories of how children think and learn, traces his work as an adult back to the trauma of his childhood:

> One of the direct consequences of my mother's poor mental health was that I started to forgo playing for serious work very early in childhood; this I did as much to imitate my father (a scholar of painstaking and critical mind who taught me the value of systematic work) as to take refuge in a private and nonfictitious world. I have always detested any departure from reality, an attitude which I related to this important influential factor of my early life, namely my mother's poor mental state.[4]

Caretaker Prodigies

Eleven of the survivors I interviewed were employed in the helping professions. Another seven were involved in extensive volunteer work. Growing up in troubled homes, what they learned to do best was take care of other people, becoming what I term "caretaker prodigies." Gifted at anticipating and meeting the needs of others—usually at the expense of their own—they are primed for professions in education, the clergy, medicine, day care, counseling, foster care, nursing and the like. Moreover, they have a high tolerance for inappropriate behavior, delayed or nonexistent gratification, crisis orientation and a sixth sense for other people's moods.

Several survivors reflected that they may have fared better than their siblings precisely because they took on so much responsibility so young. In contrast, their siblings were often in a more passive role, without distraction or structure, left to absorb the pain as best they could. Although Laura is saddened and frustrated by her brother's maltreatment of his children, she says, "I also understand that Chris is *exactly* who he was raised to be. I was told I was unlovable, and today, I work for love. I coped with the ordeal by getting busy by protecting my brothers. Chris was constantly told he couldn't do anything right—he was lazy, stupid, shiftless. So, big surprise, he's chronically unemployed. I'm not excusing it. But I've always remembered him as passive and sad."

Once a suicidal teenager, today Joan is a high school counselor with special training in dealing with suicidal adolescents. "I know where they end and I begin—my boundaries are good. If not, I'd do more harm than good. But every time one of those kids stops obsessing about suicide, I do feel like I've saved a little piece of myself."

As a hospital social worker, Rob helps patients to alleviate and manage chronic pain. "You know, that's the one piece of this that still makes me mad. If I hadn't had this violent childhood, I would have been a doctor or lawyer and made some serious money. But, no, I had to identify with the victim. At age sixteen, when I was locked up as a delinquent and dealing with horrendous probation officers, and later as a marine, I knew I'd finish school and become a therapist and work with people who suffer."

Janet became a therapist, specializing in the treatment of sexual dysfunction. "I just went back to my twenty-fifth high school reunion and my classmates reminded me that in the ninth grade, on Career Day, I announced I was going to be a sex counselor. Not only was I the shoulder everyone cried on, but I was the only one who knew what sex was. What they didn't know was that much of my education was my father's sexual violence against my mother, blatant affairs, piles of pornography, and creepy lewdness toward me."

For many, the work of taking care of others also serves the purpose of bearing witness to the harm done by family violence. Janet continues, "I knew all about battering and violence long before any of the books were written. I have an inherent knowledge of it from my childhood. Instead of feeling helpless and defeated, I was angry about what my father did to my mother and me. I'm determined to use that knowledge to help the survivors of child abuse I work with to discover and enjoy sexual pleasure free of violence."

Psychologist John Wilson has developed a useful tool, the "typology of stress response syndromes among survivor groups," which defines a wide variety of outcomes for trauma survivors. This typology includes a "prosocial-humanitarian syndrome," which aptly describes most of the survivors I interviewed:

> [The person is] altruistic and has transformed survivor guilt and other trauma-related symptoms into a nurturing humanistic orientation to others and society. Is intense and creative. Lives with existential need to work toward ends-oriented values that promote life and self-actualization. This is, perhaps, the healthiest form of coping with the stress syndrome.[5]

Laura's career as a children's rights advocate and volunteer work as a foster mother are important to her, but "other people's attitude, when they find out I'm a survivor, can be painful and unintentionally demeaning. Some people recognize me only as one damaged person helping other damaged people—like a leper caring for other lepers, thereby preventing the spread of the disease to the uncontaminated. Their attitude is that this is my job, not theirs. If survivors take care of abused children, the rest of society does not have to. No one acts as if I'd made a conscious choice of career. 'What else could she have done with her life—she probably doesn't have good relationships. She can't have children because she might beat them, so it's nice that she takes care of these kids who are already so damaged.' Of course, I can never know for sure, but I would bet I'd be doing this same work even if I'd grown up in the perfect family. I like what I do and I do it well."

Psychologist Sarah Moskovitz takes issue with attributing a survivor's good deeds to "survivor's guilt." Her book *Love Despite Hate* is a study of twenty-four adults who spent part of their childhood either in Nazi concentration camps or in hiding during World War II. After the war, these orphans were cared for by Alice Goldberger in a home in Ling-field, England. Of Goldberger's remarkable work and the humanistic work of the survivors themselves, Moskovitz writes:

> To see compassionate acts, self-sacrifice and social commitment as largely motivated by guilt for past behavior, or for survival itself, is too facile. The positive wish to act decently and express feelings of empathy, the desire to participate humanely in one's time, require no such prior acts of omission and commission. That this doubtful wisdom is often accepted by survivors themselves—who after all are not immune to what authorities say they are supposed to feel—is a special irony, imposing as a new stigma the bitter equation of compassion equals guilt.[6]

Compassion may have more to do with wisdom than guilt. Elaine works in the private sector and volunteers as a Big Sister. Her motivation is typical of healthy survivors: "If you've ever been in a position where you couldn't handle something yourself and you know you were dependent on other people, I think it's criminal not to try to help someone else in turn."

The Meaning of Work

First and foremost, work provides survivors with economic independence. As children, Vinnie and Thelma dreamed of escaping poverty. Today both are wealthy. Thelma says, "I identify with Scarlett O'Hara: 'As God is my witness, I'll never be hungry again.' I worked hard to get out of my social class, never to be impoverished again." All of the survivors I interviewed had attained at least middle-class status, and they saw their economic status as something that, unlike the abuse they had suffered, they could control. Still, Vinnie and Thelma and the other survivors who worked in the business or science sectors used their status and financial resources to help their communities. Vinnie, now a corporate attorney, has never forgotten the safe haven his Catholic summer camp afforded him from the relentless violence in his home. Today, he is a benefactor to dozens of campers from the "old neighborhood."

Work also offers social contact with minimum vulnerability. Even in the helping professions one is not required to bare one's soul—in fact, such behavior is often considered "unprofessional." Many survivors find this guarantee of invulnerability attractive. Thelma is aware that she hid behind her job: "Whatever my title was—that's who I was." Some survivors showed me their résumés, awards they had won or articles others had written about them. These actions seemed to help them regain their equilibrium after displaying their courage and vulnerability in telling me their stories. Quite understandably, they needed to return to the "safe zone" of their work and to show me "proof" that they hadn't been irreparably damaged by the traumas they'd shared with me.

Being part of a work group or being a "boss" who is responsible for the well-being of other employees can bring a sense of belonging. Yet half the survivors I interviewed were self-employed, stating that they had not enjoyed working for other people. Self-employment offered them contact with other people—on their own terms. Many described how past work situations had replicated the dynamics of their child-hoods. Some had discovered in their bosses irrational or abusive figures like their parents. Some had been victims of sexual harassment, racism and other forms of discrimination.

Glen now has his own consulting firm. He explained: "In my last job, I was so angry with my boss, I feared I would kill her. All anyone at that agency cared about was what I could do for them, how good I made them look. Me, as a person, I didn't count. Once again, I was the spoils of battle, split between warring powers. I had a difficult time remembering that they weren't *really* my family and they didn't have that kind of power over me. I decided I needed to leave. Going into business for myself was the best thing I could have done."

Others had taken on an inordinate amount of responsibility, often taking care of coworkers or employees. Eventually they came to resent the burden, and some found themselves reacting as their own troubled parents had. Laura remembers: "I was in middle management in a large social service agency. I had all the responsibility but no power. I was overwhelmed by the neediness of a staff of twenty-four. One day, after we'd moved into a larger space, one of the social workers came to me with a problem: her desk had been lost in the move. She had a perfectly legitimate need, but given the bureaucracy of the place, the lack of resources and the irrationality of my boss, I knew it would be a long time, if ever, before I could get her a desk. I remember the waves of helplessness; I felt just like my dad, who would shrug and walk away after my mother had pummeled me. And, like my mom, I really wished she didn't exist at that moment. It wasn't right. She was a good person. That was the turning point—I resigned soon after."

But Laura also found genuine healing in relationships with two of her coworkers: "They were the kind of healthy men I never would have been attracted to in a social situation. We were equals, the expectations were clear and the relationship never would be sexual. That freed me up to be more open to them. Both were incredibly trustworthy, sensitive to my feelings and fun to be with. We shared this rather intimate task—doing co-therapy with groups of abused preschoolers. I think of these men as 'work husbands.' Through our successes, I rethought my distrust of all men based on my father's betrayal of me. I had to reconsider: maybe I wasn't as terrible at long-term relationships with men as I thought—maybe the real thing wasn't beyond my reach forever."

Finally, work provides structure, something to do with our time and energy. Many survivors trace their affinity for work back to their childhoods, when it served as an antidote to chaos and a distraction from pain.

As psychologist Bryan Robinson writes in *Work Addiction:*

> Unknown to me at age ten and into my 20s, work addiction was already injecting itself into my life. It relieved pain, helped me forget, entertained me, offered me a sanctuary and gave me silent companionship when I felt all alone in the world. My greatest compulsions about work were the false sense of power and control I felt over my life.[7]

Such inordinate importance attached to work can fall into healthy obsolescence with the recognition that work's role as an organizing force of the survivor's time and energy and a source of self-esteem through mastery has become a barrier to growth and self-expression in other equally important areas of life.

Work Addiction

If survivors do not learn to balance work with attention to internal development and other areas, the salvation and healing that work offers can be undermined. Like alcohol, narcotics, sex, food, gambling, approval or the spending of money, work can be addictive and is subject to abuse.

Some survivors would agree with Jake, however. "Look, as the son of addicts, I was bound to be an addict. This addiction is more socially redeeming than the others." Certainly work addiction is more socially acceptable. We may joke to a coworker, "Yes, I'm a work addict," but we would never so cavalierly admit to binging on food or drugs. Yet many survivors have become aware of how serious the consequences of their addiction can be. When Jake's wife threatened him with divorce, he realized he had become just as unavailable to his two sons as his father had been to him. "I had abandoned Barbara to do the best she could on her own, just as my dad had done to my mom. And I used things I could buy them to prove that I loved them just as much as my mom used the food she brought home to reassure herself she was a good mother."

Psychologist Bryan Robinson believes that work addiction is "a blessed betrayal. It's the only lifeboat designed to sink. It serves you as a child when you're drowning in the disease of alcoholism or family dysfunction. You think you're saved. But you're taken hostage by a disguised form of sickness that helps you survive and then insidiously reaches out a hand and insists on your paying the price."[8]

When the work addict is not consumed with work, he or she may be flooded with dreaded feelings of depression, anxiety, rage, despair and emptiness, and perhaps memories of childhood trauma as well. The addict turns to more work to repress these thoughts and feelings, but the next time he is without work, they come back with even greater intensity. Eventually, physical health fails, relationships falter and serenity evaporates.

While society rewards the unbalanced life-style of the work addict and in fact often measures survivors' success *solely* by their ability to work, the survivor is descending into deeper emotional, physical and spiritual pain. Hitting bottom—when the work no longer works—inspired many of the survivors I spoke with to seek balance in their lives.

Don't Just Do Something—Sit There

Survivors who have learned to put work in perspective caution that the search for balance sometimes led them to put undue emphasis on other aspects of their lives. As Jake reflects, "When I finally overdosed on work—dangerously high blood pressure was my clue—I got into 'doing feelings' and 'doing therapy' and 'doing friendships' and even 'doing play' with the same determination and relentlessness I had previously done work. I finally realized my problem when I tried to 'do' my marriage. I was so goal-oriented, I had work plans for how much fun, sex and serious discussion we should be having. My wife wasn't interested in going at my breakneck pace. She just wanted to see what naturally unfolded when we spent more time together."

One step in seeking a healthy balance is to entertain the notion "I deserve to be loved, just because." Up until now, work has been the best way the survivor knows to have his needs met.

In her book *When Helping You Is Hurting Me,* social worker Carmen Berry explores the issues of "helpaholics" or "messiahs." She traces the roots of their dilemma back to dysfunctional childhoods and two powerful beliefs: "If I don't do it, it won't get done" and "Everyone else's needs take priority over mine." Of course, messiahs eventually burn out and complain that they are not getting enough out of life.

> Messiahs are emotionally undernourished, not because the banquet is sparse, but because the Messiahs have tiny little mouths that are incapable of taking in the feast. A person's longings do not indicate what life has to offer. On the contrary, the level of need indicates *what portions of life* that person is currently capable of experiencing. In all my professional and personal observations, I have never met a person who was capable of accepting more love and nurturance than he or she was currently experiencing. Should a new relationship or affair seem to promise more, it was not long before the aura faded, the relationship proved disappointing, and the person felt lonely again [emphasis added].[9]

Survivors can learn to apply work skills to other areas of life. Caretaker prodigies can learn to take care of themselves as well as they take care of other people, turning empathy and resourcefulness inward instead of outward. Esther, the therapist, learned to say the same things to herself that she would say to a client. "My compassion is a quality I value and now I give it to myself as much as I give it to others."

Psychiatrist Edwin Peck recounts the psychoanalysis he provided for a heroic homicide detective, "Jim," who had repressed memories of his father's sadistic physical abuse of him as a child. As the analysis progressed, Jim not only recovered many memories and experienced the depression inherent in grieving over the loss of a safe childhood, but also became less immersed in his previously all-consuming job.

> Jim began to see that his leaving home for work duty had been his shield against depression. I noted that Jim had unraveled community crimes with success but very little satisfaction; now he was unraveling family crimes committed against him, and in doing so, he was experiencing satisfaction and relief along with his depression.[10]

Beth found a new aspect to life in watching and playing basketball. "What a great way to relax! And it's a different use of what was the best of me in work. I've always been a team player. The game requires intelligence, a capacity for strategy and grace under pressure. It's fast and chaotic, just like I'm used to from my family and work. My favorite thing about basketball is how I can get my feelings out in the excitement and disappointments of the game."

Survivors can also learn to spread their needs around to other aspects of life. Although friends, romance, play and the like don't pay the rent, they can provide a sense of belonging, affirmation and structure to our lives. Doing or working is one of the strengths of survivors who have fared well in life. It is also one of the greatest opportunities for healing and growth, as long as it takes its rightful place alongside just *being*. Perhaps Freud's musings were incomplete. Perhaps there are *many* pillars to a happy life: not only love and work, but also self-love, play, relaxation, friendship, spirituality.

CHAPTER NINE

From Defiance to Awe: Spirituality

I believe that man will not merely
endure: he will prevail . . . because
he has a soul, a spirit capable of
compassion and sacrifice and
endurance.

—William Faulkner
*Nobel Prize acceptance speech,
December 10, 1950*

At twenty, Stefan jumped off a bridge, expecting to die. But he entered the water feetfirst, doing little damage to his body. A passerby called the police, who rescued him before he succumbed to exposure. "It was not a spiritual experience, believe me. I was angry to still be alive." Although he was misdiagnosed at the hospital—"No one ever asked me about abuse in my family; they told me I was having a hard time adjusting to adulthood, as if that alone makes people jump off eighty-foot bridges in the middle of winter"—his thwarted suicide attempt began a long journey through psychotherapies.

Stefan's parents, Theresa and Franz, met as children living on adjacent peasant farms in Hungary. Devout Catholics with a fierce sense of social justice, Theresa and her parents sheltered Hungarian Jews. In 1941 they were captured by the Nazis and sent to Buchenwald, where her mother was soon executed and her father died of exhaustion. Franz resisted the Nazi draft in 1942 and was incarcerated in the same camp, where he and Theresa began their romantic relationship.

The guards took turns sexually abusing Theresa, verbally and physically. One day a Nazi officer shot her in the back for resisting him. She was left for dead, but Franz and three others found her that evening, unconscious but still alive. They carried her to the infirmary, where she recovered by sheer will.

After the war Theresa and Franz married. In 1950 they immigrated to a Midwestern American city with a large Hungarian community. Theresa gave birth to Stefan and, three years later, his brother Peter.

There were many camp survivors in Stefan's neighborhood, but they had a pact of secrecy. "They didn't talk about the war or how they came to America. The adults' attitude was 'We are here now—the past is best left alone.'" But the world outside their neighborhood was seen as a hostile one: "My parents always believed there was another Holocaust right around the corner." Neither boy learned a word of English until they entered the first grade, after which they became their parents' translators.

"The first few years of my life were relatively all right, all things considered. I remember my mother singing us lullabies and working on her embroidery. My father did factory work. When Peter and I went to school, my mom had less to do. She started drinking and quickly became an alcoholic. Often when I came home from school, she'd have passed out while cooking and I'd run and turn the burners off."

Other times Stefan came home to an empty house. "I'd wait until dinnertime. If Mom hadn't shown up by then, I'd tell Peter, 'Lock the door and don't let anyone in until I get back.' I'd go from bar to bar, speaking Hungarian, asking if anyone knew where my mother was. I still feel humiliated from the pity in those people's eyes, looking down on this little crying boy. Once, when I was nine, I found her in a six-foot snowdrift, coat open, boots off. To this day, I can't account for how I dragged her home."

Stefan also protected his mother from his father's disgust. "I couldn't get to sleep until he came home, after midnight. He'd work double shifts just to get away from her. He'd find the place a mess, she'd be passed out and he'd wake her up to yell at her. She'd blacked out, so she didn't know what he was so upset about. Big fights would start and

I'd have to break them up. I'm still haunted by seeing my mother's face bruised and cut the morning after a fight."

Stefan didn't know what to make of all the despair and chaos around him. At first, he turned to Catholicism for answers. "Every night I prayed for my parents to be happier, for my mom to be well, for my dad to stop being mad at her." But his prayers went unanswered. His mother's alcoholism worsened and his father became more detached, yet he was unwilling to commit Theresa to a hospital, which would have meant imprisonment for her once again. School was not a refuge for Stefan as it was for so many other survivors. "In elementary school, they called me stupid because English wasn't my first language. Then, by junior high, I'd get beat up because I'd argue theology with the nuns. I was so cynical—there was no heaven or redemption. Life was tough and then you die. I read Camus's *The Stranger* when I was in the seventh grade. Very early on, I decided the world is absurd and ridiculous. Reality is a contrived invention, conceived from moment to moment."

Around the time Stefan began exploring existentialism, he also discovered the martial arts. His life changed: "My instructor became my second father. The discipline of karate is very health-oriented and anti-alcohol. I especially liked the intellectual athleticism of it. I'd always battled intangible demons—fears, apprehensions, insecurities. Karate was perfect because, in practice, you are in a fight but you don't know who you are fighting."

While Stefan was out of the house battling his demons, his brother Peter began drinking with Theresa, hoping his companionship would ease her pain. By fifteen Peter was breaking into homes, stealing money to buy more and more liquor to share with Theresa. When I met Stefan, Peter had just been released from a five-year prison term for armed robbery.

By the time Stefan was thirty, Theresa was dying of Korsakoff's psychosis—an advanced stage of physiological deterioration from alcoholism. "I'd been a wild guy since my suicide attempt. But I had kept up with karate. Through it I met many Buddhists. They had a peace about them that I longed for. So I asked to go along with them to temple. Skeptical at first, I began to like it because the whole point of the religion is to break through illusions." After visiting his mother, who was in a coma, Stefan "sat" for the first time—he meditated at a Zen temple from five in the morning until nine in the evening. "It was a direct facing of myself. I didn't eat, turn on the TV or find solace in the latest lover. I just sat still in the temple and felt terrible. All of the dark horrors I had suppressed welled up in me. My body shuddered and I wept. The pain burned and burned and burned until it passed."

Stefan finally found the serenity he had been seeking through years of philosophy, psychotherapy and the martial arts. Frequent "sitting" helped him cope with his mother's death, which came within the month.

"People from all over the country came to my mother's deathbed. I knew she had been a resistance leader before her arrest. But I didn't know about her heroism in the concentration camp. They came to thank her and to say good-bye. They told me incredible tales of her courage. This woman whom I had known mostly as an illiterate, emotionally damaged alcoholic was also a hero. They said she was a saint, that her spirit prevailed."

Stefan still finds serenity in Buddhism and karate. Like his mother in her youth, he does what he can for other people. "I love being a therapist for very troubled people—folks no one else wants to work with. I don't talk about my family or my suicide attempt, but they can feel the faith I have in them. And the hope. I want people to stop seeing their traumas as permanent scars but rather as *their* opportunities to see deeper and broader than others. There can be a breadth of vision and sense of hope that people with untroubled lives often don't have."

The First Thing to Go

There is an old saying in Alcoholics Anonymous: In the disease of alcoholism, spirituality is the first thing to go and the last thing to come back. Compared with alcohol, the troubled family may be far more efficient at committing what Alice Miller calls a "soul murder."[1]

Abused children are robbed of their faith in the goodwill of other people and their belief in a safe world. As psychotherapists Patricia Reiker and Elaine Carmen explain:

Confrontations with violence challenge one's most basic assumptions about the self as invulnerable and intrinsically worthy and about the world as orderly and just. After abuse, the victim's view of self and world can never be the same again: it must be reconstructed to incorporate the abuse experience.[2]

Spirituality, which has always been a cornerstone of civilization, helps us experience a connection to others and to nature. All spiritual systems are based on the belief that there is a power greater than the self and that faith in that power makes us better people.

Sixteen survivors I interviewed had found spirituality a great source of healing in adulthood. Their notion of spirituality is captured by physician Bernie Siegel in *Love, Medicine and Miracles:*

> Spirituality means the ability to find peace and happiness in an imperfect world, and to feel that one's own personality is imperfect but acceptable. From this peaceful state of mind come both the creativity and the ability to love unselfishly, which go hand in hand.[3]

Jenny comments: "I don't know if my spirituality enhanced my recovery or if my recovery made me more open to spirituality. Now my spirituality is how I live my everyday life. When I am in the throes of a bad memory or overwhelmed with difficult feelings, it is my belief in someone greater than myself—that I wouldn't be going through this unless there was a reason, unless I was ready—that gets me through." Like Stefan, many survivors found that spirituality took them to deeper levels of self-acceptance and peace with their past than psychotherapy had.

In *When All You've Ever Wanted Isn't Enough,* Rabbi Harold Kushner explores the differences between psychotherapy and spirituality:

> The original, literal meaning of the word "psychotherapy" is "the care and cure of souls," and it is precisely our souls that need caring for. I have personally benefited from therapy at times in my life when I was overwhelmed with problems and needed a skilled outside observer to tell me where I was making things harder for myself. I needed to be told that I was avoiding certain truths. In addition, I have used the insights of psychology and psychotherapy to inform my sermons and to counsel troubled members of my congregation. I know that therapy has value. . . . But the values of the therapeutic approach tend to be values of adjustment to what is, rather than visions of a world that does not exist.[4]

In spiritual beliefs many survivors find the safe, just world that did not exist for them in childhood.

Our First Idols

Very young children believe that their parents are all-knowing and all-powerful. A toddler walks into the living room with chocolate all over her face. Her mother says to her, "I told you to keep out of the brownies, didn't I?" The child innocently replies, "I didn't do anything." But her parent persists: "I can see that you got into the brownies."

Wow, the child thinks to herself, she knows everything. She was in the living room and I was in the kitchen, but she knows. How does she do that? If the mother deals with the incident in a caring and constructive way, the child associates her mother's omniscience and omnipotence with nurturance and protection, and the foundation for a comforting belief in a higher power is laid.[5]

In a troubled family the all-knowing and all-powerful parent is less likely to be consistent and caring. One time the child gets away with sneaking the brownie because the parent is passed out in the living room. The next time she is humiliated or slapped for a similar transgression. Jake had to stand in a corner all day, naked, for exactly this "crime." The next time it happened his father went in and ate the remaining brownies himself.

The parents' inevitable fall from grace also plays a part in how the child perceives other higher powers. Did the child learn in a gentle way that the parent was not really all-knowing and all-powerful? Was the "consolation prize" that the child could himself become powerful and wise, to ensure his own safety in the world, to find faith in himself? Was the child inclined and able to move on from the connection to the parent and believe in the same kind of connection to other entities? Or did that realization happen in the wake of a trauma or betrayal? In violent families the parent is an irrational and avenging "god." A child may not want to seek out other potentially similar gods when he can barely cope with the ones he has at home.

God the Father and Mother Nature

In spite of their parents' behavior, some survivors continued to believe in a greater power or source of knowledge. Rob remembers, "No matter how bad it got, I always knew there was something greater than myself and my dilemma."

Many described themselves as having a "spirited sense that my parents—not me—were very wrong." Jenny believes her strong spiritual presence today has its roots in her childhood. "I knew that if I would just stop standing up to my father, I wouldn't be beaten so badly or so often. But even as a little girl, I knew there was something more important than my body involved here. I was afraid that if I backed down, my spirit would break. Now I admire that spunky little girl."

As a child, Yolanda "loved the Virgin Mary. I'd study in church so she would help me learn. Then, I'd say an Our Father because I was afraid God would be jealous."

When Justin was thirteen years old, Marjorie, his protective neighbor, took him to a Pentecostal church. "I'll never forget my first sermon. The minister read from the Scriptures, John 3:16: 'God so loved the world that he gave his only begotten Son, that whosoever believeth in him should not perish, but have everlasting life.' I said to myself, 'That's who I am—a whosoever. They're talking about me.'" He accepted Christ into his life and found solace not only in Marjorie's "radiant peace" but also in the welcome of several families in the church who invited Justin to live with them during his teen years.

Jenny found a "good father" in the Baptist church. "I was eight years old, in vacation Bible camp, studying the Psalms of David: 'I will be a father to him who has no father.' I asked myself, Does that include ones who have bad fathers too? That has been the bedrock I sank my roots into." She also feels a strong connection to nature, which has given her an image of strength that she could not find in her own passive mother: "I see myself as a tree on a mountaintop, blown by fierce winds, twisted into what might be deformity, yet there is beauty in that. The roots have grown deep to withstand the winds. All of the leaves have been blown away so you can truly see this tree."

Repeatedly, the survivors interviewed described nature as "safe," "giving," "healing" and "nurturing"—more so than other human beings.

Esther found solace in the ocean, as it "was the only part of my life that was consistent. Every time we went, it was exactly the same, timeless, always safe. Its beauty and power was good. I lay on the hot sand and let the tide wash over me. You are being cleansed, healed, loved, I would tell myself."

Rita grew up next to a Navaho reservation. Her mother, a Navaho, insisted the family live in a shack in town. "My mother denied and hated her Native heritage. She forbade my brother and me to go on the reservation. I figured there must be something pretty special there and snuck over every chance I could. While on the reservation, I rode the wild ponies bareback. One summer day, when I was eight, my pony was hot, so I got off his back and started to walk him to water. Out of nowhere this elderly man I'd seen in town appeared. I'd assumed he couldn't speak English, but he told me he was a medicine man, and he thought I could become a spiritual person." For the next five years he taught Rita the spiritual lessons of her culture. "He showed me a jumping cactus. They have long, fragile roots, which are above ground. If you step on one of the roots, the cactus jumps, attacks you. He asked me if the cactus reminded me of anyone I knew. It was just like my dad, who would hit us over nothing. We talked about it and the medicine man helped me to take the violence less personally and to try to stay away from those roots."

Some survivors told me that their involvement in organized religion had compounded their trauma. Stefan explains, "I think that the Catholic Church's focus on sin and punishment made me believe even more that I deserved to be mistreated, that it was my punishment for my sins. I couldn't defy my parents, so I defied God instead—if you *really* exist, how could you allow this to happen to me?"

Abusers who claim to practice religion sometimes tell child victims that they are agents of God and that the abuse is God's will: "Honor thy father" is a commandment; "Honor thy child" is not.

Life in the Face of Death

Most children gain familiarity with death through the loss of pets and elderly relatives. When this happens, a compassionate adult will explain the concept of death, answer the child's questions, and help the child to grieve. Childhood is supposed to be a time of innocence, and ideally children are sheltered from the enormity of their own mortality until they are older and better able to tolerate despair and to understand the philosophical questions inherent in issues of life and death.

In violent families, however, threats of violence, even death, are as common as "How was school today?" is in healthier families. Nancy's stepfather's idea of normal conversation was "I'd just as soon throw you through that wall as look at you." It was not an idle comment, unfortunately.

Esther remembers: "I never knew from one day to the next if we were going to be alive. As an adult, I can now see how much melodrama and game playing there was, but I couldn't have known it when I was a child. I believed the threats. My mother told me repeatedly, 'I brought you into this world and I'm going to take you out.' Being knocked out was as close to death as I'll ever get without actually dying. Every night when I went to sleep, I was half afraid I wouldn't wake up and half wishing I wouldn't wake up."

As the result of violence, many survivors have had near-death experiences. Some become fixated on such experiences, constantly re-creating life-and-death situations to "beat the odds." In contrast, the survivors who'd embraced spirituality used it to understand and integrate these frightening experiences.

Two survivors told me they'd had psychic experiences that helped them to tolerate threats against their lives. Janet remembers: "I was afraid my father would kill me, beating me with this nightstick. One night, when I was eight, I woke up in the middle of the night. My room was filled with a white mist. It was peaceful and calm. I saw my baby-sitter—the only person who really cared about me—in a coffin in the middle of the room. I remember the sensation that she was happy and all was as it should be, for a change. Two days later she died. After that premonition I was never afraid of death again." In her early twenties she became "cynical" and "preoccupied with sex," but in her thirties she reconnected with her spiritual powers and now meditates, visualizing a "healing white light" that guides her through each day.

When Rob was twenty-two years old, his mother had just died and his father was permanently hospitalized for Huntington's chorea. "I was just out of the marines, newly sober, and overwhelmed with despair.

Worn out from my childhood, I really considered suicide. I prayed: If there's anyone up there, I really need to know. I felt myself being elevated, suspended in the air, squished comfortably, as if someone were cradling me. I had this profound sense of well-being. All things in my life made connections and seemed right, yet I could not tell you what those connections were. I was hanging out there for what seemed like an eternity. I was not alone."

Death loses its power when survivors find in spirituality the comfort and support they did not receive from their parents. Instead of "living to avoid death," they learn to live to live.

Faith over Fear

To protect their spirits when faith and trust has been shattered, children become defiant. Therapist Robert Subby, who works with adult children of alcoholics, defines defiance as "living in the world without faith."[6] Having learned to leave nothing to fate or chance, some survivors believe, "I am alone in the world: it is all up to me." Some believe in no power greater than the self.

Believing that one is in control of one's life is healthy—to a point. Certainly attributing everything that happens to divine will is a denial of personal responsibility. However, the idea that a person is completely the master of his destiny is equally problematic, reflecting the need for total control of one who is, paradoxically, out of control. The need to be in control now controls the survivor.

The serenity prayer from Alcoholics Anonymous speaks eloquently to the desired balance: "God grant me the serenity to accept the things I cannot change, the courage to change the things I can, and the wisdom to know the difference." Ironically, a lack of faith and need for control tend to make survivors as irrational as their parents once seemed to them. Yet they may fear that if they give up control, they'll be back in the position of the frightened little child, helpless before his angry gods.

Jake said: "I started to meditate for medical reasons, to reduce high blood pressure. At first I hated it—especially the mumbo jumbo about tuning in to your energy and the universe. I preferred tuning in to the sports channel. But it did help with my blood pressure. And when my wife and kids started saying I was calmer, I relaxed even more. They started to tell me what a tyrant I'd been, always running the show, telling everyone what to do. Now my motto is 'Don't just do something, sit there!' We all have more fun. I'm off the hook because I don't have to be in charge all of the time."

Many survivors experienced childhood religious training as "being in the head—it was about rules and rituals." Yet they returned to religion as adults, experiencing it as more "heartfelt." As a child, Jenny benefited from the affirmations she found in the Scriptures. As a young adult with a battering spouse and recovering from the car accident that caused the amputation of her right leg, she tried harder and harder to control her life. Finally, in 1966, she had come to the end of herself: "I was divorcing my second husband, his business had burned down, I was stuck paying for two mortgages, I'd just lost my job due to my disability and I was raising our three children. One day, I visualized myself as walking uphill, on my crutches, with two houses and three children hanging onto my back. Just as when I was a little girl, I had to keep going, had to do it all, no matter how worn out I was. Then I realized that I wasn't God. Somebody else was. I let go of trying to control everything. I accepted that I am whole and loved by a mighty Creator."

Jenny's life changed dramatically. Eventually she regained financial solvency and became an activist in services for handicapped people. After a while she went back to graduate school for training as a pastoral counselor. She has kept the best of her perseverance and resourcefulness as a child and tempered these strengths with faith, self-acceptance and a sense of family she takes from the Pentecostal church.

Jenny's faith and that of so many of the spiritually oriented survivors I interviewed is best expressed by an old story.

An old man has a farm and relies on his horse to plow his field. One day the horse runs away and his neighbors lament, "Oh, it is so terrible that your horse ran away. Don't you feel awful?" He replies, "We'll see."

His horse returns to the farm with five wild horses. "Oh, isn't this wonderful!" rejoice his neighbors. The old farmer replies, "We'll see."

While breaking in a wild horse, the farmer's son is thrown and shatters his leg in several places. "What a tragedy!" wail the neighbors. Again, all the farmer has to say is "We'll see."

The next week the government drafts all of the young men in town to go to war. The farmer's son is exempt from service because of his leg.

"You are so lucky!" exclaim the neighbors. "We'll see," says the farmer.

The farmer has faith—the same kind of faith that has helped survivors to feel less alone in the world and less responsible for everything that happens. The powerlessness they experienced as children was genuine and terrifying, but trying to be powerful and in control all of the time is not the answer. Faith transforms powerlessness into a state of grace, an accepting attitude—a perennial "We'll see" that allows the survivor to transcend the ego. With faith, vulnerability no longer means a guarantee of injury: it can also be an opportunity for healing.

Faith is an antidote to fear. Guided by a belief in some power greater than the self, many have transformed their fear of living into an awe of life. Rabbi Harold Kushner describes the difference:

> The feeling of awe is similar to fear in some ways. We feel a sense of being overwhelmed, of confronting someone or something much more powerful than ourselves. But awe is a positive feeling, an expansive feeling. Where fear makes us want to run away, awe makes us want to draw closer even as we hesitate to get too close. Instead of resenting our smallness or weakness, we stand openmouthed in appreciation of something greater than ourselves. To stand at the edge of a steep cliff and look down is to experience fear. We want to get out of that situation as quickly and as safely as we can. To stand securely on a mountaintop and look around us is to feel awe. We could linger there forever.[7]

The perception of having climbed a mountain rather than teetering on the edge of a cliff is important. None of the survivors I talked with would say they have reached the summit yet, but they do see themselves as hearty climbers who are on their way to the top. How different from being a victim about to fall into the abyss!

Forgive But Don't Forget

Some survivors who fear their rage at their abusive and nonprotective parents turn to spirituality to help them forgive. Thelma recognizes that she uses forgiveness "as a detour around my anger. I forgive people almost immediately just to get away from my anger. I not only forgive them, but then I pat myself on the back, telling myself what a wonderful person I am because I can forgive. But none of this really makes me feel any better."

As we've seen, survivors must first forgive themselves for being helpless and innocent and cease denial and minimization before they can begin to forgive others. Psychiatrist Scott Peck reminds us that this is very hard work: there are no shortcuts, spiritual or otherwise. To truly forgive, to be fair and just in our forgiveness, he believes that we must conduct a trial in our minds, with opening statements, briefs for the prosecution and for the defense, witnesses and cross-examination, evidence presented and closing arguments. Only after a verdict of guilty can there be a pardon. If there is a hung jury, mistrial or acquittal, we must start again. After such a process, which requires rigorous thinking and deep emotional exploration—since the survivor plays all the parts—one can accept and make peace with an unfair and unfortunate part of the past.[8]

Rita found that "genuine forgiveness came naturally at the end of my grief work. Before that, I used to say, 'Oh, it wasn't my parents' fault. They were alcoholic or they were abused kids too or they hurt us because racism hurt them.' But that wasn't forgiveness—it was rationalization. Only when I got toward the end of my own pain could I really see their pain and begin to forgive."

Therapists Wendy Maltz and Beverly Holman address the forgiveness of survivors of child sexual abuse in *Incest and Sexuality*:

> Survivors often wonder whether they should feel forgiveness toward the offender and other members of the family. Forgiveness in the sense of releasing others from responsibility for their harmful actions and believing their actions were justified is not healthy. But if forgiveness can be defined in a way that emphasizes understanding a person's humanness, limitations, and history, then it may be very beneficial. This second style of forgiveness is self-affirming. It can allow and encourage the survivor to accept her own humanness, develop compassion toward herself, remove remaining self-blame and release herself from constantly experiencing negative feelings toward old family members.[9]

Forgiving others unclutters one's own life. Rob describes it as letting go of what gets in the way of his life: "My parents told me repeatedly I was unlovable and I believed them. Today, I don't believe it anymore.

They are still accountable for having said it, but I don't hold on to it anymore."

As Claudia Black states, "Forgiving is not forgetting. It is remembering and letting go."[10]

Rituals of Healing

Joan's African-Portuguese culture is rich with rituals. As she neared the end of her therapy she bought a doll who resembled her to symbolize the little girl who had killed her mother: "I put her in a box, with a letter to my mother, telling how much I loved her and missed her. I buried the doll at my mother's grave site, with a ceremony, leaving behind my guilt and torment."

While individual approaches to spiritual healing are vital, I believe that we are still in need of a collective and inclusive ritual of healing. My colleagues who treat post-traumatic stress disorder in Vietnam veterans believe there have been two distinct eras in their work: "before the Wall" (the Vietnam War Memorial in Washington, D.C.) and "after the Wall."[11] The Wall represents a "spiritual breakthrough" because it gave veterans a common meeting ground where they could remember and grieve together. Just as important, the Wall marked the end of this country's denial of its experience and a sanction of mourning over the war. Today the Wall is a sacred place for veterans and their families where healing rituals can be performed—finding the names of buddies and loved ones, taking home an imprint of a name, leaving letters, flowers, medals and the like.

I believe that with respect to childhood abuse, we are now where we were fifteen years ago with Vietnam veterans. We largely deny the experience. Aside from group therapy and support groups, which are usually more for the mind and heart than for the soul, there is no sacred place for survivors to come together to mourn their losses, to feel less alone. Our society does not sanction the mourning of childhood trauma.

We need a wall for survivors of childhood trauma. There we could remember and not be alone. We could grieve in good company. Lacking such a memorial to the horrors of childhood trauma, we have, instead, living memorials in the survivors who "prove" the myth of "Once damaged goods, always damaged goods": criminals, addicts, and abusive parents. They remind us of how bad it is, lest we forget. Their presence is a rebuke to our belief that children are safe in their homes in America.

Attitude Is Gratitude

None of the survivors I interviewed believed that their abuse was the will of a god, punishment for their sins, or, in more mystical terms, bad Karma, retribution for despicable deeds done in a past life, or, worse yet, a "choice" the victim made in order to learn spiritual lessons. They recognized such belief systems as yet another elaborate control mechanism in which inappropriate guilt masquerades as faith.

Yolanda studies shamanism, Eastern religions and Native American spiritual beliefs. She rejects the idea that childhood abuse and neglect are heaven-sent: "I think it has no meaning, should never have happened and had no value. Abuse is abuse is abuse. To give meaning to it is to excuse it, as if to say to abusive parents, 'It is good that you are hurting your child because she will find great meaning in it.' When people tell me I chose my childhood because there were lessons I needed to learn from it, I tell them to go have themselves beat up if they think it is so meaningful."

But once they understood, "It's not my fault," many turned to spirituality to find an answer to the next question: "Then *why* did it happen?" Rabbi Harold Kushner offers one explanation:

Pain is the price we pay for being alive. . . . When we understand that, our question will change from 'Why do we have to feel pain?' to 'What do we do with our pain so that it becomes meaningful and not just pointless, empty suffering? How can we turn all the painful experiences of our lives into birth pangs or into growing pangs?' We may not ever understand why we suffer or be able to control the forces that cause our suffering, but we have a lot to say about what the suffering does to us, and what sort of people we become because of it. Pain makes some people bitter and envious. It makes others sensitive and compassionate. It is the result, not the cause, of pain that makes some experiences of pain meaningful and others empty and destructive.[12]

Making the best of a bad situation, many could readily identify "gifts" or "lessons"—skills, interests, creativity, heightened talents—that developed in the shadow of the abuse. Native American beliefs taught Rita to find the "gifts in the abuse so that it would not control me. This is something the white culture does not understand. My sensitivity is a good thing that has come out of the abuse. Knowing and embracing that puts the abuse in perspective and takes away its negative power over me. But I would never say that I chose violent parents so I could be a sensitive person."

Stefan has found the "gift of my sense of humor from the hell I've been through. I have this talent for seeing the absurdity in any situation. It saved my life because as long as it's absurd, as long as it's surreal, then it couldn't be my fault. My humor brings me closer to other people and it's helped me to keep my perspective."

Janet believes she wouldn't have the optimism she has today if she had not been tested so severely: "It's only been by triumphing over hundreds of ordeals that I have this gift, which I offer to others as well. Life is good and it does get better as you get older."

Elaine's best childhood memory is "sitting at this old upright piano in the basement, playing for hours. I could see the grass outside the little basement window, and the dust particles shone in the stream of sunlight." She taught herself to compose intricate sonatas in her head. "I remember being eight years old and falling asleep on a long family trip in the car. I was aware of the steady rhythm of the car going over bumps, so I wrote and heard music for a quartet, based on that rhythm, in my head. All through my childhood, I composed music to keep my mind off my troubles. I am so grateful for my talent."

Such survivors share a remarkable lack of bitterness and a sense of outrage at their childhood abuse that has taken on a universal perspective: "How could that happen to anyone? How could any adult do that to any child?" In contrast, survivors who lack belief in anything beyond themselves tend to be more self-absorbed and therefore more bitter: "How could that happen to *me*?" The connection to others who have suffered the same fate is lost, and, as a result, their isolation is heightened.

The survivors I spoke with also had remarkable compassion for their "brothers and sisters" who had been, at least for the time being, defeated by the trauma. Most felt that "but for the grace of God, I could have been in the same situation." Some remembered with humility that they had been in similar situations, and counted themselves fortunate to have been able to get out. As Paul explains, "I look at the criminal on television or the mentally ill street person or the parent beating his kid in the supermarket, and I remember the fear, rage, distrust, repulsion I felt when I was a little kid being beaten. I think they want me to remember, to understand how they feel. I hope that other people look at them and know a little bit more about how it feels, what it is like, how it can turn out, to be a hurt kid."

These survivors believe that the peace and serenity they find today offsets the harm done to them in the past. As Paul puts it, "I know my past is there but I don't like to dwell on it. I look around me, at how beautiful my children are, the power of a river, the coziness of the hills that surround me, the colors in a sunset, and I think, Life is good. Here in the country, we stack cords of wood for the winter. In my mind, I think of all the horrific things that happened to me as a kid as being about as big as one cord of wood. But as an adult, I've made friends, I have lots of interests, lots of love in my life and I have fun. I believe these things are just as important and have been put in my path for a reason. The good things pile up to be about two cords of wood. Don't misunderstand me—it's not that I ignore that one awful cord. It's there. It's just that I know the balance has tipped and that keeps me going."

Time and time again, I was impressed with these survivors' ability to make a little go a long way, to interweave the good with the bad to make a whole life. Laura sees her life as a quilt. "I started with a heap of old rags, but I've taken the little scraps of good that I got as a kid—my cat who loved me, teachers who said I was smart, my secret alone place, Nancy Drew novels, a week at my grandparents' house when I was ten years old—and I made that into a quilt. Like the gorgeous old quilts you see in exhibitions, there are tears and faded parts and seams that show. That's the violence that plagued my childhood. The rest of it is so beautiful that the quilt can accommodate those imperfections. In fact, it gives the quilt character. I can wrap the quilt around me and it keeps me warm."

Raised in hell, these survivors have created heaven within their daily lives. To be more precise, they see the world not as perfect but as simply "good enough." Transcending their egos, they surrender to yet another source of healing. "This is my last frontier," Beth explains. "My spirituality, my meditation and trust in fate, gives me a sense of belonging in this world and a peace of mind that all the therapy and friends I have been blessed with could not give me."

Welcome Home

Courage can be just as infectious
as fear.

—ALICE MILLER
For Your Own Good

T he survivors who so eloquently spoke to me of the hope and health
in their lives challenge any narrow assumptions about the "inevitable" outcomes of childhood trauma. The obstacles they have overcome
are not merely those of the past; nor are they solely internal or intrapsy-
chic. Projected deficiency has plagued each of them. They feared that
people's perception of them would change—for the worse—if they
disclosed their childhoods. Grateful as they are for the help they have
received, all believe they could have used more help along the way. They
are healing *in spite of* the society they live in. They found no "haven in
a heartless world" in their families of origin, yet most found an unwel-
coming environment in the world outside the home, where they had
to strive to recover as best they could.

Christina says: "My greatest barrier is not the fact that I am disabled:

it is other people's assumptions about me. A lot of people believe that once you've been through childhood abuse, you are ruined for life. Couple that with being deaf-blind, and it's 'Forget it.' I end up feeling like I'm not worth the effort, not salvageable. As I continue to heal and thrive, it is as if I am doing it illegally, getting away with something."

Many people know better than to stereotype people based on race, religion, age, disability, gender, socioeconomic class or sexual preference. The list of those deserving "equal opportunity" needs to include those who have been traumatized in childhood. Too often, knowing that a friend or coworker is a survivor changes our perceptions of them, diminishes their humanness in our eyes. We may view them as a "human time bomb waiting to go off." We may become impatient with their suffering, cajoling them with "It could have been worse," or trying to reassure them that "the worst is over." Why, we wonder, do they hang on to obsolete coping skills? We fail to recognize how our denial, minimization and pseudoscientific projections of blame for trauma parallel the abusers' defenses and thinking errors, how our insensitivity keeps alive just those defense mechanisms that need to be discarded. Sadly, our stereotypes of survivors help ensure that the "large and secret club" Gloria Steinem identified remains secret.

This "safety in secrecy" stance is not unique to survivors of childhood abuse and neglect. In her conclusions about the child Holocaust survivors she interviewed, Sarah Moskovitz notes:

> For them, the problem of stigma is everywhere . . . the isolating quality of their experiences magnified and made more difficult to endure. . . . So it is the feeling of being an outsider, engendered by uprooting, persecution and murder of one's family, are too often reinforced by attitudes of suspicion, "self-protective disinterest," or pathology-seeking by those who would not consciously wish the survivor harm, but isolate him nevertheless. No wonder survivors have often withdrawn or formed their own groups, in which they can speak freely, integrating the past without being stigmatized. Yet, for this, the psychiatric literature has seen survivors as being able to relate only among themselves. Many psychiatrists, *themselves unable or unwilling to deal with survivors' experiences,* bear a responsibility for having popularized too narrow a vision in attributing "alienation" of survivors to pathological preoccupation with the past [emphasis added].[1]

It is not just psychiatrists who silence and isolate survivors. We all do it. Nor is the ostracism Moskovitz describes the artifact of a unique point in history. Child abuse and neglect have thrived for centuries and continue to thrive precisely because we will not squarely face their deleterious effects. Alice Miller reminds us:

> We are still barely conscious of how harmful it is to treat children in a degrading manner. Treating them with respect and recognizing the consequences of their being humiliated are by no means intellectual matters; otherwise, their importance would long since have been generally recognized. To empathize with what a child is feeling when he or she is defenseless, hurt or humiliated is like suddenly seeing in a mirror the suffering of one's own childhood, something many people must ward off out of fear while others can accept it with mourning. People who have mourned in this way understand more about the dynamics of the psyche than they could ever have learned from books.[2]

But where and how to mourn? Like survivors of the Holocaust, many survivors of childhood trauma find a welcoming atmosphere in self-help and activist groups made up of other survivors. Daryl knows that "the world is not a straight world. I used to think, If I had been raised in more safety and security, I would be happier. Now I know better. If I had been raised free of trauma, I would be very naive, without deep feelings about a lot of things. The downside is that we become lopsided. I don't cry at funerals, the way other people do. To me, death is a part of life. Yet I cry at the uncovering of truth, at justice prevailing. This sometimes sets me apart from others who are not survivors and cannot understand or accept the intensity of my feelings."

Stefan and other survivors spoke of the wisdom or depth their experiences have given them. Yet not all survivors have a greater breadth of vision or capacity for empathy. Certainly the survivors I've interviewed are transforming their experiences into a greater appreciation of life, compassion for themselves and caring for others. Many of them had periods of their lives where they were immersed in their childhood traumas. The only friends they had—perhaps the only people they trusted—were other survivors. They dedicated their lives to learning about trauma and expressing their feelings in therapy. But they did not stop there.

Today, some of their friends and loved ones are survivors, some aren't. They are still open to learning about trauma *and* they are intellectually curious about many other matters as well. Some of their feelings and passions have roots in childhood trauma, but not all. Diving deep into their pasts was a way station, an intermediate point on a journey; it was not the final destination. Each has an identity beyond that of "survivor."

As Paul says, he wants to participate in life, just like anyone else. "I've paid my dues—the hard way. Now I want membership in the club."

He is talking about a homecoming, a welcoming. Having overcome daunting internal obstacles and learned to integrate their traumas, survivors deserve our efforts to remove the external obstacles that prevent them from being integrated into society. Perhaps every human being who has endured profound suffering anticipates the day of homecoming. Viktor Frankl writes of the Nazi concentration camp survivors:

> But for every one of the liberated prisoners, the day comes when, looking back on his camp experiences, he can no longer understand how he endured it all. As the day of his liberation eventually came, when everything seemed to him like a beautiful dream, so also comes the day when all his camp experiences seem to him nothing but a nightmare.[3]

For survivors like those who have spoken on these pages, who had the courage and the determination to prevail, the nightmare is over. Welcome home.

NOTES

Preface

1. Gloria Steinem, "Ruth's Song (Because She Could Not Sing It)," *Outrageous Acts and Everyday Rebellions* (New York: Holt, Rinehart & Winston, 1983), p. 162.
2. Aaron Antonovsky, *Health, Stress and Coping: New Perspectives on Mental and Physical Well-being* (San Francisco: Jossey-Bass, 1979).
3. Aaron Antonovsky, "The Salutogenic Perspective: Toward a New View of Health and Illness," *Advances,* Vol. 4, No. 1, 1987, p. 47.
4. James Garbarino, Edna Guttmann and Janis Wilson Seeley, *The Psychologically Battered Child* (San Francisco: Jossey-Bass, 1986), p. 8.

Chapter One

1. Sarah Moskovitz, *Love Despite Hate: Child Survivors of the Holocaust and Their Adult Lives* (New York: Schocken Books, 1983), p. 237.
2. J. Kirk Felsman and George Vaillant, "Resilient Children as Adults: A 40-Year Study," in E. James Anthony and Bertram J. Cohler, eds., *The Invulnerable Child* (New York: Guilford Press, 1987), p. 298.
3. Rosalie Cruise Jesse, *Children in Recovery: Healing the Parent-Child Relationship in Alcoholic/Addictive Families* (New York: W. W. Norton & Co., 1989), p. 137.
4. David Finkelhor, "Foreword," in James Leehan and Laura Pistone Wilson, *Grown Up Abused Children* (Springfield, Ill.: Charles Thomas Publishers, 1985), p. v.
5. Personal communications with A. Nicholas Groth, PhD., Orlando, Fla.
6. Linda Meyer Williams and David Finkelhor, "The Characteristics of Incestuous Fathers: A Review of Recent Studies," in W. L. Marshall, D. R. Laws and H. E. Babaree, *The Handbook of Sexual Assault: Issues, Theories and Treatment of the Offender* (New York: Plenum, 1988).
7. Susan Okula, "Abusive child-parent theory dispelled," Associated Press, September 1987.

8. Martin Seligman, *Helplessness: On Depression, Development and Death* (New York: Freeman Press, 1975), p. 21.

9. Ibid., p. 24.

10. Edward Gondolf and Ellen Fisher, *Battered Women as Survivors: An Alternative to Treating Learned Helplessness* (Lexington, Mass.: Lexington Books, 1988), p. 14.

11. Ibid., p. 92.

12. Norman Garmezy, PhD., The Susan B. Wise Memorial Lecture, sponsored by the Boston Psychoanalytical Society and Institute, May 13, 1989.

13. D. W. Winnicott, "Ego Integration in Child Development," in *The Maturational Processes and the Facilitating Environment* (New York: International Universities Press, 1962), pp. 56–63.

14. Viktor Frankl, *Man's Search for Meaning: An Introduction to Logotherapy* (New York: Simon and Schuster, Inc., 1959), p. 55.

15. Manfred Bleuher, *The Schizophrenic Disorders* (New Haven, Conn.: Yale University Press, 1978), p. 409.

16. Felsman and Vaillant, op. cit., p. 304.

17. Lois Barclay Murphy and Alice Moriarty, *Vulnerability, Coping and Growth* (New Haven, Conn.: Yale University Press, 1976), p. 202.

18. Harold Kushner, *When Bad Things Happen to Good People* (New York: Schocken Books, 1981), p. 133.

Chapter Two

1. Personal communications with Frank Pescosolido, M.S.W., Providence, Rhode Island.

2. Brandt Steele, "Notes on the Lasting Effects of Early Childhood Abuse," *Child Abuse and Neglect*, Vol. 10, 1986, p. 283.

3. Florence Rush, *The Best-Kept Secret* (New York: McGraw-Hill, 1980).

4. *The Diagnostic and Statistical Manual of Mental Disorders (III-R)* (Washington, D.C.: American Psychiatric Association, 1989), pp. 247–50.

5. *The Random House Dictionary of the English Language* (New York: Random House, 1987).

6. Lenore Terr, "Chowchilla Revisited: The Effects of Psychic Trauma Four Years After a School Bus Kidnapping," *American Journal of Psychiatry*, Vol. 140, 1983, pp. 1543–50.

Chapter Three

1. Thank you to David Marion, PhD., who first introduced me to this formulation during clinical supervision in 1984.

2. Jane Middleton-Moz and Lorie Dwinell, *After the Tears: Reclaiming the*

Personal Losses of Childhood (Pompano Beach, Fla.: Health Communications Press, 1986), p. 75.

3. E. James Anthony, "The syndrome of the psychologically vulnerable child," in E. J. Anthony and C. Koupernik, eds., *The Child in His Family: Children at Psychiatric Risk* (New York: Wiley, 1974), p. 540.

4. E. James Anthony, "High Risk Children Growing Up Successfully," in Anthony and Cohler, op. cit., p. 161.

Chapter Four

1. Personal communications with Sharon Wegscheider-Cruse, Rapid City, S.D.

2. Personal communications with Terry Hunt, EdD.

3. Claudia Black, *It Will Never Happen to Me* (Denver, Colo.: MAC Publishers, 1981), p. 31.

4. I first heard of this concept from Carole Keller of Denver, Colo., speaking of Spirituality and Adult Children of Alcoholics, On-Site, Rapid City, S. D., August 7, 1985.

5. Rokelle Learner, lecture on "Healing the Child Within," National Adult Children of Alcoholics Conference, Orlando, Fla., February 28, 1988.

6. Frank Herbert, *Dune* (Radnor, Pa.: Chilton Book Company, 1965), p. 8.

7. Gershen Kaufman, *Shame: The Power of Caring* (Rochester, Vt.: Schenkman Books, 1980), p. 9.

8. Gershen Kaufman, *The Psychology of Shame: Theory and Treatment of Shame-Based Syndromes* (New York: Springer Publishing Company, 1989), p. 33.

9. Karen Paine-Gernee and Terry Hunt, *Emotional Healing* (New York: Warner Books, 1990), pp. 20–23.

10. Personal communications with Terry Hunt, EdD, Boston, Mass.

11. D. W. Winnicott, "Fear of Breakdown," *International Review of Psychoanalysis,* Vol. 1, 1974, p. 104.

12. Elisabeth Kübler-Ross, *On Death and Dying* (London: Collier-Macmillan, Ltd., 1969).

13. Judith Viorst, *Necessary Losses* (New York: Random House, 1986), pp. 274–5.

Chapter Five

1. Interview with James Ritchie, LICSW, Boston, Mass., April 14, 1989.

2. Bessel van der Kolk, *Psychological Trauma* (Washington, D.C.: American Psychiatric Press, 1987), pp. 63–89.

3. Hans Selye, *Stress Without Distress* (New York: Signet, 1974), pp. 24–27.

4. Bessel van der Kolk, "The Compulsion to Repeat the Trauma," *Psychiatric Clinics of North America*, Vol. 12, No. 2, June 1989, p. 396.

5. Personal communications with John Prebble, Orange County, Calif.

6. Bernie Siegel, *Love, Medicine and Miracles* (New York: Harper and Row, 1986), p. 69.

Chapter Six

1. Alice Miller, *Prisoners of Childhood, The Drama of the Gifted Child and the Search for the True Self* (New York: Basic Books, 1981), p. 6.

2. Nicolas Etcheverry, "Discovering the Healthy Core, or There Are No Dumb Symptoms," presented at the Andras Angyal Association Conference, Brandeis University, Waltham, Mass., April 20, 1985.

3. Andras Angyal, *Neuroses and Treatment* (New York: John Wiley & Sons, 1965).

4. Middleton-Moz and Dwinnell, op. cit., pp. 1–17.

5. Personal communications with Terry Kellog, Minneapolis, Minn.

6. Arthur Miller, *After the Fall* (New York: Viking Penguin Inc., 1964), pp. 21–22.

Chapter Seven

1. Louise Kaplan, *Oneness and Separateness: From Infant to Individual* (New York: Simon and Schuster, 1978), p. 28.

2. Viorst, op. cit., p. 43.

3. Kaplan, op. cit., p. 47.

4. Ritchie, op. cit.

5. D. W. Winnicott, "Aggression in Relation to Emotional Development," in *Collected Papers* (London: Tavistock Publications, 1958), p. 216.

6. Jean Baker Miller, MD, and her associates at the Stone Center of Wellesley College, Wellesley, Mass., are the leaders in this line of thought.

7. Paine-Gernee and Hunt, op. cit, p. 192.

8. Viorst, op. cit., p. 33.

9. Jesse, op. cit., p. 92.

10. Ibid., p. 105.

11. Robert Ackerman, *Same House, Different Homes* (Pompano Beach, Fla.: Health Communications Inc., 1986).

Chapter Eight

1. Kellog, op. cit.
2. Personal communications with Nicholas D. Etcheverry, Lincoln, Mass.
3. William Plummer, "No Ring Violence Can Equal What Donny Lalonde Knew at Home," *People Weekly,* November 7, 1988, pp. 71–77.
4. Jean Piaget, "Autobiography," in E. Boring, H. Langfeld, H. Werner and R. Yerkes, *A History of Psychology in Autobiography,* Volume 4 (Worcester, Mass.: Clark University Press, 1952), p. 237.
5. John Wilson and Sheldon Zigelbaum, "Post-traumatic Stress Disorder and the Disposition to Criminal Behavior," in Charles Figley (editor), *Trauma and Its Wake: Theory, Research and Intervention* (New York: Brunner/Mazel, 1986), p. 308.
6. Moskovitz, op. cit., p. 224.
7. Bryan E. Robinson, *Work Addiction: Hidden Legacies of Adult Children* (Pompano Beach, Fla.: Health Communications Inc., 1989), p. 24.
8. Ibid.
9. Carmen Renee Berry, *When Helping You Is Hurting Me: Escaping the Messiah Trap* (New York: Harper and Row, 1988), pp. 98–99.
10. Edwin C. Peck, Jr., "The Traits of True Invulnerability and Posttraumatic Stress in Psychoanalyzed Men of Action," in E. James Anthony and Bertram Cohler, eds., op. cit., p. 331.

Chapter Nine

1. Alice Miller, *For Your Own Good: Hidden Cruelty in Child-Rearing and the Roots of Violence* (New York: Farrar, Straus & Giroux, 1983), p. 231.
2. Patricia P. Reiker and Elaine Carmen, "The Victim to Patient Process: The Disconfirmation and Transformation of Abuse," *American Journal of Orthopsychiatry,* 56, 1986, p. 360.
3. Siegel, op. cit., p. 178.
4. Harold Kushner, *When All You've Ever Wanted Isn't Enough: The Search for a Life that Matters* (New York: Simon and Schuster, 1986), p. 21.
5. Carole Keller, op. cit.
6. Robert Subby, Plenary Session, Adult Children of Alcoholics National Convention, Nashville, Tenn., February 28, 1989.
7. Kushner, *When All You've Ever Wanted Isn't Enough,* p. 131.
8. M. Scott Peck in lectures on *The Road Less Traveled.*
9. Wendy Maltz and Beverly Holman, *Incest and Sexuality: A Guide to*

Understanding and Healing (Lexington, Mass.: Lexington Books, 1987), p. 31.

10. Claudia Black, *It's Never Too Late to Have a Happy Childhood: Inspirations for Adult Children* (New York: Random House, 1989).

11. Personal communications with Bessel van der Kolk, Boston, Mass.

12. Kushner, *When Bad Things Happen to Good People,* p. 64.

Afterword

1. Moskovitz, op. cit., p. 229.

2. Alice Miller, *For Your Own Good,* p. 177.

3. Frankl, op. cit., p. 99.

APPENDIX:
METHODOLOGY AND
DEMOGRAPHY

The basis of this book was a nonempirical study of twenty survivors. Interviews lasted an average of three hours and consisted of each survivor's open-ended answers to twenty questions.

To recruit volunteers for the interview, a request for study volunteers was sent to over one hundred psychotherapists, researchers and self-help leaders, stating, in part, "I would like to interview adults who are over thirty years old, gainfully employed (or committed to volunteer work), have meaningful connections with others which would include friendships and possibly (but not necessarily) a partner." Thirty-six survivors, mostly current or past clients of psychotherapists, volunteered and were qualified to be interviewed. Twenty were chosen for the most extensive cross-section possible.

The screening criteria addressed many common problems associated with the "once damaged goods, always damaged goods" myth. A minimum of seven years was required since the last episode of self-abuse (suicide attempts, cutting, burning); substance abuse (alcohol or drugs); eating disorders (anorexia or bulimia); psychiatric hospitalizations; criminal behavior, including physical assaults against peers or children. Furthermore, an "active recovery" program—psychotherapy and/or the Anonymous self-help groups—was required if the volunteer had experienced any of those problems in young adulthood. A history of sexual offenses of any kind rendered the subject ineligible for the study.

Among the twenty survivors chosen for the study, six never had any of the above stated problems. Of the remaining fourteen, four had been psychiatrically hospitalized more than fifteen years before, all for suicide attempts. One of those four survivors had engaged in cutting behavior more than twelve years ago. Eight survivors had a minimum of seven years of sobriety and active recovery from substance abuse; six identified themselves as alcoholic or "almost alcoholic" and two were daily marijuana smokers. No one had a history of anorexia or bulimia; two men had previously been overeaters and one woman identified overeating as a current problem for her. Two men disclosed prior criminal activity: one had been an adjudicated juvenile delinquent with a propensity toward fistfights as a young adult, although fifteen years have passed since his last fight. The other had been a gambler, and had engaged in one undetected incident of theft in college. None had physically abused children.

If the potential interviewee had been a victim of physical or sexual assault within the past three years, I recommended that the interview, at this time, was most likely not in his or her best interest because of the possibility of triggering powerful memories and affect. One woman in this study had been a battered wife twenty-three years ago. Another woman had been an acquaintance rape victim ten years ago. Both had sought and completed specialized psychotherapy for this adult trauma.

Confidentiality was guaranteed by a signed agreement. All names, geographic locations of the survivors' families of origin, and details of their current occupations have been changed for this book. In some cases, the survivor requested that his or her ethnic origins be altered.

The youngest survivor was thirty-five years old at the time of the interview. Seven of the survivors are in their late thirties; eleven are in their forties; one is fifty-four years old and the oldest had celebrated her sixtieth birthday just four days before the interview.

Eleven women and nine men were interviewed. Two survivors are black, one is Hispanic, one is Native American and the remaining sixteen are Caucasian. Unfortunately, in spite of much effort, I was unable to locate an Asian American survivor who was willing to be interviewed. This is an important lack, which I regret.

One gay man and two lesbians were included in this study. Another three survivors spoke of significant homosexual relationships in their past. Seventeen survivors identified their current sexual orientation as heterosexual.

Two survivors were disabled: one has been deaf since birth and also has a degenerative eye disease and is now legally blind; the other survivor became an amputee in adulthood. She had recently been successfully fitted for a leg prothsesis and was no longer in need of a wheelchair. The remaining eighteen survivors are currently able-bodied. Three of these survivors grew up with disabled siblings.

Two of the survivors were only children. For the remaining survivors, size of family of origin ranged from two to seven children. Ten had brothers or sisters who had significant problems in adulthood resulting in incarceration, mostly for crimes of violence; abuse and neglect of their own children so severe that child protection agencies had removed the children; suicide;

chronic substance abuse; or chronic mental illness requiring full-time supervision. Another two survivors had siblings whom they identified as "problem drinkers" even though those siblings were relatively functional at work.

All twenty survivors were at least currently middle-class socioeconomically. However, in terms of family of origin, three grew up in poverty; seven were working poor; seven were middle-class and three grew up in economic wealth.

Three of the survivors have always been single; five are still with their original spouses; three have lived with a partner for more than five years; four are divorced and currently single; and the remaining five are divorced and remarried.

Ten of the survivors are parents to birth or adopted children; one is a foster parent. There are twenty-one children among the ten parents.

OUT IN THE OPEN
A Guide For Young People Who Have Been Sexually Abused
Ouanié Bain and Maureen Sanders

'It sets out to break the loneliness felt by many victims. . . and helps them survive the pain, anger and fear which follows' – *Daily Express*

'The most surprising thing for me was to find out that it wasn't some weird thing that happened just to me'

If you have ever experienced any kind of sexual abuse, this book is for you. Plain-speaking and sympathetic, it cuts through the terrible loneliness and silence and talks frankly about the range of feelings sexually abused young people experience. Including other people's stories and discussing honestly what can happen once the truth is told, it also offers practical advice and encouragement to young people on the road to recovery. Ultimately this is an optimistic book, arguing and believing that despite the pain, anger, fears and setbacks, once things are out in the open, victims *can* become survivors.

MY FATHER'S HOUSE
A Memoir of Incest and Healing
Sylvia Fraser

'*My Father's House* has the tension and pace of a detective novel – except that the detective is a part of the narrator's self, and so is the murder victim. A beautifully written, heart-wrenching and ultimately healing story by an amazing and courageous woman' - *Margaret Atwood*

She was a beautiful blonde child, a quintessential Canadian teenager: she loved Saturday film matinees, giggled at pyjama parties, ran for student president, led the cheerleading squad, went steady with the right boy and married him, her proud father at her side. But from the age of seven Sylvia Fraser shared her body with a 'twin' who lived a separate life from her. This other self was created to do the things Sylvia was too frightened, too ashamed, too repelled to do – the things her father made her do. As an adult, she had no recollection of a sexual relationship with her father, yet some connection always remained – pain, terror, and guilt were never far from the surface. With tremendous power, candour, and eloquence, Sylvia Fraser breaks through her amnesia to discover and embrace the self she left behind. *My Father's House* is at once a terrible account of a woman's coming of age and a lyric story of love and forgiveness.

CRY HARD AND SWIM
The Story of an Incest Survivor
Jacqueline Spring

'The stark eloquence of the betrayed child lingers long after the book has been closed' - *Helen Torlesse, Daily Telegraph*

'This is the true story of the childhood and therapy of an incest survivor – myself.' Jacqueline Spring (a pseudonym) was the youngest of seven children, born into a Glaswegian family that appeared conventionally at ease both emotionally and materially. But the picture that emerges here in letters to her mother, in poems and narration is one of pain and immense bewilderment caused by her father's sexual advances. The frightened, compliant child was pressured by family silence never to refer to what was going on inside or outside the family. It was only years later, in therapy – an experience that was to be profoundly transforming – that she began to confront her own psychological mutilation. Her therapist, Eve, through her warmth and acceptance, helped Jaqueline to rid herself of her guilt and self-hatred. And she began to learn how common her feelings and conflicts were in talking to other women in incest survivors' groups. It is for them and for the many workers who deal with survivors that she has described what was for her this 'beautiful and ultimately healing journey'.

NEARI PRESS TITLES

The NEARI Press
New England Adolescent Research Institute
70 North Summer Street
Holyoke, MA 01040
Phone (413) 540-0712

Forthcoming! 2005. **Current Perspectives: Working with Sexually Aggressive Youth and Youth with Sexual Behavior Problems** by R. E. Longo & D. S. Prescott (Editors). NEARI Press. **ISBN# 1-929657-26-9**

Enhancing Empathy by Robert E. Longo and Laren Bays (1999). NEARI Press. Paperback, 77 pages. **ISBN#1-929657-04-8**

Growing Beyond by Susan L. Robinson (2002). NEARI Press. Paperback, 216 pages. **ISBN# 1-929657-17-X**

Growing Beyond Treatment Manual by Susan L. Robinson (2002). NEARI Press. Paperback, 42 pages. **ISBN# 1-929657-15-3**

Lessons from the Lion's Den: Therapeutic Management of Children in Psychiatric Hospitals and Treatment Centers by Nancy S. Cotton, Ph.D. (2005). NEARI Press. Paperback, 354 pages. **ISBN# 1-929657-24-2**

Men & Anger: Understanding and Managing Your Anger by Murray Cullen and Robert E. Longo (1999). NEARI Press. Paperback, 125 pages. **ISBN#1-929657-12-9**

Moving Beyond Sexually Abusive Behavior: A Relapse Prevention Curriculum by Thomas F. Leversee (2002). NEARI Press. Paperback, 88 pages. **ISBN# 1-929657-16-1**

Moving Beyond Student Manual by Thomas F. Leversee (2002). NEARI Press. Paperback, 52 pages. **ISBN# 1-929657-18-8**

New Hope For Youth: Experiential Exercises for Children & Adolescents by Robert E. Longo & Deborah P. Longo (2003). NEARI Press. Paperback,150 pages. **ISBN# 1-929657-20-X**

Paths To Wellness by Robert E. Longo (2001). NEARI Press. Paperback, 144 pages. **ISBN#1-929657-19-6**

Power Struggles: A Book of Strategies for Adults Who Live and Work with Angry Kids. by Penny Cuninggam (2003). NEARI Press. Paperback, 112 pages. **ISBN# 1-929657- 23-4**

Respecting Residential Work With Children by James R. Harris (2003). NEARI Press. Hardcover, 163 pages. **ISBN# 1-929657-21-8**

Standards of Care for Youth in Sex Offense Specific Residential Treatment by S. Bengis, A. Brown, R. Longo, B. Matsuda, K. Singer, and J. Thomas (1997, 1998, 1999). NEARI Press. Paperback, 71 pages. **ISBN# 1-929657-05-6**

Strong at the Broken Places: Building Resiliency in Survivors of Trauma (2005).by Linda T. Sanford. NEARI Press. Paperback, 208 pages. **ISBN# 1-929657-25-0**

The Safe Workbook for Youth by John McCarthy and Kathy MacDonald (2001). NEARI Press. Paperback, 210 pages. **ISBN# 1-929657-14-5**

Who Am I and Why Am I In Treatment by Robert E. Longo with Laren Bays (2000). NEARI Press. Paperback, 85 pages. **ISBN#1-929657-01-3**

Why Did I Do It Again & How Can I Stop? by Robert E. Longo with Laren Bays (1999). NEARI Press. Paperback, 192 pages. **ISBN#1-929657-11-0**

Using Conscience as a Guide: Enhancing Sex Offender Treatment in the Moral Doamin by Niki Delson (2003). NEARI Press. Paperback, 102 pages. **ISBN# 1-929657-22-6**

Using Conscience as a Guide: Student Manual by Niki Delson (2003). NEARI Press. Paperback, 50 pages. **ISBN# 1-929657-19-6**

~ ~

For prices and shipping information, or to order, please call:
Whitman Distribution 800.353.3730

Find us on line at: www.neari.com